Blueprints

Clinical Cases in Obstetrics & Gynecology

Aaron B. Caughey, MD, MPP, MPH (Series Editor)

Arzou Ahsan, MA, MD

Linda Margaret Hopkins, MD

Juan E. Vargas, MD

O. W. Stephanie Yap, MD

Blackwell
Publishing

© 2002 by Blackwell Science, Inc.
a Blackwell Publishing Company

Editorial Offices:
Commerce Place, 350 Main Street, Malden, Massachusetts 02148, USA
Osney Mead, Oxford OX2 0EL, England
25 John Street, London WC1N 2BS, England
23 Ainslie Place, Edinburgh EH3 6AJ, Scotland
54 University Street, Carlton, Victoria 3053, Australia

Other Editorial Offices:
Blackwell Wissenschafts-Verlag GmbH, Kurfürstendamm 57, 10707 Berlin, Germany
Blackwell Science KK, MG Kodenmacho Building, 7-10 Kodenmacho
    Nihombashi, Chuo-ku, Tokyo 104, Japan
Iowa State University Press, A Blackwell Science Company, 2121 S. State Avenue,
    Ames, Iowa 50014-8300, USA

Distributors:

The Americas
    Blackwell Publishing
    c/o AIDC
    P.O. Box 20
    50 Winter Sport Lane
    Williston, VT 05495-0020
    (Telephone orders: 800-216-2522;
    fax orders: 802-864-7626)

Australia
    Blackwell Science Pty, Ltd.
    54 University Street
    Carlton, Victoria 3053
    (Telephone orders: 03-9347-0300;
    fax orders: 03-9349-3016)

Outside The Americas and Australia
    Blackwell Science, Ltd.
    c/o Marston Book Services, Ltd.
    P.O. Box 269
    Abingdon
    Oxon OX14 4YN
    England
    (Telephone orders: 44-01235-465500;
    fax orders: 44-01235-465555)

Acquisitions: Beverly Copland
Development: Angela Gagliano
Production: Jennifer Kowalewski
Manufacturing: Lisa Flanagan
Marketing Manager: Kathleen Mulcahy
Cover design: Hannus Design
Interior design: Julie Gallagher
Typeset by International Typesetting and Composition
Printed and bound by Capital City Press

Printed in the United States of America
02 03 04 05 5 4 3 2 1

Library of Congress Cataloging-in-Publication Data

Blueprints clinical cases in obstetrics and gynecology / edited by Aaron B. Caughey ...[et al.].
    p. ; cm. — (Blueprints clinical cases)
    ISBN 0-632-04611-2 (pbk.)
  1. Obstetrics—Case studies. 2. Obstetrics—Examinations, questions, etc.
3. Gynecology—Case studies. 4. Gynecology—Examinations, questions, etc.
5. Physicians—Licenses—United States—Examinations—Study guides.
    [DNLM: 1. Obstetrics—Case Report. 2. Obstetrics—Examination Questions.
3. Genital Diseases, Female—Case Report. 4. Genital Diseases, Female—Examination
Questions. 5. Pregnancy Complications—Case Report. 6. Pregnancy Complications—
Examination Questions. WQ 18.2 B658 2002] I. Caughey, Aaron B. II. Series.
    RG106 .B585 2002
    618'.076—dc21   2001007475

Notice: The indications and dosages of all drugs in this book have been recommended in the medical literature and conform to the practices of the general community. The medications described and treatment prescriptions suggested do not necessarily have specific approval by the Food and Drug Administration for use in the diseases and dosages for which they are recommended. The package insert for each drug should be consulted for use and dosage as approved by the FDA. Because standards for usage change, it is advisable to keep abreast of revised recommendations, particularly those concerning new drugs.

Blueprints

Clinical Cases in Obstetrics & Gynecology

AUTHORS

Aaron B. Caughey, MD, MPP, MPH (Series Editor)
Fellow in Maternal-Fetal Medicine
Department of Obstetrics and Gynecology
University of California, San Francisco
San Francisco, California

Arzou Ahsan, MA, MD
Chief Resident in Obstetrics and Gynecology
University of California, San Francisco
San Francisco, California

Linda Margaret Hopkins, MD
Chief Resident in Obstetrics and Gynecology
University of California, San Francisco
San Francisco, California

Juan E. Vargas, MD
Chief Resident in Obstetrics and Gynecology
University of California, San Francisco
San Francisco, California

O. W. Stephanie Yap, MD
Clinical Instructor, Department of Obstetrics and Gynecology
Stanford University School of Medicine
Fellow, Gynecologic Oncology, Department of Obstetrics and Gynecology
Stanford University Medical Center
Stanford, California
and
University of California, San Francisco
San Francisco, California

Susan H. Tran, MD (Contributing Editor)
Resident in Obstetrics and Gynecology
Kaiser, San Francisco
San Francisco, California

DEDICATION

We would all like to thank the staff at Blackwell particularly Bev Copland and Angela Gagliano for their untiring work on this project. We would also like to thank our family, friends, and colleagues including the residents and faculty in the Departments of Obstetrics and Gynecology at UCSF and the Brigham and Women's Hospital, Drs. A. Eugene Washington, Mary E. Norton, Miriam Kuppermann & Peter Callen. I also extend my appreciation to the students, staff and faculty at UC Berkeley's Health Services and Policy Analysis program and the Department of Economics, and as always my mother, father, Ethan, Samara, Big & Mugsy, my grandparents Theodore Schraft and Elizabeth Caughey, and of course, Susan, whose patience and support during all of my projects keeps me on task and productive.

Aaron

For Strayer, Oriane and Judas

Arzou

To my ever supportive partner—Jim. Thank you.

Love, Linda

For Holly, for everything and beyond

Juan

To my parents, Piek Yong and Fook Loi, for their invaluable support

Thank you, Stephanie

CONTENTS

CONTENTS

PREFACE

The *Blueprints* Clinical Cases series has been developed to complement clinical rotations during the third and fourth years of medical school, and for use as a review when preparing for in-service and Board exams. The cases describe common and important presentations of patients seen in the outpatient and inpatient settings. The design of the cases is meant to parallel the clinical thought process; because the diagnosis is not revealed immediately, students must think through the presentations as they unfold. Once the diagnosis is made, a discussion of treatment and other management issues follows.

Blueprints Clinical Cases in Obstetrics and Gynecology has been designed to take you, the student clinician, through a variety of settings in the clinic, triage, labor and delivery, emergency department, and operating room. The book has two sections with the first half consisting of obstetric cases and the second, gynecologic cases. The presentations are mostly common complaints seen from our patients and cover the gamut of most obstetric issues, gynecologic cancers, and general gynecology. There are a few other variations between this book and the rest in the series, as well as additional considerations you need to make while reading these cases.

These cases have been designed to take you through the thought process of assessing and diagnosing a patient presenting with the given chief complaint. The emphasis is on common patient complaints, and prevalent or important disease processes. Case-based learning is an effective and enjoyable educational tool, but requires a different approach from conventional learning methods. Following is a description of the overall format of the cases and suggestions on how to get the most out of this book.

Title/CC: The case titles and chief complaints (CC) are based on common presenting symptoms, signs, and lab or diagnostic test findings. In general, they represent the common reasons physicians are consulted to see patients, and suggest a broad differential diagnosis to begin the case.

HPI (HPP): The history of present illness (HPI) contains additional descriptive history regarding the patient's chief complaint. In addition, it usually includes a brief review of pertinent systems. At the end of the HPI, you should consider the differential diagnosis, what to look for on the physical exam, and which diagnostic tests should be ordered. Some of these items have been formalized in the thought questions.

The HPI in obstetrics is also known as the HPP, history of present pregnancy. Obstetric patients are always presented with their gravidity and parity as well as their gestational age and pregnancy dating criteria. Gravidity refers to the number of pregnancies a patient has had and parity to the number of births. Parity is further broken down into term, preterm, aborted, and living children resulting in a four digit description. Multiple gestations only count as a single pregnancy and birth, but obviously result in more living children. Aborted pregnancies include spontaneous and elective abortions as well as ectopic pregnancies. When the difference between these three is significant, additional descriptors are supplied. Dating of the pregnancy is done utilizing the patient's last menstrual period and confirmed with physical exam and ultrasound. Ultrasound dating can vary by 8% to 12%, thus the variation from the actual dating increases as the pregnancy progresses.

Past Hx: The past medical, surgical, and social histories along with medications and allergies further supplement the HPI. In some cases, this section contains crucial information regarding the patient's baseline medical status or social situation. Consider how these issues in conjunction with current medications impact the differential diagnosis and eventual treatment plans. In addition to the past medical and surgical history, obstetrician-gynecologists include sections of past obstetric (POBHx) and past gynecologic history (PGynHx). The POBHx includes the number of pregnancies and births, gestational age at delivery, birthweight, mode of delivery and any complications. Included in PGynHx are frequency and regularity of menses, menarche, age of onset of menopause, pelvic infections and history of any gynecologic surgeries.

PREFACE

VS/PE: The vital signs (VS) and physical exam (PE) provide further clarifying information regarding the patient's illness. In these cases, only the pertinent positive and negative findings are mentioned. If a system or finding is not described, it can be assumed to be normal, and does not contribute to the final diagnosis. Information gained from the physical exam should further narrow the differential diagnosis and list of desired diagnostic tests. In many of our patients who are young and healthy, the PE noted in these cases will focus on the abdominal and pelvic exam. Please note that while your notes in an actual clinical setting should reflect a full physical exam, only the pertinent positives and negatives are presented here to save space.

Labs/X-ray: Again, we have included only the pertinent positive and negative findings. Common abbreviations are used as well as the standard format for the complete blood count (CBC) and electrolyte panels. We have included photos and radiographic images in many of the cases to further enhance the skill of incorporating these visual tools into diagnosis. Certainly the most common imaging modality used in OB/Gyn is ultrasound. Real time ultrasound allows the clinician to visualize the uterus and ovaries in our patients and of course the fetus and placenta in obstetric patients. The images included with cases are representative of common images seen and you should familiarize yourself with these images as well as the strengths and limitations of the different imaging modalities.

Thought Questions and Answers: These open-ended questions are meant to stimulate ideas regarding diagnosis, pathophysiology and treatment, and to help plan further workup. In order to get the most out of these questions, spend some time reflecting on possible answers. We suggest writing the answers down, or if working in a group, discussing the possibilities with other students. The answers to the thought questions follow immediately, so try not to read ahead. The thought questions often follow the HPI or the PE, but are occasionally used throughout the cases to help stimulate thought regarding how to proceed in the workup.

Case Continued: These sections may give further bits of diagnostic information in the middle of a case, or give the final diagnosis, and often treatment or follow-up, at the end of the case.

Multiple Choice Questions: There are four MC questions at the end of every case. These are meant to be in-service or Boards-style questions, and should be done at the end of each case. These questions and answers provide additional information about the case diagnosis, and often address other important conditions in the differential diagnosis.

Obstetrics: While gynecology is truly a surgical subspecialty and patients can be considered in a similar way to those in medicine and surgery, obstetric patients are unique within medicine. There are several key differences that need to be considered when caring for obstetric patients. First, the baseline physiology is different from all other patients, and it may change throughout pregnancy. Second, there are two patients to consider: the mother and the fetus. Thus both the diagnosis and treatment may differ from nonpregnant patients. Finally, pregnancy itself is not an illness. In general, these patients are well, and therefore, need to be treated and considered in that light. For educational purposes, many of the patients in our cases undergo complications of pregnancy, but for the majority of patients, pregnancy is an uncomplicated process.

We hope you enjoy and benefit from the cases we have created. We believe that these cases, questions and answers will be useful to the novice student, the more experienced sub-intern and even junior physicians in training.

Aaron B. Caughey, MD, MPP, MPH
Arzou Ahsan, MA, MD
Linda Margaret Hopkins, MD
Juan E. Vargas, MD
O. W. Stephanie Yap, MD

ABBREVIATIONS/ACRONYMS

A	aborta (abortions)
ABG	arterial blood gas
ACE	angiotensin-converting enzyme
ACS	antenatal corticosteroids
ACTH	adrenocorticotropic hormone
ADA	*American Diabetes Association*
ADH	antidiuretic hormone
AF	anteflexed
AFI	amniotic fluid index
AFLP	acute fatty liver of pregnancy
AFP	α-fetoprotein
AGUS	atypical glandular cells of undetermined significance
AIDS	acquired immunodeficiency syndrome
All	allergies
ALT	alanine transaminase
approx	approximately
ARC	AIDS-related conditions
AROM	artificial rupture of the membranes
ASCUS	atypical squamous cells of unknown significance
AST	aspartate transaminase
AV	anteverted
BC	birth control
β-hCG	beta human chorionic gonadotropin
BID	*bis in die* (two times a day)
BME	bimanual exam
BP	blood pressure
bpm	beats per minute
BPP	biophysical profile
BSO	bilateral salpingo-oophorectomy
BUN	blood urea nitrogen
BV	bacterial vaginosis
BX	biopsy
Ca	calcium
CAH	congenital adrenal hyperplasia
cAMP	cyclic adenosine monophosphate
CBC	complete blood count
cc	cubic centimeter
CC	chief complaint
CCE	no clubbing, cyanosis, and edema
CF	cystic fibrosis
CMT	cervical motion tenderness
CMV	cytomegalovirus
CNS	central nervous system
Cor	coronary
CPP	chronic pelvic pain
Cr	creatine
C/S	cesarean section
CST	contraction stress test
CT	computed tomography
CTAB	*clear to auscultation bilaterally*
Ctxns	contractions
CVAT	costovertebral angle tenderness
CVS	chorionic villus sampling
D&C	dilation and curettage
D&E	dilation and evacuation

DES	diethylstilbestrol
DEXA	dual x-ray absorptiometry
DHEAS	dihydroepiandrosterone sulfate
DHT	dihydrotestosterone
DMPA	medroxyprogesterone acetate
DUB	dysfunctional uterine bleeding
dx	diagnosis
EBL	estimated blood loss
EFW	estimated fetal weight
EGA	estimated gestational age
EGBUS	external genitalia, Bartholin's, urethra, and Skene's
ESR	erythrocyte sedimentation rate
EtOH/ETOH	ethanol use
FDA	Food and Drug Administration
FHR	fetal heart rate
FHT	fetal heart tracing
FHx	family history
FIGO	International Federation of Gynecology and Obstetrics
FSBG	finger stick blood glucose
FSH	follicle-stimulating hormone
FTP	failure to progress
G	gravida (pregnancies)
GA	gestational age
GBS	Group B *Streptococcus*
GDM	gestational diabetes mellitus
Gen	general
GERD	gastroesophageal reflux disease
GI	gastrointestinal
GLT	glucose loading test
GnRH	gonadotropin-releasing hormone
GTD	gestational trophoblastic disease
GTT	glucose tolerance test
GU	genitourinary
HA	headache
Hb	hemoglobin
hCG	human chorionic gonadotropin
Hct	hematocrit
HEENT	head, ears, eyes, nose, throat
HELLP	hemolysis, elevated liver enzymes, low platelets syndrome
HGSIL	high-grade squamous intraepithelial lesion
HIV	human immunodeficiency virus
h/o	history of
HPI	history of present illness
hPL	human placental lactogen
HPV	human papillomavirus
HR	heart rate
HRT	hormone replacement therapy
HSG	hysterosalpingogram
HSM	hepatosplenomegaly
HSV	herpes simplex virus
Hx	history
ID	identification
Ig	immunoglobulin

ABBREVIATIONS/ACRONYMS

IHCP	intrahepatic cholestasis of pregnancy
IM	intramuscular
IOL	induction of labor
IUD	intrauterine device
IUGR	intrauterine growth restriction
IUI	intrauterine insemination
IUP	intrauterine pregnancy
IUPC	intrauterine pressure catheter
IV	intravenous
IVDA	intravenous drug abuse
IVF	in vitro fertilization
IVH	intraventricular hemorrhage
KOH	potassium hydroxide
labs	laboratory tests
LAD	lymphadenopahty
lbs	pound(s)
LDH	lactate dehydrogenase
LEEP	loop electrosurgical excision procedure
LFT	liver function test
LGA	large for gestational age
LGSIL	low-grade squamous intraepithelial lesion
LH	leuteinizing hormone
LLQ	lower left quadrant
LMP	last menstrual period
LOT	left occiput transverse
MCV	mean corpuscular volume
Meds	medicines/drugs
$MgSO_4$	magnesium sulfate
MIF	müllerian-inhibiting factor
mIu	milli international units
MoM	multiples of the median
MRI	magnetic resonance imaging
MRKH	Meyer-Rokitansky-Kuster Hauser
MSAFP	maternal serum α-fetoprotein
mu	milliunits
MV	Montevideo units
NAD	no acute distress
ND	no distension
NKDA	no known drug allergies
NPO	*nil per os* (nothing by mouth)
NSAID	nonsteroidal anti-inflammatory drug
NST	nonstress test
NSVD	normal spontaneous vaginal delivery
NT	nontender
NTD	neural tube defect
N/V	nausea and vomiting
OCP	oral contraceptive pill
OCT	oxytocin challenge test
Δ OD 450	deviation of optical density at 450
OR	operating room
P	para (births of viable offspring)
Pap smear	Papanicolaou smear
PCOS	polycystic ovary syndrome
PCR	polymerase chain reaction
PE	physical examination
PGE_{1M}	prostaglandin E_{1M} (Cytotec/misoprostol)
PGE_2	prostaglandin E_2
$PGF_{2\alpha}$	prostaglandin F_2-alpha
PID	pelvic inflammatory disease
PIH	pregnancy-induced hypertension
Plts	platelets
PMDD	premenstrual dysphoric disorder
PMHx	past medical history
PNV	prenatal vitamins
PO	*per os* (by mouth, orally)
POb/GynHx	past obstetric and/or gynecologic history
POC	products of conception
POP	pelvic organ prolapse
PPD	purified protein derivative
PPH	postpartum hemorrhage
PPROM	preterm premature rupture of the membranes
PRL	prolactin
PRN	*pro re nata* (as needed)
PROM	premature rupture of membranes
PSHx	past surgical history
PT	prothrombin time
PUBS	percutaneous umbilical blood sampling
PUPPP	pruritic urticarial papules and plaques of pregnancy
QID	*quater in die* (four times a day)
RBC	red blood cell
RDS	respiratory distress syndrome
RLQ	right lower quadrant
ROS	review of systems
RPR	rapid plasma reagin
RR	respiratory rate
RR&R	regular rate and rhythm
RUQ	right upper quadrant
S > D	size greater than dates
SAB	spontaneous abortion
SC	subcutaneous
SCA	sickle cell anemia
SEM	systolic ejection murmur
SGA	small for gestational age
SHx	social history
SLE	systemic lupus erythematosus
SQ	subcutaneous
SROM	spontaneous rupture of the membranes
SSE	sterile speculum exam
STD	sexually transmitted disease
STI	sexually transmitted infections
SVE	sterile vaginal examination
TAB	therapeutic abortion
Tbili	total bilirubin
TCA	trichloroacetic acid application
Temp	temperature
TOA	tubo-ovarian abscess
TOC	tubo-ovarian complex
Toco	(related to labor)
TOLAC	trial of labor after cesarean
TSH	thyroid-stimulating hormone
UA	urinalysis
UC	uterine contraction
URI	upper respiratory infection
US	ultrasound
UTI	urinary tract infection
V/Q	ventilation/perfusion ratio
VAS	vibroacoustic stimulation
VBAC	vaginal birth after cesarean
VIN	vulvar intraepithelial neoplasia
VS	vital signs
VZV	varicella zoster virus
WBC	white blood cell
WNL	within normal limits

CASES

ID/CC: 29-year-old G_1P_0 woman presents for her first prenatal visit.

HPI: This is a desired pregnancy for P. C. who is at 18 weeks from her last menstrual period (LMP). She had a positive home pregnancy test 12 weeks ago. She is worried because she has not felt any quickening (fetal movement) yet.

PMHx/PSHx: None   **Meds:** Prenatal vitamins (PNV)   **All:** No known drug allergies (NKDA)

POb/GynHx: Irregular menses, every 45 to 60 days

SHx: Denies use of tobacco, ethanol, or recreational or intravenous drugs.

FHx: 25-year-old brother is mentally retarded with autistic behavior. She is Italian, and the father of the baby is Greek American.

VS: Temp afebrile, BP 110/62, HR 86

PE: *Gen:* pleasant adult female in no acute distress. *Abdomen:* soft, nontender, gravid, with uterus palpable 4 cm below the umbilicus. *Pelvic:* long and closed cervix, gravid uterus. No palpable adnexal masses. *Doppler:* positive fetal heart tones in the 160s.

Labs: Urine dipstick: no proteinuria, no glucosuria

THOUGHT QUESTIONS

- Which antenatal diagnostic evaluation is appropriate for this patient?
- Should an obstetrical ultrasound be ordered? Why?
- Given the patient's family history, which inherited disorders should be considered?

All pregnant women should undergo routine prenatal testing as well as any additional testing that may be indicated based on personal and family history and/or ethnic background. Routine prenatal laboratory tests on the first visit should include complete blood count (CBC), blood group and Rh, antibody screen, rapid plasma reagin (RPR), hepatitis B surface antigen, rubella titer, Papanicolaou (Pap) smear, purified protein derivative (PPD), cervical studies for *Neisseria gonorrhoeae* and *Chlamydia trachomatis,* HIV, and urinalysis. Subsequent tests include maternal serum triple screen at 15 to 18 weeks; and a repeat of hematocrit, RPR, and glucose screens at 24 to 28 weeks. In this case, because of the patient's and the father of the baby's ethnic backgrounds, they should be screened for β thalassemia, which can be done simply by obtaining a CBC in both parents. A normal MCV in at least one of the parents rules out the possibility of β thalassemia major in their baby, the homozygous state of this recessive disorder.

Because this patient has irregular menses, her dates are uncertain. An ultrasound is therefore needed to verify gestational age. Obstetric ultrasound performed in the first trimester can estimate gestational age (GA) via a crown–rump length measurement, which has an error of less than ±7 days. In the second trimester, GA can be estimated to within 10 to 14 days when based on calculations using the biparietal diameter and femur length measurements. Thereafter, intrinsic and extrinsic factors contribute to greater variation of growth in the fetus, making estimation of GA by ultrasound less accurate.

Given this patient's family history of mental retardation, chromosomal abnormalities and fragile X as well as other inherited disorders should be considered. Ideally, information about the patient's brother would be most helpful in establishing a diagnosis and deciding which, if any, testing is indicated for your patient.

CASE CONTINUED

Obstetrical ultrasound reveals a single live fetus at 16 weeks GA. Routine prenatal labs are normal except for a mild microcytic, hypochromic anemia. Review of records from the patient's brother revealed normal karyotype performed when he was 5 years old. Maternal serum triple screen correlated with the ultrasound dating is normal.

QUESTIONS

1. The most appropriate next step in the management of this patient's mild anemia with low MCV is:
   A. Do nothing because this represents physiologic anemia of pregnancy
   B. Iron sulfate 325 mg BID, repeat CBC in 4 to 6 weeks
   C. Hemoglobin electrophoresis, CBC in father of baby
   D. Amniocentesis, DNA testing for β thalassemia
   E. None of the above

2. Given this patient's family history, you recommend which of the following?
   A. Repeat chromosome analysis and DNA for fragile X testing on her brother.
   B. If her brother cannot be tested, amniocentesis with genetic testing may be offered.
   C. No further workup needed because ultrasound findings and triple screen are normal.
   D. Chromosome analysis of the mother.
   E. A and B are both correct.

3. Which of the following statements concerning gestational age assessment is INCORRECT?
   A. Maternal perception of fetal movements first occurs between 16 to 20 weeks.
   B. At 20 weeks gestation, the uterine fundus should be palpable at the level of the umbilicus (approximately 20 cm above the symphysis pubis).
   C. An intrauterine pregnancy cannot be seen by transvaginal ultrasound before 6 weeks GA.
   D. The uterine fundus can usually be palpated at the symphysis pubis at 12 weeks.
   E. Fetal heart tones can be heard with Doppler after 11 or 12 weeks.

4. Which of the following prenatal screening evaluations should be offered to the populations described?
   A. Cystic fibrosis, Canavan disease, and Tay-Sachs disease in Ashkenazi Jews
   B. Cystic fibrosis in a Hispanic couple with no family history of cystic fibrosis
   C. Sickle cell anemia in African-Americans
   D. A and C are correct
   E. A, B, and C are correct

ID/CC: 36-year-old G_4P_2 woman at 9 weeks GA by LMP presents with complaint of menstrual-like bleeding and cramping.

HPI: S.A. is now 9 weeks into her current pregnancy (dated by an LMP) and had a positive self-administered urine pregnancy test about 3 weeks ago. She notes that she had been doing well and actually has felt less nausea over the past week than the preceding few weeks until this evening, when she started having some abdominal cramping. About an hour later she noted that she was having vaginal spotting, which increased to menstrual-like flow over the past couple of hours.

PMHx/PSHx: None   **Meds:** PNV   **All:** NKDA

POb/GynHx: Two prior term vaginal deliveries, uncomplicated, 4 and 6 years ago. 1 first trimester TAB (therapeutic abortion) 13 years ago. Regular menses, every 29 to 30 days. No STIs, no pelvic surgery, no infertility.

SHx: Lives with husband and two children; no domestic violence. No tobacco or recreational drug use; social ethanol use.

VS: Temp 98.8°F, BP 118/72, HR 84, RR 16

PE: *Abdomen:* soft, nontender, no distension, no peritoneal signs. *SSE:* cervix closed, small amount of blood coming from os. *BME:* uterus anteverted (AV) and anteflexed (AF), approx 7 to 8 weeks in size and slightly tender; no cervical motion tenderness (CMT); no palpable adnexal masses.

Labs: Urine pregnancy test positive; Hct 37.4; β-hCG 24,122 mIU/mL

US: Pending

THOUGHT QUESTIONS
- What is in this patient's differential diagnosis?
- How does the beta human chorionic gonadotropin (β-hCG) value help, other than confirming the positive urine pregnancy test?
- How will the results of the pelvic ultrasound help in the diagnosis?

Mrs. A's differential diagnosis includes ectopic pregnancy, complete spontaneous abortion (SAB), and threatened abortion. She has no risk factors for ectopic pregnancy, but this remains the most dangerous possible diagnosis. It is estimated that approximately 15% to 20% of known pregnancies result in SAB (known to the layperson as a miscarriage); the percentage of all pregnancies that result in SAB is probably even higher. The primary etiology for first trimester SABs is abnormal karyotype, the most common of these being 45,XO, Turner syndrome. Other known etiologies for first trimester SAB include uterine abnormalities (e.g., bicornuate uterus, submucosal fibroids), luteal phase defect (believed to be due to corpus luteum progesterone production that is inadequate to maintain pregnancy), thrombophilias (e.g., antiphospholipid antibody syndrome, systemic lupus erythematosus), infections (e.g., cytomegalovirus, varicella zoster virus, herpes simple virus), and balanced translocation of a chromosome in one of the parents. Despite these numerous possible etiologies as well as extensive testing, most SABs are idiopathic.

The value of the β-hCG helps to guide what can be seen on ultrasound. With transvaginal ultrasound, an intrauterine pregnancy can be seen with a β-hCG of 1600–2000 and fetal heart motion can be seen with a β-hCG of 5000–6000. Thus, in this patient with a β-hCG of greater than 20,000, the pregnancy should be easily seen by ultrasound, provided it is normal. If an intrauterine pregnancy is seen, it rules out ectopic pregnancy, except in the extremely rare case of heterotopic pregnancy (one pregnancy in the uterus and one ectopic). Fetal heart motion should also be seen; if it is present, the risk of miscarriage is decreased to less than 5%.

CASE CONTINUED

US: Intrauterine gestational sac seen (Figure 2). However, no fetal pole is identified. No adnexal masses and no free fluid in the cul-de-sac.

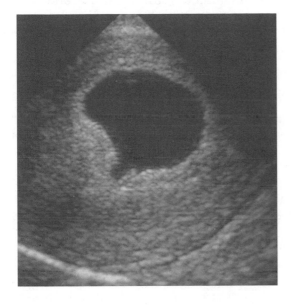

FIGURE 2 An intrauterine gestational sac that, although large enough, has no evidence of fetal pole. (Image provided by Departments of Radiology and Obstetrics & Gynecology, University of California, San Francisco.)

Upon returning from ultrasound, the patient has an increase in vaginal bleeding. Now when examined, the cervix is slightly dilated and there is continued bleeding from the os. A dilatation and curettage (D&C) is performed and the bleeding stops at the end of the procedure. Tissue is sent for pathology, which reveals trophoblastic tissue, but no fetal tissue.

QUESTIONS

5. Upon initial presentation with a closed cervix and a nonviable pregnancy, this patient's diagnosis was:
   A. Missed abortion
   B. Complete abortion
   C. Incomplete abortion
   D. Inevitable abortion
   E. Threatened abortion

6. When she returned from ultrasound with a dilated cervix, her diagnosis was:
   A. Missed abortion
   B. Complete abortion
   C. Incomplete abortion
   D. Inevitable abortion
   E. Threatened abortion

7. If the patient had not begun to dilate upon returning from ultrasound, which of the following management options would *not* be reasonable?
   A. Expectant management at home
   B. Dilation and curettage (D&C)
   C. Schedule D&C for 1 week later
   D. Misoprostol given vaginally
   E. Expectant management in the hospital

8. Given that this patient has now had one SAB, what is the probability of having another SAB in her next pregnancy?
   A. 15% to 20%
   B. 25%
   C. 30%
   D. 35%
   E. 40%

CASE 3 / HYPEREMESIS IN PREGNANCY

ID/CC: 21-year-old G_2P_1 woman at approximately 11 weeks GA by sure LMP complains of irregular vaginal bleeding, nausea, and vomiting.

HPI: M.P. is excited and happy about this pregnancy but notes worsening nausea and vomiting over the last 2 weeks, which is unlike her prior pregnancy. She feels nauseous most of the day and is unable to keep anything down other than the occasional water and saltine crackers. She also reports the onset of vaginal spotting and bleeding over the last few days. She denies any abdominal or back cramps.

PMHx: Hypothyroidism   **PSHx:** None   **Meds:** L-thyroxine, PNV   **All:** NKDA

POb/GynHx: One normal vaginal delivery (2 years ago). Regular menses every 28 days. No STIs or prior pelvic or abdominal surgery.

SHx: She is married and lives with her husband and son. No use of ethanol, tobacco, or recreational drugs.

VS: Temp 97.8°F, BP 120/65, HR 90, RR 20

PE: *Neck:* supple, mobile, no masses. *Abdomen:* soft, nontender, no distension. *Pelvic:* no cervical polyp or lesion. 15-week size uterus, nontender, no adnexal masses. *Doppler:* no fetal heart sounds by Doppler tones.

Labs: hCG 270,000 mIU/mL   **US:** Pending

THOUGHT QUESTIONS

- What does the differential diagnosis include for this patient?
- Which diagnostic tests would be most useful?
- Does the hCG value help?

The differential diagnosis of larger than expected uterine size and bleeding includes multiple gestation, inaccurate dating, uterine leiomyomas (fibroids) or adenomyosis, and gestational trophoblastic disease (GTD). If the uterus is enlarged because of fibroids or baseline adenomyosis, the differential diagnosis should include threatened miscarriage, ectopic pregnancy, and normal intrauterine pregnancy. An hCG level and a transvaginal ultrasound would help evaluate the state of the pregnancy. An abnormally high hCG level and a "snowstorm" pattern on ultrasound are diagnostic of GTD. Thyroid function tests would rule out hyperthyroidism as a cause of the hyperemesis.

CASE CONTINUED

The radiologist calls you with the findings of no evidence of a fetus, but a "snowstorm" pattern of swollen chorionic villi within the uterine cavity. You tell the patient that she has a molar pregnancy and explain some of the differences between a complete and an incomplete molar pregnancy (Table 3). Her thyroid function tests are normal, and a chest x-ray is negative for metastases. You arrange for a suction curettage to be performed.

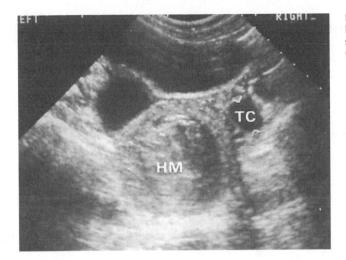

FIGURE 3 Complete molar pregnancy on ultrasound. Note the hydropic villi (seen as black lucent areas) and the general snowstorm appearance. (Chamberlin G. Lecture Notes on Obstetrics. 7th ed. Oxford: Blackwell Science, 1996.)

TABLE 3. Differences Between Complete and Incomplete Molar Pregnancies

FACTOR	COMPLETE	INCOMPLETE
Proportion	90%	10%
Karyotype	Diploid, usually 46,XX	Triploid, usually 69,XXY
POCs	No fetus, hydropic trophoblast	Associated fetus, hydropic trophoblast
Malignancy	15–23% of cases	4% of cases

QUESTIONS

9. What is the most common presenting symptom of a complete molar pregnancy?
   A. Hyperemesis
   B. Tachycardia
   C. Vaginal bleeding
   D. Dyspnea and tachypnea
   E. Abdominal distension and pain

10. The diagnosis of a complete hydatidiform mole has been confirmed following the suction curettage. What is the most appropriate management for this patient now?
    A. Weekly and then monthly hCG testing
    B. Repeat D&C if the hCG value is elevated
    C. Transvaginal ultrasonographic examination
    D. Chemotherapy

11. At 5 and 6 weeks after evacuation of the molar pregnancy her hCG levels are 10,900 and 12,100 mIU/mL, respectively. You are now worried about malignant GTD. Which of the following is *not* acceptable in her management?
    A. Single-agent chemotherapy with methotrexate
    B. Transvaginal ultrasound to evaluate the uterine cavity
    C. Repeat chest x-ray, abdominal-pelvic CT
    D. Hysterectomy and then chemotherapy
    E. Radiologic imaging of the brain

12. What hormone is proposed as the cause of hyperemesis associated with a molar pregnancy?
    A. Estrogen
    B. hCG
    C. Progesterone
    D. Total T_4
    E. Leuteinizing hormone (LH)

ID/CC: 40-year-old G_2P_0 woman at 7 weeks GA by LMP at her first prenatal visit.

HPI: A.M. spontaneously conceived after 2 years of trying. She is excited about the pregnancy but at the same time is concerned about potential risks for herself as well as the baby related to her age. Her husband is 52 years old, healthy, and has fathered two children from a prior marriage. The week prior to the visit, she experienced spotting that lasted 3 days and then resolved. Currently she has no complaints.

PMHx/PSHx: None **POb/GynHx:** Regular menses, every 30 days

Meds: PNV and folic acid **All:** NKDA

SHx: Lawyer and active tennis player, lives with husband and two cats. Denies tobacco or alcohol use.

FHx: Noncontributory **Labs:** Normal prenatal labs

THOUGHT QUESTIONS

- What adverse perinatal outcomes are associated with advanced maternal age? Advanced paternal age?
- Is advanced maternal age associated with increased maternal morbidity?
- What would be the appropriate test for fetal evaluation for this patient?

The risk of aneuploidy increases with age, increasing exponentially after age 35 years. As a result, there is an increased risk for spontaneous abortion, fetal demise and stillbirth, and a live-born child with chromosomal abnormality. Advanced paternal age is associated with an increased risk for autosomal dominant conditions due to spontaneous mutations. Because chronic illnesses such as hypertension, obesity, and diabetes mellitus type II are age related, there is increased maternal morbidity associated with advanced maternal age (>35 years). In addition, advanced maternal age has been associated with increased risk for preeclampsia, gestational diabetes, and cesarean birth. It is unclear whether these risks are purely associated with the risk for comorbidity from medical illness, or whether age is an independent risk factor.

Invasive genetic testing, either amniocentesis at 16 to 18 weeks GA or chorionic villus sampling (CVS) between 9.5 and 11 weeks GA, is routinely offered to women 35 and older. The a priori risk for a 35-year-old woman to have a fetus with aneuploidy at the time of amniocentesis is approximately 1 in 200. The risk of pregnancy loss secondary to the amniocentesis is estimated at 1 in 200. CVS has the advantage of providing a diagnosis 6 weeks earlier than amniocentesis, which may have psychological advantages for the woman. In addition, termination procedures are technically simpler and associated with less morbidity at earlier gestational ages. However, CVS has a slightly higher procedure-related pregnancy loss rate (approximately 0.5% to 1.0%) than 16-week amniocentesis.

CASE CONTINUED

The patient was offered an amniocentesis at 16 weeks GA but she declined due to the concern for miscarriage. Instead, she chose to have a level II ultrasound (detailed ultrasound survey of fetal anatomy) and maternal serum screening.

Her estriol, hCG, and α-fetoprotein (AFP) were low. At 18 weeks from her LMP, ultrasound showed a fetus consistent with 16 weeks size, increased amniotic fluid, club foot, omphalocele, choroid plexus cyst, and possible heart defect.

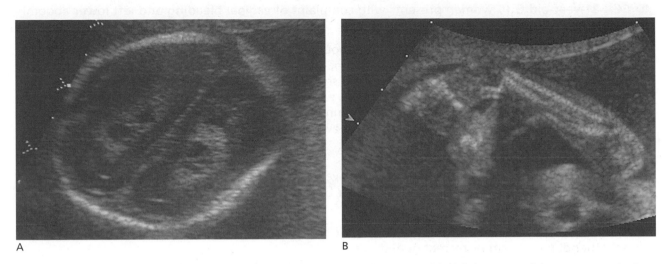

A   B

FIGURE 4 (A) Choroid plexus (CP) cyst located in the lateral ventricles of the brain. **(B)** Club foot. Note that you can see the leg straight on, but the foot is off at an angle. (Image provided by Departments of Radiology and Obstetrics & Gynecology, University of California, San Francisco.)

QUESTIONS

13. Based on the patient's history and data provided what is the most likely diagnosis?
    A. Trisomy 21
    B. Trisomy 13
    C. Trisomy 18
    D. X-linked ichthyosis
    E. Beckwith-Wiedemann syndrome

14. The risks of amniocentesis include which of the following?
    A. Alloimmunization of an Rh-negative woman carrying a Rh-positive fetus
    B. Small risk of fetal injury with the needle
    C. Premature rupture of membranes
    D. All of the above
    E. None of the above

15. Which of the following statements regarding ultrasound for the detection of chromosomal abnormalities is *false*?
    A. Ultrasound has a sensitivity of 50% for the detection of Down syndrome when done between 18 and 24 weeks.
    B. Nuchal translucency has a sensitivity of greater than 60% when used between 10 to 14 weeks for the detection of trisomy 21.
    C. A normal level II fetal ultrasound excludes the possibility of trisomy 21.
    D. Increased nuchal thickness, short femur, pyelectasis, and echogenic cardiac foci are sonographic variants that are seen more frequently in fetuses with Down syndrome.

16. Which of the following conditions are associated with advanced paternal age?
    A. 47,XXX
    B. Neurofibromatosis I
    C. Trisomy 21
    D. Cystic fibrosis
    E. Patau syndrome

ID/CC: 21-year-old G_1P_0 woman presents with complaint of vaginal bleeding and left lower abdominal pain for 1 day.

HPI: E.P. was in her usual state of health until about 18 hours prior to presenting to the emergency department. At that time she noted that she had begun vaginal spotting and had some crampy, non-radiating, left lower quadrant abdominal pain. As she was several weeks late for her period, she assumed that it was beginning. However, over the ensuing 12 to 18 hours, the pain became worse than her normal menses, while the bleeding remained spotting. She notes some mild nausea, no vomiting, and no anorexia; no fever or chills, no bowel symptoms, no dysuria.

PMHx/PSHx: None   **Meds:** None   **All:** NKDA

POb/GynHx: Menarche age 12, regular menses every 28 days until this cycle. Currently sexually active in a monogamous relationship; condoms for birth control (BC); normal Pap smear 7 months ago.

SHx: Junior at local university, lives in college dormitory; half-pack per day cigarette smoker; recreational ethanol use; no other recreational drugs.

VS: Temp 98.2°F, BP 110/58, HR 76, RR 16

PE: *Abdomen:* soft with mild tenderness in lower left quadrant, no peritoneal signs, no distension. *SSE:* cervix closed, small amount of old blood in vault. *BME:* uterus AV/AF, slightly enlarged and slightly tender. No CMT. No palpable adnexal masses, but some mild left adnexal tenderness.

Labs: Urine pregnancy test positive   **Blood:** Pending   **US:** Pending

---

THOUGHT QUESTIONS

- What is included in the differential diagnosis at this point?
- What is the most dangerous possible diagnosis in this patient?
- What lab tests are the most important in this patient?
- What findings on the ultrasound will help sort out the diagnosis?
- What further history might be helpful?

This young woman's differential diagnosis includes ectopic pregnancy, spontaneous abortion, threatened abortion, and ruptured corpus luteum. The most dangerous diagnosis she could have is that of ectopic pregnancy. Because the quantitative β-hCG level will help determine what should be seen on pelvic ultrasound, it is an important test to obtain. A CBC is important to ensure that she is not anemic from internal bleeding.

Patients who are pregnant and bleeding with abdominal pain should be treated as if they might have ectopic pregnancies until it is ruled out by an intrauterine pregnancy (IUP) being shown on ultrasound. A viable IUP will confirm pregnancy and make the diagnosis of threatened abortion. An IUP that is not viable or has partially passed confirms the diagnoses of missed abortion and incomplete abortion, respectively. An IUP plus moderate free fluid in the cul-de-sac is consistent with a hemorrhagic cyst—usually the corpus luteum.

In patients who are ruled out as ectopic pregnancy candidates, it is essential to obtain a history of possible ectopic risk factors and to carefully tease out the gestational age using LMP dating. Ectopic pregnancy occurs in approximately 1% to 2% of all pregnancies and has increased in incidence over the past few decades. Ectopic risk factors include prior ectopic pregnancy, pelvic inflammatory disease (PID), prior tubal or pelvic surgery, infertility, assisted reproduction, age <25, cigarette smoker, and current intrauterine device (IUD) use.

CASE CONTINUED

Labs: β-hCG 824; WBC 9.7; Hct 35.4

US: No IUP seen, no adnexal masses seen, small amount of free fluid in cul-de-sac

Upon further questioning, the patient reports PID at age 17. Her LMP was 7 weeks ago. Since the diagnosis of ectopic pregnancy cannot be ruled out for this patient, and she is hemodynamically stable and unsure whether this is a desired pregnancy, it is appropriate to discharge the patient with instructions to return in 2 days for another quantitative β-hCG test or to return sooner if the pain increases.

She returns in 2 days and her β-hCG is now 1462. Her vitals signs are normal. Repeat ultrasound is identical to the first one and she continues to have mild lower left quadrant pain. With the normal rise in her β-hCG (it should approximately double every 48 hours), the plan is made for her to return again in 48 hours for repeat testing.

QUESTIONS

For questions 17 and 18, select from the following diagnoses and corresponding management:
- A. Rule out ectopic, uterine aspiration
- B. Rule out ectopic, treat with methotrexate
- C. Normal pregnancy, follow up in 48 hours
- D. Spontaneous abortion, dilatation and evacuation (D&E)
- E. Spontaneous abortion, expectant management

17. If her second β-hCG had increased to 1026, what would be the diagnosis and plan?

18. If her second β-hCG had fallen to 422, what would be the diagnosis and plan?

19. If a patient presents similarly to the patient above with the exception of having the pelvic ultrasound shown in Figure 5 in addition to cervical motion tenderness, which of the following is the most appropriate management if it is a desired pregnancy?
- A. Exploratory laparotomy
- B. Exploratory laparoscopy
- C. Treat with methotrexate
- D. Expectant management
- E. Dilatation and curettage (D&C)

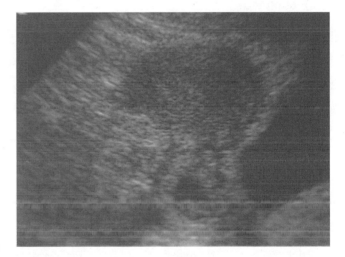

FIGURE 5

20. A patient presents with a β-hCG of 1160, hematocrit of 36, moderate lower left quadrant pain, but no peritoneal signs and an ultrasound that shows no IUP, but a small 1-cm adnexal mass distinct from the ovary. A D&C is performed which reveals no villi. The next step in her management is:
- A. Exploratory laparotomy
- B. Exploratory laparoscopy
- C. Treat with methotrexate
- D. Treat with methotrexate and misoprostol
- E. Treat with misoprostol

CASE 6 / ELEVATED MSAFP

ID/CC: 22-year-old G_1P_0 woman at 16 weeks GA by LMP has an elevated level of maternal serum α-fetoprotein (MSAFP).

HPI: N.T. receives a phone call from her obstetrician regarding the results of the triple screen test performed 5 days before. The study showed a MSAFP level of 4.1 MoM (multiples of the median). She initiated prenatal care at 10 weeks gestation, and was started on prenatal vitamins. Her physical exam 5 days prior was unremarkable, with a fundal height of 13 cm and positive fetal heart tones on Doppler.

PMHx/PSHx: None **Meds:** PNV **All:** Sulfas

POb/GynHx: Regular menses, every 27 to 29 days.

SHx: Lives with boyfriend who is supportive. No tobacco or ethanol use.

THOUGHT QUESTIONS

- What are the components of the triple screen and how is it interpreted?
- What are common causes of elevated MSAFP?
- What is the next step in the management of this case?

The triple screen, also known as the expanded AFP test, is a screening test for neural tube defects (NTDs) and fetal aneuploidy. Unlike invasive diagnostic tests, such as amniocentesis and chorionic villus sampling, the triple screen is a noninvasive screening test that involves evaluation of maternal serum levels of AFP, unconjugated estriol, and hCG. Because these serum levels depend on gestational age, the triple screen should be performed between 15 to 20 weeks GA. The levels of the individual markers are altered characteristically depending on the defect, as depicted in Table 6.

TABLE 6. Triple Screen Table

	TRISOMY 21	TRISOMY 18	TRISOMY 13	NTDs
MSAFP	Decreased	Decreased	Depends on defects	Increased
Estriol	Decreased	Decreased	Depends on defects	Normal
β-hCG	Elevated	Decreased	Depends on defects	Normal

Callahan T, Caughey A, Heffner L. Blueprints in Obstetrics and Gynecology. 2nd ed. Malden, MA: Blackwell Science, 2001:10.

α-Fetoprotein is a protein structurally similar to albumin that is synthesized by the fetal liver. Elevated MSAFP is used as a screening test primarily for the detection of neural tube defects. A decreased MSAFP is a marker for aneuploidy including trisomy 21. The more common causes of elevated MSAFP include incorrect dating, fetal demise, multiple gestation, neural tube defects, ventral abdominal wall defects (gastroschisis and omphalocele), placental abnormalities, and congenital nephrosis. Pregnancies in which there is no explanation for the increased AFP level, described as unexplained elevated MSAFP, are associated with an increased risk for adverse perinatal outcomes including intrauterine growth restriction (IUGR) and placental abruption. An ultrasound should be ordered after an abnormal level of MSAFP is detected. Because the serum AFP varies with gestational age, if the gestational age derived by ultrasound is different than by dates, the MSAFP value of multiples of the median (MoMs) is recalculated.

CASE CONTINUED

An obstetric ultrasound revealed a single, live fetus, with biometry consistent with 16 weeks GA (concordant with LMP). A 3-cm lumbosacral myelomeningocele was detected (Figure 6A). In addition, the banana and the lemon sign were present (Figure 6B), but no other fetal anomaly was identified. The patient was counseled and opted to terminate the pregnancy via dilatation and evacuation (D&E). Karyotype of the fetus revealed normal 46,XY.

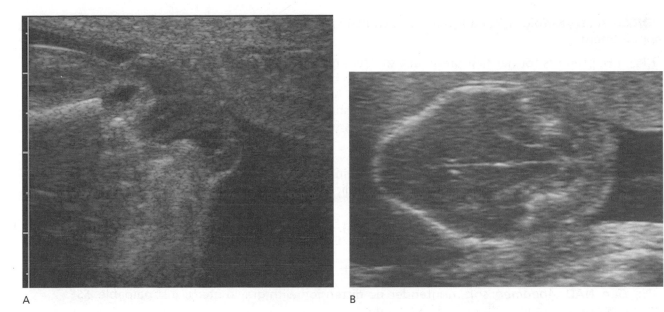

A   B

FIGURE 6 (A) In this transverse image of the lower spine, note that the skin is open and the myelomeningocele is coming through the opening. **(B)** The cerebral findings of neural tube defects include a bilateral indentation of the frontal bones (lemon sign) and an outward bowing of the cerebellar hemispheres (banana sign). (Image provided by Departments of Radiology and Obstetrics & Gynecology, University of California, San Francisco.)

QUESTIONS

21. The incidence of NTDs is associated with which of the following medications used in pregnancy?
    A. Valproic acid
    B. Lithium
    C. Fluoxetine
    D. Prednisone
    E. Tylenol

22. The recurrence of NTDs can be decreased by the administration of:
    A. 1 mg of folic acid from the time of missed LMP
    B. 4 mg of folic acid 1 month prior to conception until 12 weeks GA
    C. 0.4 mg of folic acid from conception through the end of the pregnancy
    D. Diet rich in leafy vegetables periconceptionally
    E. The recurrence of NTDs cannot be decreased

23. Unexplained elevated MSAFP is associated with all of the following except:
    A. Abruptio placentae
    B. Preeclampsia
    C. Intrauterine growth retardation
    D. Gestational diabetes

24. A 24-year-old patient is screened as positive for Down syndrome by MSAFP. Which of the following statements is false?
    A. The risk of trisomy 21 is increased when a couple has had an affected offspring with trisomy 21 if the affected offspring was conceived prior to maternal age 30 years.
    B. A normal ultrasound does not rule out Down syndrome.
    C. The likelihood of having trisomy 21 on a 16-week amniocentesis is smaller than having a live-born child with trisomy 21.
    D. It is important to obtain a karyotype of a child with Down syndrome because the genetic information may be predictive of recurrence in future pregnancies.

ID/CC: A 28-year-old G_4P_2 Caucasian woman at 13 weeks GA presents for her first prenatal care appointment.

HPI: F.H. presents for her first prenatal visit. Her pregnancy is at 13 weeks GA by a regular LMP. She notes that, in her last pregnancy, she was found to be Rh D-negative with antibodies to Rh D and was followed serially without requiring amniocentesis. At birth, that child was tested and found to be Rh D-negative as well. Both her first child and her husband, who is the father of both children, are Rh D-positive. She wants to know what the outlook is for this pregnancy.

PMHx/PSHx: None   **Meds:** PNV   **All:** NKDA

POb/GynHx: Two term, normal spontaneous vaginal deliveries. As above, first child Rh-positive, second child Rh-negative; neither child with complications of alloimmunization. One SAB between the two births.

SHx: Lives with Caucasian husband and two children; no domestic violence; social ethanol use; no tobacco or recreational drug use.

VS: Temp 97.8°F, BP 108/64, HR 78, RR 16; Weight: 154 lbs

PE: *Gen:* NAD. *Abdomen:* soft, nontender, no distension with gravid uterus just palpable. *SSE:* parous cervix, no abnormalities. *BME:* size = dates.

THOUGHT QUESTION

- Other than her initial prenatal laboratory tests, is there any other testing that should be done for this patient at this point?

As part of the prenatal laboratory tests, an antibody screen is done and a titer if the screen is positive. With this patient's history of being alloimmunized, she is likely to have a positive titer. At 13 weeks, no other particular testing should be done in this patient at this time. However, in many cases it is a good idea to offer genetic counseling about the issue of Rh D alloimmunization to the patient and her partner and to offer blood typing and DNA testing to the partner to determine zygosity. Because of the common occurrence of uncertain paternity, it is a good idea to address this issue in private with the patient as well.

CASE CONTINUED

Labs: O-negative blood type, Anti-D titer 1:8

At the patient's next visit at 16 weeks GA, she asks about the possibility of getting a blood type on the fetus. You discuss with her that at this point, as the antibody titer is less than 1:16, there is no reason to risk an invasive procedure. She subsequently has antibody titers drawn at both 16 and 20 weeks GA, which both return 1:8. However, at 24 weeks, the antibody titer rises to 1:32.

> **THOUGHT QUESTION**
> • What is the next step in the management of this patient?

At this point, with a titer that is at or above 1:16, there is a risk for developing hemolytic anemia in the fetus. Thus, an amniocentesis to assess the amniotic fluid for breakdown products of bilirubin should be performed. At the time of this amniocentesis, if there is even the slightest doubt about the likely blood type of the fetus, fetal cells can be collected and typed. The amniotic fluid is tested using a spectrophotometer, which measures light absorption of the fluid, expressed as the Δ OD 450. This measurement is plotted versus gestational age on a graph known as the Liley curve. The graph is divided into three sections: Zones I, II, and III. Values in Zone I and low-Zone II can be followed every 2 to 3 weeks with repeat amniocentesis. Values in mid-Zone II or a trend upward should be followed more frequently every week. Values in Zone III or a rapid ascension to high-Zone II warrants direct assessment of fetal hematocrit using percutaneous umbilical blood sampling (PUBS).

CASE CONTINUED

Ms. H. undergoes an amniocentesis that shows the Δ OD 450 to be in mid-Zone II. The ultrasound performed at the same time is entirely normal. She is scheduled to return in 1 week for a repeat amniocentesis and ultrasound. When she returns at 25 weeks GA, the ultrasound now shows some scalp thickening and a small collection of fluid in abdomen.

QUESTIONS

25. What is the next step in the management of this patient?
    A. Repeat amniocentesis
    B. PUBS to check fetal hematocrit
    C. PUBS for fetal transfusion
    D. Emergent delivery

26. Which of the following are *not* signs of fetal hydrops on ultrasound?
    A. Scalp thickening
    B. Ascites
    C. Pericardial effusion
    D. Pleural effusion
    E. Cystic hygroma

27. Based on this patient's history, her husband's Rh status is:
    A. Homozygous dominant (DD)
    B. Homozygous recessive (– –)
    C. Heterozygous (D–)
    D. 0.5 chance of D–, 0.5 chance of DD
    E. 0.33 chance of D–, 0.67 chance of DD

28. Given that the gene frequency of the D-negative allele is 0.4 among Caucasians, what is the probability that a fetus born to two Caucasian parents will be Rh negative?
    A. 0.48
    B. 0.16
    C. 0.36
    D. 0.0256
    E. 0.1216

CASE 8 / ELEVATED GLUCOSE LOADING TEST

ID/CC: 32-year-old G_2P_0 woman at 28 weeks GA with glucose level of 157 mg/dL after a 1-hour 50-gram oral glucose loading test (GLT).

HPI: This is a desired and uncomplicated pregnancy. G.D. has no complaints and reports normal fetal movements.

PMHx/PSHx: None   **Meds:** PNV   **All:** NKDA

SHx: Married. Denies tobacco, alcohol, or recreational drug use.

FHx: Mexican-American origin, no family history of diabetes.

VS: Temp afebrile, BP 110/68, HR 88. Weight 164 lbs, Height 5'4"

PE: *Gen:* 20-lbs weight gain since first visit at 10 weeks GA. *Abdomen:* soft, nontender, gravid. Fundal height 29 cm. *Doppler:* positive fetal heart tones. *Extremities:* trace edema, left = right.

Labs: Urine dipstick: no proteinuria, positive glucosuria

THOUGHT QUESTIONS

- Who should be screened for diabetes during pregnancy and when?
- What is the appropriate next step in management for this patient?

Screening for gestational diabetes mellitus (GDM) among only those with risk factors would miss about 50% of GDM women. Risk factors for GDM include age greater than 30 years, obesity, race/ethnicity (Hispanics, Native Americans, and Pacific Islanders), prior history of GDM, history of large for gestational age infant, history of fetal demise of unknown etiology, and first-degree relative with diabetes mellitus. The current recommendation is to screen all pregnant women between 24 and 28 weeks GA. Women at increased risk for GDM should be screened at the first prenatal visit with a fasting glucose; again at 16 to 20 weeks GA; and finally with a GLT at 26 to 28 weeks GA.

In this patient with an abnormal 1-hour GLT of 157 mg/dL (normal: <140 mg/dL), a 3-hour glucose tolerance test (GTT) with 100 grams of glucose is indicated; GDM is diagnosed if either two or more values are elevated, or the fasting glucose is >95 mg/dL.

TABLE 8A. Glucose Screening Tests During Pregnancy

TEST	NORMAL GLUCOSE LEVEL (mg/dL)
Fasting	<105
1 hour after 50-gram glucose load	<140
2 hours after 100-gram glucose load	<165

Callahan T, Caughey A, Heffner L. Blueprints in Obstetrics and Gynecology. 2nd ed. Malden: Blackwell Science, 2001:76.

TABLE 8B. Three-Hour Glucose Tolerance Test: Venous and Plasma Criteria for GDM

TIMING OF GLUCOSE MEASUREMENT	NORMAL WHOLE VENOUS BLOOD GLUCOSE (mg/dL)	NORMAL PLASMA GLUCOSE (mg/dL)
Fasting	90	105
1 hour	165	190
2 hour	145	165
3 hour	125	145

Callahan T, Caughey A, Heffner L. Blueprints in Obstetrics and Gynecology. 2nd ed. Malden, MA: Blackwell Science, 2001:77.

CASE CONTINUED

You order a glucose tolerance test (GTT), which reveals a fasting glucose of 93 mg/dL, 1-hour at 198 mg/dL, 2-hour at 167 mg/dL, and 3-hour at 134 mg/dL.

> *THOUGHT QUESTION*
>
> - Based on this testing you diagnose her as having gestational diabetes. What treatment and follow-up examinations would you recommend?

With confirmation of her diagnosis, treatment should be initiated, ideally in consultation with a perinatologist and a dietitian who have experience with diabetics. Ninety percent of GDM patients are well-controlled with diabetic diet alone. In contrast to nonpregnant type II diabetic patients, weight loss during pregnancy is not recommended. Daily home monitoring of finger stick blood glucose (FSBG) levels (specifically for fasting, and 1-hour or 2-hour postprandial levels) in addition to assessment after 1 week of dietary changes is typically recommended for GDM patients. Targeted glucose levels for GDM patients should be as close as possible to levels of the non-GDM population (fasting less than 95 mg/dL, 1-hour postprandial less than 140 mg/dL, 2-hour postprandial less than 120 mg/dL).

You start her on an ADA diet and instruct her on home glucose monitoring of fasting and 1-hour postprandial FSBG levels. She returns for a follow-up evaluation in 1 week. Her FSBG values the day prior to follow up are pre-breakfast, 105 mg/dL; 1-hour post breakfast, 154 mg/dL; 1 hour post lunch, 171 mg/dL; and 1-hour post-dinner, 168 mg/dL, all of which are consistent with her values on prior days. The patient states that she has been compliant with her diet.

QUESTIONS

29. What would be the most appropriate next step in management?
    - A. Hospitalize the patient to ensure she follows a strict ADA diet
    - B. Continue diabetic teaching and reevaluate in 1 week
    - C. Begin oral hypoglycemic agent titrating dose to achieve adequate metabolic control
    - D. Start insulin and continue FSBG monitoring at home
    - E. Hospitalize to begin diabetic teaching and initiation of insulin therapy until metabolic control is obtained

30. Which of the following complications is *not* associated with GDM?
    - A. Macrosomic infant
    - B. Increased risk for shoulder dystocia and brachial plexus injury
    - C. Neonatal polycythemia
    - D. Neonatal hypoglycemia
    - E. Increased risk for major malformations

31. Which of the following is correct with regard to peripartum management and delivery of GDM patients?
    - A. Antenatal testing should be started between 32 to 34 weeks GA only in diabetic patients on insulin.
    - B. NPH insulin should continue to be administered throughout labor and delivery.
    - C. Glucosuria is a reliable indicator of poor metabolic control among GDM patients.
    - D. GDM patients should not be induced prior to 41 weeks, regardless of their glucose control.

32. She has a normal spontaneous vaginal delivery (NSVD) at term of a 3.9-kg female infant. For her postpartum management you recommend:
    - A. Continue ADA diet and follow FSBG for 48 hours
    - B. Continue insulin drip for 48 hours postpartum
    - C. Regular diet, follow-up testing 6 weeks postpartum with a fasting and 75-gram glucose loading test
    - D. Regular diet, check fasting glucose once a year starting at age 35
    - E. Continue with ADA diet; decrease insulin to one-half the antepartum dose

ID/CC: 24-year-old G_3P_2 woman at 28 weeks GA by LMP presents with complaint of low backache for 3 hours.

HPI: P.L. works part-time at a nursery school and cares for her own two young children. She awoke this morning with mild low back pain and cramping that has grown progressively worse since she went to work. Despite lying down while waiting to be seen by the doctor, she continues to have this pain and has felt abdominal tightening approximately every 5 to 10 minutes. She noticed a small amount of vaginal spotting after wiping, but has not had any loss of fluid. She confirms normal fetal movement and denies having any dysuria, nausea, or vomiting, fever or chills, or any change in bowel movements.

Ms. L notes that this pregnancy has been uncomplicated, though she has had to miss many of her prenatal appointments due to her busy schedule. Her triple marker screen was negative, her 1-hour glucola test (50-gram glucose load) for diabetes was 88 (<140 is within normal limits), and her original urine and cervical cultures were negative.

PMHx/PSHx: None   **Meds:** PNV   **All:** NKDA

POb/GynHx: 1 prior term vaginal delivery, 1 prior preterm vaginal delivery at 32 weeks GA.

SHx: Lives with husband and 2 children.

VS: Temp 98.0°F, BP 104/64, HR 90, RR 16. Weight: 110 lbs

PE: *Abdomen:* soft, nontender; contractions palpable. *FHT* (fetal heart rate tracing): 140s, no decelerations. *Toco:* uterine contractions every 5 minutes. *SVE:* 1-cm dilation, 25% effacement, midposition, soft, −3 station. GBS culture and vaginal swabs obtained.

Labs: Urine: specific gravity 1.030, nitrite and esterase negative. Wet prep: positive clue cells, no *Trichomonas*

THOUGHT QUESTIONS

- What are this patient's risk factors and possible causes for preterm labor?
- Is this patient in preterm labor?
- What should be done immediately to help stop this patient's contractions?
- What agents are used for stopping contractions and how do they work?

This patient's risk factors/potential causes for preterm labor include bacterial vaginosis (BV), prepregnant maternal weight of <110 lbs, and a previous preterm delivery. The latter is her most significant risk factor, increasing her risk threefold over the existing baseline risk in the population of 7% to 8%. In addition, the patient is dehydrated with an elevated urine specific gravity, which can lead to preterm contractions. Theoretically, this is thought to be due to the elevated levels of antidiuretic hormone (ADH) that arise in response to dehydration and subsequently cross-react with the oxytocin receptor.

Although contractions do occur normally in pregnancy before term, contractions that cause cervical change are abnormal and define preterm labor. Given this patient's risk factors for preterm labor and her frequent contractions, intravenous hydration should be initiated. Many practitioners will also consider giving a dose of SQ terbutaline to see whether the contractions can be easily resolved.

Many agents are used for tocolysis. However, only one, ritodrine, is actually FDA approved for this purpose. There are currently five classes of tocolytics: β-mimetics (terbutaline, ritodrine), calcium channel blockers (nifedipine), prostaglandin inhibitors (indomethacin), oxytocin receptor antagonists, and magnesium sulfate. Most tocolytics essentially work by decreasing the availability of intracellular calcium, which is needed to initiate uterine contractions.

CASE CONTINUED

The patient continues to contract despite the SQ terbutaline and IV fluids. The repeat cervical exam 1 hour later reveals her cervix to be 2-cm dilated with 50% effacement. She is admitted to the hospital and immediately receives betamethasone 12 mg IM, and a 6-gram bolus of magnesium sulfate ($MgSO_4$) followed by a 2-gram/hour maintenance rate of $MgSO_4$. As part of her management she is given Flagyl to treat the BV and also started on IV penicillin. After 48 hours of magnesium sulfate, the infusion is stopped. She remains acontractile for the ensuing 24 hours with no further cervical change past 2-cm dilated and 50% effacement. There is much debate about the usefulness of a fetal fibronectin screen in this patient, but in the end a fetal fibronectin test is performed with a negative result.

QUESTIONS

33. Why does this patient receive penicillin?
    A. As prophylaxis for chorioamnionitis
    B. As treatment for bacterial vaginosis
    C. To help prevent rupture of membranes
    D. As prophylaxis for Group B *Streptococcus* (GBS)

34. When should she receive her second dose of betamethasone?
    A. 6 hours later
    B. 12 hours later
    C. 24 hours later
    D. 48 hours later

35. What is the mechanism by which magnesium sulfate works to decrease contractions?
    A. It is a calcium antagonist and membrane stabilizer.
    B. It increases cAMP thus decreasing free calcium ions.
    C. It blocks calcium channels.
    D. It is a prostaglandin inhibitor decreasing levels of intracellular calcium.

36. What is the utility of a fetal fibronectin test in preterm labor?
    A. It has a good positive predictive value in helping to determine who will deliver prematurely.
    B. It has a good negative predictive value in helping to determine who will not deliver prematurely.
    C. It has a high sensitivity in determining who has had premature rupture of membranes.
    D. It has a high sensitivity for determining who has chorioamnionitis.

ID/CC: 22-year-old G_1P_0 woman at 28 weeks GA presents with new onset abdominal pain and fever.

HPI: A.A. reports gradual, progressive pain over the last 12 hours that is localized to the right lateral/flank area without radiation. The pain is now 8/10, constant with occasional exacerbations, and worse with walking. She also notes anorexia, and feeling "warm." She denies any nausea or vomiting. Her last bowel movement was 2 days ago. She reports increased urinary frequency over the last month but no dysuria or hematuria. She has felt some "tightening" of the uterus over the last couple of hours.

PMHx/PSHx: None **Meds:** PNV **All:** NKDA

POb/GynHx: Regular menses. *Chlamydia* infection at age 16 years, no other history of STIs.

SHx: Single, lives with father of baby. Denies tobacco, ethanol, or recreational drug use.

VS: Temp 38.3°C, BP 102/54, HR 110, RR 18, O_2 saturation 99% on RA.

PE: *Gen:* Caucasian female, appears ill. *HEENT:* unremarkable except for mildly dry mouth and lips, neck supple, no lymph adenopathy. *Cor:* unremarkable. *Abdomen:* soft, mildly tender to deep palpation and worse at periumbilical area lateral to the uterus; subtle, localized rebound tenderness, no guarding; bowel sounds present. No costovertebral angle tenderness (CVAT). The uterus is soft and nontender, with a fundal height of 26 cm. *Pelvic exam:* long and closed cervix, minimal vaginal discharge, and moderate tenderness in the right adnexal region without palpable mass. *Rectal exam:* tender. *Doppler:* fetal heart tones in 150s.

Labs: Stool guaiac negative

THOUGHT QUESTIONS

- What is the differential diagnosis for this patient?
- Which initial studies would you order?
- How should this patient be managed initially?

The differential for acute abdominal pain and fever is broad and includes gastrointestinal (GI), obstetric/gynecologic (Ob/Gyn), and genitourinary (GU) origins. With regard to Ob/Gyn causes, torsion of adnexal mass, ruptured ovarian mass, and degenerating fibroid should be considered, but the clinical presentation described is not typical for these. Chorioamnionitis is another obstetric etiology. GU causes include pyelonephritis and urinary tract stones. Careful physical examination and urinalysis (UA) are important in excluding these diagnoses. GI causes include appendicitis, cholecystitis, and pancreatitis. Of these, appendicitis should be strongly considered, given the patient's presentation. In pregnancy, the diagnosis of appendicitis is often delayed, possibly due to the different localization of the appendix secondary to displacement by the gravid uterus, and also because of the relative decrease in peritoneal signs as compared to nonpregnant patients.

CBC with differential, liver transaminases, amylase, lipase, and UA tests should be obtained for diagnostic purposes. In addition, electrolytes, blood urea nitrogen (BUN), and creatinine (Cr) should be ordered to assess her fluid/renal status. Ultrasound of the abdomen and pelvis or spiral CT of the abdomen and pelvis are important tools to narrow the differential diagnosis. A nonstress test (NST) should be obtained on arrival to assess fetal well-being and to clarify uterine activity. An amniocentesis to rule out chorioamnionitis at this moment does not appear indicated. This patient should be admitted for close observation, made NPO, given IV fluids, pain control, and correction of electrolyte abnormalities. A surgical consultation should be obtained.

CASE CONTINUED

You decide to admit the patient for the above management. Her initial laboratory studies show a WBC of 16.2 with left shift, Hb 11.7, and platelets 180K. Liver transaminases are within normal limits; amylase 32. UA shows a specific gravity of 1.020 but is otherwise negative. She is seen by general surgery who request a spiral CT of the abdomen and pelvis.

QUESTIONS

37. Over the next 2 hours her pain is persistent, and on exam she is tachycardic and has localized rebound tenderness. The next step in management is:
    A. Laparoscopy
    B. Exploratory laparotomy
    C. IV antibiotics
    D. Repeat CT scan of abdomen and pelvis
    E. IV fluid bolus of crystalloids

38. If the patient goes to surgery for a possible appendectomy, which of the following would be your recommendation for tocolysis?
    A. Prophylactic IV tocolysis with magnesium sulfate
    B. Tocolytics only for the development of regular uterine contractions and/or cervical change
    C. Tocolysis not indicated, given her cervical exam on admission
    D. Prophylactic tocolysis with IV ritodrine (β_2-agonist)
    E. Use of Demerol for painful uterine contractions

39. Regarding the use of corticosteroids for fetal lung maturity in this patient, which of the following is the *best* answer?
    A. Should never be used in the setting of an acute infection.
    B. Have little or no effect in reducing respiratory distress syndrome (RDS) at this gestational age therefore not indicated.
    C. Should be used if there is concern for premature delivery prior to 34 weeks GA.
    D. Steroids cause WBC elevation and hence would make follow up of her clinical condition difficult.
    E. The fetus is already "stressed" due to the maternal infection and therefore corticosteroids are not recommended.

40. Four days after her surgery, the patient develops painful uterine contractions and progressive cervical change, despite tocolytics. Which of the following is correct regarding intrapartum management?
    A. Allow for trial of vaginal delivery if cephalic presentation.
    B. Vaginal delivery is contraindicated due to risk of anterior abdominal wall defect secondary to recent laparotomy.
    C. Early epidural anesthesia should be used.
    D. Encourage vaginal delivery for breech presentation.
    E. Cesarean section is contraindicated because of the risk of wound infection.

ID/CC: 32-year-old G_1P_0 woman at 29 weeks GA presents with complaint of leakage of fluid for 2 days.

HPI: R.M. has had an uncomplicated pregnancy until 2 days ago when she noted a moderate amount of fluid on her underwear. She felt a gush of fluid at that time and has since noted leakage of small amounts of clear fluid. She is uncertain whether it is urine, as she has at times had difficulty controlling her bladder, especially during active fetal movement. She has not noticed any contractions, cramps, vaginal bleeding, fevers, or chills. She denies having dysuria but has had urinary frequency.

PMHx: Migraine headaches **PSHx:** Appendectomy **Meds:** PNV **All:** NKDA

POb/GynHx: Unremarkable. No STIs or PID.

SHx: Works as an accountant. Lives with father of baby. No ethanol, tobacco, or recreational drug use.

> *THOUGHT QUESTIONS*
> - What type of vaginal exam should you do?
> - How can you distinguish between urine and amniotic fluid?
> - What is the difference between PROM and PPROM?
> - If the bag of water is ruptured, what might be the plan of management?

If this patient has ruptured membranes, you do not want to increase her risk of infection by performing a digital vaginal exam. Therefore, an exam using a sterile speculum is performed. On this exam you will look for evidence of rupture—a pool of fluid in the vagina which has a basic pH (a "positive nitrazine test") and reveals a ferning pattern when dried on a slide. Urine may have a basic pH, but will not fern on a slide. PROM is premature rupture of membranes ("premature" meaning prior to the onset of labor); PPROM is preterm premature rupture of the membranes (preterm meaning prior to 37 weeks gestation). SROM is spontaneous rupture of the membranes, which means the membranes rupture of their own accord, as opposed to AROM (artificial rupture of the membranes), which means a clinician intentionally ruptures the membranes, usually performed with an amniotomy hook.

There are two particularly important neonatal outcomes that can result from PPROM: preterm delivery with the risks of prematurity and neonatal infection/sepsis from chorioamnionitis. The management of PPROM is therefore a balance, weighing the risk of prematurity with the risk of the development of perinatal infection. Thus, at very early gestational ages (<32 to 34 weeks), if there is no overt sign of chorioamnionitis, a course of antenatal corticosteroids (ACS), usually betamethasone or dexamethasone, is given to help reduce the incidence of respiratory distress syndrome (RDS) in preterm neonates by enhancing fetal lung maturity. In addition, there is evidence that ACS reduces other morbidity associated with prematurity including intraventricular hemorrhage and necrotizing enterocolitis. At gestational ages beyond 34 weeks, the risks of prematurity are less; therefore, ACS is not administered and delivery is allowed to occur, and in certain cases is even induced. At all gestational ages, if chorioamnionitis develops, labor is induced or augmented to decrease the risk of neonatal infection/sepsis.

CASE CONTINUED

VS: Temp 98.0°F, BP 100/62, HR 80, RR 16

PE: *Gen:* NAD. *Abdomen:* soft, nontender. Fundal height 28 cm. *SSE:* cervix appears closed, positive pooling of clear yellow fluid, positive nitrazine, positive ferning. *FHT:* 130s, reactive. *Toco:* uterine contractions every 20 minutes.

Labs: Urine: Specific gravity 1.010; pH 6.0; negative nitrite/esterase/blood; WBC 10.0. Sonogram: vertex presentation, AFI 6.0.

Given the sterile speculum exam findings and the low AFI (a normal AFI at this GA is >8), this patient has ruptured membranes. Her nontender abdominal exam, normal temperature, lack of significant contractions, and normal white blood cell count suggest that she has not developed chorioamnionitis. She is admitted to the hospital for expectant management of PPROM. She is given 12 mg IM of betamethasone with a repeat dose 24 hours later and is started on an ampicillin and erythromycin IV. On hospital day 2 she develops infrequent contractions, uterine tenderness, and a fever to 101.9°F. She is started on Pitocin and makes rapid progress through labor. She delivers a viable 1200-gram male infant.

QUESTIONS

41. What is the primary reason this patient is given ampicillin and erythromycin?
    A. Group B *Streptococcus* prophylaxis
    B. To increase the latency period to the onset of labor
    C. To prevent the development of chorioamnionitis
    D. To help prevent a bladder infection

42. In most cases of PPROM, the cause is:
    A. preterm contractions
    B. amniocentesis
    C. unknown, possibly a subclinical infection
    D. sexually transmitted infections

43. Given the early gestational age of this fetus, why is Pitocin begun rather than a tocolytic?
    A. To help prevent the development of chorioamnionitis
    B. To help prevent neonatal sepsis
    C. To help prevent abruption
    D. To help prevent fetal distress

44. Beyond which gestational age would PPROM without overt chorioamnionitis be a reason for immediate delivery through induction?
    A. 28 weeks
    B. 30 weeks
    C. 32 weeks
    D. 35 weeks

CASE 12 / SIZE LESS THAN DATES

ID/CC: 34-year-old $G_4P_2S_1$ woman at 28 weeks GA by LMP with size less than dates.

HPI: G.R. has a scheduled prenatal office visit with you. She denies any symptoms except mild ankle swelling. Her blood pressures have remained in the 130–140/70–90 range since you switched her from benazepril to labetalol at her first prenatal visit (8 weeks GA), and she states that she has been compliant with her medications. She has been charting "kick counts" since you instructed her to begin 3 weeks ago; they are normal. She has no complaints of headache, visual changes, right upper quadrant pain, or increased edema.

PMHx: Chronic hypertension diagnosed after her last pregnancy 2 years ago.

PSHx: None   **Meds:** PNV; labetalol 100 mg BID   **All:** NKDA

POb/GynHx: 2 full-term NSVD resulting in 2 viable infants, both >7 lbs; pregnancies were complicated by pregnancy-induced hypertension (PIH).

SHx: Lives with husband and 2 children. No tobacco, ethanol or recreational drug use.

VS: BP 142/89, HR 92

PE: *Gen:* NAD. *Cor:* RR&R, 1/6 SEM, no S_3, no S_4. *Abdomen:* soft, nontender, no distension, gravid with a fundal height (measured from the pubic symphysis to the top of the uterine fundus) of 24 cm, a 1-cm increment from her prior visit 4 weeks ago. *Extremities:* mild bilateral ankle edema, 2+ DTR bilaterally.

Labs: Urine dipstick: negative proteinuria. Normal prenatal labs, Rh positive.

US: At 16 weeks GA, confirmed a single, live fetus with a normal fetal anatomy survey, and size equal to dates.

THOUGHT QUESTIONS

- How is uterine fundal measurement used?
- What are the causes of size less than dates?
- What is the next best step in the management of this case?
- Why was the ACE-inhibitor changed to labetalol?

Measuring the uterine fundus and documenting its continual growth is a very simple method to monitor fetal growth. In general, the uterus is expected to increase by approximately 1 cm per week, and beyond 20 weeks GA, the fundal height in centimeters should equal the GA in weeks. The most common causes for size less than dates are incorrect dating, small for gestational age (SGA) fetus (estimated fetal weight below the 5th or 10th percentile), transverse fetal lie, and oligohydramnios (from premature rupture of the membranes or decreased/absent fetal production of urine). Clinical estimation of fetal size is not very accurate and cannot usually differentiate between the above causes.

The next step in management is to obtain an ultrasound for estimated fetal weight (EFW). If the EFW is less than 5% to 10%, the fetus is termed SGA. In general, possible causes for an SGA fetus include incorrect dating, chromosomal abnormalities, fetal anomalies, maternal/fetal infections, abnormal placentation, and maternal vascular diseases (rheumatologic, cardiovascular, or long-standing diabetes).

Because ACE inhibitors can lead to severe fetal renal dysfunction and death, especially when used in the second and third trimester, their use is contraindicated during pregnancy. Labetalol, a β-blocker that also offers some alpha blockade, is commonly used for blood pressure management in pregnancy.

CASE CONTINUED

Ultrasound at 28 2/7 weeks GA (based on dates by 16-week sonogram) shows an active, male, cephalic fetus. The placenta is posterior, with no evidence of previa. The amniotic fluid volume, measured by the amniotic fluid index (AFI), is low-normal at 8.9 (normal AFI: 5 to 20). A detailed survey of fetal anatomy did not reveal any abnormalities. Fetal growth is at the 19th percentile for GA. A biophysical profile (BPP) is 8 out of 8, and umbilical cord Doppler flow is within normal limits. You discuss these findings with the patient and recommend continuing her current antihypertensive regimen and daily kick counts, with the addition of modified bedrest, a weekly blood pressure check and urine dipstick, and weekly antenatal testing with nonstress test (NST) and AFI. You schedule a repeat ultrasound in 3 weeks to check for fetal growth, which subsequently shows no interval fetal growth, and a decreased AFI of 3.0; umbilical cord Doppler flow evaluation shows absent end-diastolic flow.

QUESTIONS

45. The most appropriate next step in management is:
    A. Hospitalize, continuous FHT monitoring, induction of fetal lung maturity with corticosteroids and plan for delivery in 48 hours
    B. Daily NST and plan delivery at 34 weeks if blood pressures remain stable
    C. Continue with pregnancy until 37 weeks if there is no evidence of preeclampsia
    D. Optimize blood pressure control and reassess fetal growth in 2 weeks
    E. Cesarean section

46. While the patient is on the FHT monitoring, the fetal heart rate drops to 60 beats per minute (bpm). Despite conservative measures (oxygen and changing patient position), it remains in the 60s for the next 6 minutes. Her BP is 154/98, and her cervix is 1 cm open and 3 cm long. She is not contracting. The next step in management is:
    A. Amnioinfusion
    B. Begin Pitocin induction
    C. Emergent cesarean section
    D. Hydralazine, 5 mg IV
    E. Administer betamethasone

47. Which of the following is not associated with intrauterine growth restriction (IUGR)?
    A. Antiphospholipid antibody syndrome
    B. Turner syndrome
    C. Chronic hypertension
    D. Gestational diabetes
    E. Congenital cytomegalovirus (CMV)

48. Which of the following is the best predictor of fetal mortality in a high-risk patient at 31 weeks GA?
    A. Nonreactive NST
    B. 6 out 10 BPP
    C. Reverse diastolic flow in umbilical cord Doppler
    D. Positive oxytocin challenge test (OCT)
    E. Zero kick counts in 1 hour

CASE 13 / SIZE GREATER THAN DATES

ID/CC: 32-year-old G_1P_0 woman at 26 weeks GA by LMP, size greater than dates.

HPI: T.G. is a 32-year-old kindergarten teacher who has had an uncomplicated, planned pregnancy. She prefers to minimize testing and declined the serum screen in the second trimester. She notes rapid breathing but is not short of breath. She reports approximately one to two Braxton-Hicks contractions per hour during the past week. No other complaints.

PMHx/PSHx: None   **Meds:** None   **All:** NKDA

SHx: Lives with her husband in a large urban area. Emigrated to the United States 4 years ago from Eastern Europe.

FHx: Noncontributory   **VS:** BP 110/60, HR 94, RR 24

PE: *Gen:* NAD. *Lungs:* clear to auscultation. *Cor:* RR&R, no murmurs. *Abdomen:* soft, nontender, gravid. Fundal height 31 cm. *Doppler:* positive fetal heart tones. Probable vertex presentation by Leopold's. *SVE:* closed and long, vertex presentation, −3 station.

Labs: Normal prenatal labs except rubella nonimmune, Hb 11.2, MCV 90

THOUGHT QUESTIONS

- What is the differential diagnosis for size greater than dates (S > D)?
- What is the next best step in management?
- What steps should be taken regarding her rubella nonimmune status?

Incorrect dating, large for gestational age (LGA) fetus (>90%), polyhydramnios, multiple gestation, and large uterine fibroids are the more common causes of S > D. Obesity is often associated with S > D due to difficulty in evaluating the uterine fundus. In addition, obesity is associated with GDM and LGA infants even in the absence of diabetes.

Ultrasound is helpful in determining GA, multiple gestations, fetal weight, amniotic fluid volume, as well as evaluation of the uterus and adnexa. In cases where polyhydramnios is identified, a detailed fetal anatomy survey (level II ultrasound) is required to exclude fetal and placental causes of increased amniotic fluid. Prior to the routine use of obstetric ultrasound, 50% of twin pregnancies were not diagnosed until delivery.

The patient is rubella nonimmune, but because she is greater than 20 weeks in pregnancy her risk of congenital rubella syndrome is quite small. She should be vaccinated immediately postpartum, as there is a small, theoretical (no cases reported) risk of transmission of this live attenuated virus to the fetus.

CASE CONTINUED

Ultrasound reveals a dichorionic–diamniotic twin pregnancy (Figure 13), vertex–vertex presentation, and concordant growth at 26 weeks by anthropometrics (fetal measurements such as biparietal diameter, femur length, and abdominal circumference). Amniotic fluid is normal and the placentas are posterior and fundal.

Two weeks later, she complains of painful uterine contractions every 3 to 4 minutes. She notes no bleeding and no loss of fluid, and the fetuses are very active. Her cervical exam is 2-cm dilated, 80% effaced, vertex at −2 station.

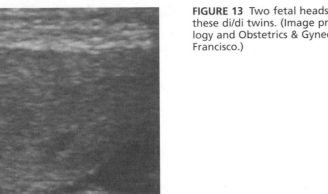

FIGURE 13 Two fetal heads separated by a thick membrane in these di/di twins. (Image provided by Departments of Radiology and Obstetrics & Gynecology, University of California, San Francisco.)

QUESTIONS

49. The most appropriate management in this case includes which of the following?
    A. Tocolysis, betamethasone (12 mg, 2 doses, 24 hours apart), ampicillin
    B. Ampicillin, prepare for imminent delivery
    C. Epidural anesthesia, prepare for delivery
    D. Tocolysis, erythromycin
    E. Trendelenburg position, cervical cerclage

50. The patient received one of the above therapies and developed gradual onset of shortness of breath and low O_2 saturations. What is the most likely diagnosis?
    A. Pulmonary embolism
    B. Amniotic fluid embolism
    C. Pulmonary edema
    D. Myocardial infarction
    E. Deep venous thromboembolism

51. In the management of twins, which of the following is *incorrect*?
    A. Amniocentesis should routinely be offered to women over the age of 32 with twin gestations.
    B. The single most important cause of perinatal mortality in twins is related to malformations.
    C. Serial ultrasounds are recommended to assess fetal growth.
    D. Preeclampsia is more common in twin than singleton gestations.
    E. Dichorionic–diamniotic twins can be either monozygotic or dizygotic.

52. Which of the following statements is *incorrect* regarding amniotic fluid disorders?
    A. Fetal duodenal atresia is frequently associated with polyhydramnios.
    B. Maternal diabetes mellitus is associated with polyhydramnios.
    C. Therapeutic (reduction) amniocentesis is indicated for maternal respiratory distress.
    D. Fetal neurologic disorders that affect swallowing cause oligohydramnios.
    E. Twin-to-twin transfusion syndrome results in polyhydramnios and oligohydramnios of the recipient and donor twins, respectively.

ID/CC: 26-year-old G_2P_1 Hispanic woman at 33 weeks GA presents complaining of a decrease in her baby's movements.

HPI: F.T. states that her baby is usually quite active in the mornings and evenings. Last evening she noticed a few movements before she fell asleep, but this morning she felt no movement after awakening. She ate breakfast and laid down on her couch to concentrate on the movements. During the following hour she felt the baby move only twice. She states that she has otherwise been feeling well. She denies having any contractions, loss of fluid, or vaginal bleeding. Ms. T presented late for prenatal care at 24 weeks gestation but has otherwise had an uncomplicated pregnancy. She is dated by a 24-week ultrasound as her LMP was uncertain.

PMHx: Migraine headaches   **PSHx:** None   **Meds:** PNV   **All:** NKDA

POb/GynHx: 1 uncomplicated NSVD at 36 weeks GA, 5 lbs 8 oz. Menarche age 12, regular menses every 28 days. Denies STIs, PID. Normal Pap smears.

SocHx: Lives with father of baby and her daughter. Denies use of tobacco, EtOH, or recreational drugs.

THOUGHT QUESTIONS

- What is the differential diagnosis for decreased fetal movement? Which diagnosis is most common?
- What is a normal amount for a fetus to move? Should they be moving all the time?
- What are some ways to test for fetal well-being?

The differential diagnosis for decreased fetal movement includes fetal sleep-cycle, oligohydramnios, fetal effects of maternal drug use (e.g., opiates, steroids), fetal distress or lack of well-being (e.g., uteroplacental insufficiency), and fetal demise. In addition, perhaps the most common reason for decreased movement is simply that the mother is unaware that movement is occurring. For example, the baby may move into a particular position that makes sensation of fetal movement difficult.

Regarding normal fetal movement, it is difficult to give a specific answer as each fetus and mother are different. Generally, in the middle to late third trimester, a mother should feel two periods of good fetal activity each day. During these periods of activity, the fetus should move or kick at least 4 to 6 times in an hour. Women are often instructed to do "kick counts" to ensure fetal well-being. To accomplish this, the patient is instructed to sit quietly once or twice a day after a meal and count fetal movements. If fewer than 4 to 6 movements are felt in an hour she is to contact her care provider.

There are many ways to test for fetal well-being. They may include 1) kick counts; 2) nonstress test (NST) of the fetal heart rate; 3) modified biophysical profile (BPP) which includes an NST and a calculation of the amniotic fluid volume; 4) a formal BPP to look at fetal movement, tone, breathing, amniotic fluid, and NST; and 5) an oxytocin challenge test (OCT) also known as a contraction stress test (CST). Of note, the contraction stress test can also be initiated using nipple stimulation, which increases circulating levels of oxytocin in the patient. However, as oxytocin levels cannot be controlled with this method, there is a greater risk of having uncontrolled, prolonged, or tetanic contractions.

CASE CONTINUED

VS: Temp 98.0°F, BP 110/64, HR 90, RR 18

PE: *Abdomen:* soft, nontender. Fundal height 32 cm. *FHT:* 130s, nonreactive without decelerations. *Toco:* no contractions.

Labs: Urine dipstick: SG 1.010, negative nitrites/esterase, negative ketones, negative glucose. Sonogram: AFI 16.2, vertex presentation.

Because the NST is not reactive, vibroacoustic stimulation (VAS) is performed; a VAS unit is placed against the maternal abdomen and emits a noise meant to stimulate the baby. The fetus responds to the VAS with one small heart rate acceleration, which is only a minimally reassuring response. Thus, a biophysical profile is performed. The fetus is evaluated by sonogram for 30 minutes; in this case, it reveals a cephalic fetus with several pockets of amniotic fluid each measuring more than 4 cm. During this observation period, the fetus, which has its hips and knees flexed, extends an arm and a leg several times each and has three large discrete body movements. One episode of breathing >30 seconds is also noted. After the BPP, the patient is placed back on the monitor and now has a reactive NST.

QUESTIONS

53. What score does the fetus receive for the biophysical profile?
    A. 4/10
    B. 6/10
    C. 8/10
    D. 10/10

54. What is the most appropriate next step for this patient?
    A. Repeat the NST in 1 week
    B. Repeat the NST in 24 hours
    C. Observation for 24 hours
    D. Immediate delivery
    E. No further testing

55. What is the definition of a reactive fetal heart rate tracing for a fetus in the late third trimester?
    A. One acceleration greater than 10 bpm lasting at least 10 seconds in 10 minutes
    B. Two accelerations greater than 15 bpm lasting at least 15 seconds in 10 minutes
    C. Two accelerations greater than 15 bpm lasting at least 15 seconds in 20 minutes
    D. Two accelerations greater than 15 bpm lasting at least 15 seconds in 30 minutes

56. What is the criteria for a completed contraction stress test (CST) or oxytocin challenge test (OCT)?
    A. Two contractions in 10 minutes
    B. Three contractions in 10 minutes
    C. Two contractions in 20 minutes
    D. Three contractions in 20 minutes

ID/CC: 27-year-old G_1P_0 woman at 35 weeks GA presents with complaint of 6 hours of worsening right upper quadrant pain.

HPI: H.S. has had an entirely normal antepartum course until she woke up this morning with mild right upper quadrant pain. She ate a normal breakfast that neither aggravated nor alleviated the pain. The pain increased over the morning and this brought her into the labor ward. She also complains of increased swelling of her feet, such that her shoes no longer fit. She has no headache, no visual symptoms, no nausea or vomiting, and no other GI complaints. On review of systems she notes that her rings no longer fit on her fingers.

PMHx/PSHx: None   **Meds:** PNV   **All:** NKDA

POb/GynHx: G_1; Regular menses every 28 days.

SHx: Lives with father of baby; no domestic violence. No use of EtOH, tobacco, or recreational drugs.

VS: Temp 98.3°F, BP 156/93, HR 72, RR 16

PE: *Gen:* NAD. *Lungs:* CTAB. *Abdomen:* mild RUQ tenderness, otherwise soft, no distension, with gravid uterus size = dates. *LE:* 3+ pitting edema. *Reflexes:* 3+ B LE, 2+ B UE, no clonus. *SVE:* cervix is long, closed, −3 station. *FHT:* 140s, reactive, moderate variability, no decelerations.

Labs: Urine 2+ protein; Hct 38.9; WBC 9.4; Plts 92K; ALT 94; AST 107; LDH 786; Cr 0.4; Tbili 0.2; uric acid 7.4.

THOUGHT QUESTIONS

- Prior to the physical exam, what was the patient's differential diagnosis?
- Prior to the lab results what was the patient's differential diagnosis?
- What is the most likely diagnosis after obtaining lab results?
- What is the next step in management of this patient?

By history, the patient had right upper quadrant pain, which can be caused by inflammation of the liver or gall bladder, gastritis, musculoskeletal, HELLP (hemolysis, elevated liver enzymes, low platelets) syndrome, hepatitis, or even a right lower lobe pneumonia. However, with no exacerbation or alleviation by eating, gall bladder disease and gastritis are unlikely. Furthermore with no symptoms of upper respiratory infection, pneumonia is unlikely. HELLP syndrome is a variant of severe preeclampsia. The patient's elevated blood pressure and brisk reflexes on physical exam support this diagnosis. Furthermore, the lab results are all consistent with a diagnosis of *H*emolysis (increased LDH), *E*levated *L*iver enzymes (increased ALT and AST), and *L*ow *P*latelets (<150,000). Hepatitis is less likely with normal bilirubin and relatively mild LFT elevations.

Preeclampsia is the triad of elevated blood pressure, proteinuria, and nondependent (facial and hand) edema. It is differentiated into mild and severe preeclampsia, with mild preeclampsia being the classic triad in the absence of any of the features of severe preeclampsia. The diagnosis of severe preeclampsia is made if the patient develops any of the following: headache, right upper quadrant pain, scotomata, blood pressures >160/110 for two readings at least 6 hours apart, oliguria (<30 cc per hour for several hours), pulmonary edema, proteinuria >5 grams in 24 hours, and HELLP syndrome. The only treatment for preeclampsia is stabilization of any acute issues and delivery of the fetus. The management of preeclampsia depends on the severity of illness plus the gestational age at diagnosis. If expectant management is used between 24 and 34 weeks GA, antenatal corticosteroids (ACS), generally betamethasone, are given to accelerate fetal lung maturity. The following are general management guidelines for different gestational ages (Table 15).

TABLE 15. Management of Mild and Severe Preeclampsia Based on Gestational Age

GESTATIONAL AGE	MILD PREECLAMPSIA	SEVERE PREECLAMPSIA
<24 weeks	Expectant mgmt vs. TAB	TAB is recommended
24–34 weeks	Expectant mgmt w/ACS	Expectant mgmt w/ACS*
34–36 weeks	Expectant mgmt	Induction of labor
36 weeks to term	Expectant mgmt vs. IOL	Induction of labor

*Expectant management in severe preeclamptics is only reasonable until the development of symptoms such as headache, right upper quadrant pain, visual symptoms, LFT > 2 times normal, Plts < 100,000, blood pressures that cannot be controlled with two agents, pulmonary edema, oliguria, or seizure.

CASE CONTINUED

Because of her diagnosis of HELLP syndrome, the patient is begun on magnesium sulfate, and prostaglandin gel is placed intravaginally for cervical ripening for induction of labor.

After 6 hours, laboratory results are rechecked and the LFTs have increased further to ALT/AST = 112/134 and the platelets have decreased to 76. On exam, the cervix is now 1.5-cm dilated and 60% effaced, and the patient is begun on Pitocin. She contracts regularly on Pitocin, and delivers vaginally 12 hours later. Samples for lab tests are drawn 20 minutes prior to birth.

QUESTIONS

57. What are the most likely lab results?
    A. ALT/AST 76/84; Plts 54
    B. ALT/AST 134/146; Plts 132
    C. ALT/AST 76/84; Plts 132
    D. ALT/AST 134/146; Plts 54
    E. ALT/AST 276/292; Plts 18

58. The magnesium sulfate, which is given for seizure prophylaxis, is continued for:
    A. 6 hours postpartum
    B. 24 hours postpartum
    C. 48 hours postpartum
    D. Blood pressures normalize
    E. Until patient is discharged

59. An exacerbation of what systemic disease most resembles severe preeclampsia?
    A. Rheumatoid arthritis
    B. Ulcerative colitis
    C. Scleroderma
    D. Diabetes
    E. Lupus

60. A patient presents 72 hours after delivery to the emergency department having had a seizure at home. She should be begun on:
    A. Phenytoin
    B. Tegretol
    C. Magnesium sulfate
    D. Valium
    E. Phenobarbital

ID/CC: 22-year-old G_2P_0 Central American woman at 33 weeks GA by LMP presents with generalized itching.

HPI: Three days ago C.P. began itching on her palms and soles. The pruritus is mainly nocturnal and is now generalized but predominantly occurs over her abdomen, palms, and soles, with her face spared. She now has difficulty sleeping. She has not noticed any skin changes or lesions. She reports no change in use of detergents or soaps, or new clothing or jewelry. She denies any use of medications.

PMHx: History of transient cholestasis associated with the use of oral contraceptives. History of hepatitis as child in Nicaragua.

PSHx: D&C   **Meds:** None   **All:** NKDA

POb/GynHx: Regular menses, history of first trimester SAB 1 year ago.

SHx: Single, father of baby supportive. Denies use of tobacco, EtOH, or recreational drugs.

FHx: Noncontributory   **VS:** Temp 36.8°C, BP 120/72, HR 88

PE: *Gen:* NAD. No skin lesions except a few excoriations on arms and abdomen secondary to scratching. No lymphadenopathy. *HEENT:* no icterus, unremarkable. *Abdomen:* soft, nontender, gravid. Unable to assess hepatic border or spleen due to gravid uterus. No uterine contractions, normal fetal movements.

THOUGHT QUESTIONS

- What is the differential diagnosis?
- What diagnostic studies would you recommend?

The clinical course presented is most compatible with intrahepatic cholestasis of pregnancy (IHCP). The presentation of the pruritus with no associated skin lesions is typical. Liver function tests are usually normal or show mild elevation of AST and alkaline phosphatase. Approximately 10% to 30% of patients with IHCP have jaundice. Pruritic urticarial papules and plaques of pregnancy (PUPPP) can also cause intense itching but are accompanied by erythematous papules and plaques that usually arise first on the abdomen. Cholestasis from either intrahepatic or extrahepatic obstruction produces pruritus similar to the pattern of IHCP. Multiple skin disorders, parasitoses, and malignancies can be associated with pruritus.

In a patient with these classic presenting symptoms of IHCP, initial studies should include CBC with differential, liver function tests, and serum bile acids. If there is icterus, viral hepatitis studies and abdominal ultrasound should be ordered to exclude cholelithiasis and pancreatic abnormalities. In the setting of no other source for pruritus, the diagnosis may be made clinically for IHCP. In addition, bile acids greater than three times normal are also diagnostic.

CASE CONTINUED

Two weeks later the patient has persistent pruritus despite treatment with Benadryl. Her physical exam is unchanged except for a few excoriations secondary to scratching.

Labs: WBC 7.9; Hct 34; Plt 234K; AST 44; Alk Phos 430; cholic acid 66 μM; Tbili 0.8; PT 1.1; hepatitis A IgG (+); IgM (–); hepatitis B and C (–).

US: Abdominal—normal, single, live, vertex, intrauterine pregnancy, size equals dates.

QUESTIONS

61. Based on the data provided, you recommend which of the following?
    A. Treat pruritus and continue with pregnancy until term
    B. Begin antenatal testing, therapy for pruritus, and deliver after confirmation of fetal lung maturity after 36 weeks GA
    C. Liver biopsy
    D. Administer S-adenosyl-L-methionine and repeat liver panel
    E. Administer vitamin K and repeat liver panel

62. In regards to IHCP, which of the following statements is *false*?
    A. 10% chance of major malformations in the offspring
    B. Recurrence risk of 1/3 in subsequent pregnancies
    C. Pruritus and jaundice promptly normalize after delivery
    D. Potential cholestasis triggered by oral contraceptive use in patients with a history of IHCP
    E. Increased risk for preterm delivery and perinatal mortality

63. A week later the patient complains of malaise, anorexia, and intractable vomiting. Lab studies indicate liver failure and hypoglycemia. Of the following, the most likely diagnosis and treatment plan is:
    A. HELLP syndrome, steroids
    B. Acute fatty liver of pregnancy, supportive measures and prompt delivery
    C. Severe IHCP, ursodeoxycholic acid therapy
    D. Acute fatty liver of pregnancy, plasmapheresis
    E. HELLP syndrome, induction of labor

64. All of the following are characteristics of pruritic urticarial papules and plaques of pregnancy (PUPPP) *except*:
    A. It rarely recurs in subsequent pregnancies.
    B. High-potency topical corticosteroids are usually effective in relieving pruritus.
    C. It usually appears in third trimester and the lesions begin on the abdomen.
    D. It is associated with late intrauterine fetal death.
    E. It resolves spontaneously during pregnancy or after delivery.

ID/CC: 27-year-old G_3P_1 woman at 28 weeks GA brought in by ambulance complains of vaginal bleeding more than her period.

HPI: P.P. was at home playing with her 3-year-old son, when she felt liquid trickle from her vagina. Thinking it was likely urine, but concerned about amniotic fluid, she went to the bathroom, where she was shocked to discover that she was bleeding and had passed several golf ball-sized clots. She immediately called 911 and was brought into the hospital. She notes that she had no contractions at home, but has had some mild cramping since she arrived at the hospital. The fetus has been active throughout. She is not lightheaded and has no other complaints. Her antepartum course has been entirely normal. She had normal labs in the first trimester, a normal serum triple screen, and, by her report, a normal ultrasound at 19 weeks.

PMHx/PSHx: None   **Meds:** PNV   **All:** NKDA

POb/GynHx: Term C/S for breech fetus (3 years ago), SAB (4 years ago)

SHx: Lives with husband; no domestic violence. No use of EtOH, tobacco, or recreational drugs.

VS: Temp 98.0°F, BP 116/73, HR 94, RR 20

PE: *Gen:* NAD. *Lungs:* CTAB. *Abdomen:* soft, nontender, no distension with gravid uterus, size = dates. *SSE:* approx 50 cc of old blood and clots in vault; no active bleeding from cervix. *FHT:* 140s, reactive, moderate reactivity, no decelerations. *Toco:* contractions on monitor every 3 to 4 minutes.

Labs: WBC 7.6; Hct 33.4; Plts 249K; Kleihauer-Betke: pending

THOUGHT QUESTIONS

- What is your differential diagnosis at this point?
- What further history and physical would you like?
- What is the significance of the Kleihauer-Betke test?
- How would an obstetric ultrasound help with the possible diagnoses?

The differential diagnosis of third trimester vaginal bleeding includes placental abruption, placenta previa, vasa previa, cervical bleeding (trauma, polyp, cancer), vaginal bleeding (trauma), and rectal bleeding (hemorrhoids, anal fissure). History and physical can be used to differentiate between uterine versus nonuterine causes of bleeding. On history, recent intercourse may be the cause for cervical bleeding. On physical exam, a site of bleeding may be seen on the cervix, vaginal wall, or in the perirectal region with associated hemorrhoids. The Kleihauer-Betke test is used to determine the presence of fetal blood in the maternal circulation. A positive test is suggestive of a fetomaternal hemorrhage, which is consistent with placental abruption.

Uterine sources of bleeding can sometimes be identified on ultrasound. During ultrasound examination, the site of placentation should be identified and a diagnosis of previa should be given if the placenta inserts over the internal os of the cervix. Although a fresh retroplacental clot of 300 cc or greater can usually be recognized on ultrasound as a sonolucent region behind the placenta, it should be noted that ultrasound is not sensitive for the detection of placental abruption. Finally, vasa previa, a blood vessel in the membranes near or over the cervix, is a difficult diagnosis to make. Concern for vasa previa should be raised if there is a succenturiate lobe (an accessory placenta with a vascular connection to the main placenta) on one side of the cervix and the rest of the placenta on the other, because the vascular connection may traverse the internal os. The diagnosis can only be made prior to labor by the use of Doppler flow to identify a blood vessel next to the cervix.

CASE CONTINUED

Ms. P has not had intercourse in the past several days and has had no problems with constipation or hemorrhoids. On physical exam, she has no evidence of cervical, vaginal, or rectal bleeding. She continues with mild contractions and the ultrasonographer arrives to perform an obstetric ultrasound.

US: A posterior placenta that inserts just past the internal os of the cervix. Otherwise, normal fetus, normal amniotic fluid, no evidence of abruption.

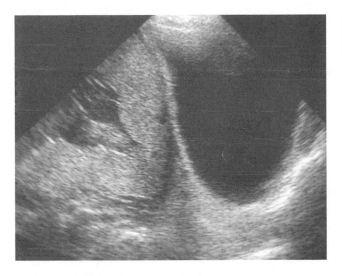

FIGURE 17 In this image of a complete placenta previa, the placenta previa is central, completely covering the cervix. (Image provided by Departments of Radiology and Obstetrics & Gynecology, University of California, San Francisco.)

QUESTIONS

65. Which of the following is part of the initial care for a patient with a known placenta previa who presents with bleeding and contractions at 28 weeks GA?
    A. Magnesium sulfate and betamethasone
    B. Terbutaline and betamethasone
    C. Betamethasone and immediate cesarean delivery
    D. Betamethasone and glucose loading test
    E. Magnesium sulfate, betamethasone, and glucose loading test

66. Which of the following is *not* a risk factor for placenta previa?
    A. Multiple fundal fibroids
    B. Prior cesarean section
    C. Bicornuate uterus
    D. Fetal macrosomia
    E. Multiple gestation

67. Placenta previa, particularly with a history of a prior cesarean delivery, is associated with an increase in:
    A. Placental abruption
    B. Placenta accreta
    C. Uterine rupture
    D. Successful vaginal birth after cesarean (VBAC)
    E. Female fetus

68. Which of the following is a likely reason the placenta previa was not seen on the initial scan?
    A. No previa at the time, and it has grown over the cervix since.
    B. The bladder was full, which pushed the placenta up during the ultrasound.
    C. Fetal movement.
    D. Sonographer error.
    E. It is not usually seen so early in pregnancy.

ID/CC: 27-year-old G_1P_0 woman at 41 3/7 weeks GA who presents for antenatal testing.

HPI: M.O. has had an uncomplicated pregnancy except for nausea and vomiting that lasted until 18 weeks gestation. Since that time she has been fine and has gained 28 lbs during the pregnancy. She was most recently seen 4 days earlier for antenatal testing and at that time had a reactive non-stress test (NST) with no decelerations and an amniotic fluid index (AFI) of 11. She presents today with occasional contractions, more at night, normal fetal movement, and no complaints of vaginal bleeding or leaking fluid.

PMHx/PSHx: Mild asthma   **Meds:** PNV, albuterol MDI   **All:** NKDA   **POb/GynHx:** G_1P_0

SHx: Lives with husband; no domestic violence. No use of ethanol, tobacco, or recreational drugs.

VS: Temp 98.4°F, BP 122/74, HR 84, RR 16

PE: *Abdomen:* soft, nontender, no distension with gravid uterus, fundal height is 40 cm. *SVE:* 1 cm, long, −2 station, midposition, firm. *FHT:* 140s, reactive, no decelerations. *Toco:* one contraction seen.

US: AFI 3.2.

THOUGHT QUESTIONS

- Is her testing reassuring or nonreassuring?
- As far as the cervix is concerned, is it inducible? What is the Bishop score?

Ms. O has presented for her antenatal testing at 41 3/7 weeks gestation. There are a variety of regimens used for antenatal testing around the country, but most involve one or more of the following:

1. Nonstress test (NST). This is a FHT assessment that is considered reactive (reassuring) if it has two accelerations of greater than or equal to 15 bpm over the baseline lasting for at least 15 seconds.

2. Biophysical profile (BPP). Can be considered with or without the NST, the ultrasound component of the BPP consists of evaluation of fetal movement, fetal tone, fetal breathing movements, and amniotic fluid. Each component is worth 2 points each and no partial credit is given.

3. Modified BPP. An NST plus a check of the amniotic fluid is usually done as an amniotic fluid index (AFI). The AFI is the sum of four measurements, one taken in each quadrant of the patient's abdomen of the largest vertical pocket of fluid (measured in cm) in that quadrant. Normal AFI ranges from 5 to 20. Less than 5 is considered oligohydramnios and greater than 20 is considered polyhydramnios.

4. Oxytocin challenge test (OCT) or a contraction stress test (CST). This involves giving the patient intravenous oxytocin until she experiences three contractions in 10 minutes and then observing the FHT for fetal heart rate decelerations associated with contractions. A negative/reassuring test will have no decelerations and is indicative of a fetus who can presumably tolerate labor.

In the case of Ms. O, she has a reactive NST, which is reassuring. However, she has oligohydramnios, which is nonreassuring, and she should be delivered. Her cervix is unfavorable, which is defined as a cervix that has a low probability of successful induction and may therefore need agents to effect pre-induction cervical ripening. One scale that is used to assess the cervix is the Bishop scoring system (Table 18). If the Bishop score is 4 or less, the cervix is considered unfavorable; a score of 5 to 9 is moderately favorable; and 10 or greater is very favorable. Using this table, Ms. O's Bishop score is +1 for dilation, +1 for station, and +1 for position for a total of 3.

TABLE 18. Determining the Bishop Score

POINTS GIVEN	0	1	2	3
Dilatation (cm)	closed	1–2	3–4	≥5
Effacement (%)	0–30	40–50	60–70	≥80
Station	–3	–2	–1 or 0	≥+1
Position	posterior	mid	anterior	
Consistency	firm	medium	soft	

Note: The Bishop score is the sum of the five categories.

CASE CONTINUED

Because of oligohydramnios, you counsel Ms. O to undergo an induction of labor. Because of her unfavorable cervix, you discuss the possibility of using a prostaglandin for cervical ripening, to which she agrees. A prostaglandin gel is placed in the vagina two times, 4 hours apart, during which time the fetus is monitored and has a reassuring heart tracing. Her cervix changes to 1 cm, 50%, –2 station, midposition, soft consistency. Her Bishop score is now 6 and Ms. O is begun on IV Pitocin and achieves a contraction pattern of every 2 to 3 minutes upon reaching a continuous infusion of 12 mu/min. Two hours later, her exam is 3-cm dilated, and you perform an artificial rupture of the membranes (AROM) to further augment her labor, which reveals moderately thick meconium-stained fluid.

QUESTIONS

69. Which of the following is *not* associated with meconium-stained fluid?
    A. Endomyometritis
    B. Meconium aspiration syndrome
    C. Oligohydramnios
    D. Preterm labor
    E. Post-dates pregnancy

70. Which of the following point deductions from the biophysical profile (BPP) is most consistent with a long-standing issue?
    A. Absent fetal movement
    B. Absent fetal tone
    C. Fetal breathing movement
    D. Amniotic fluid
    E. Nonreactive NST

71. Which of the following prostaglandin preparations is *not* used for cervical ripening?
    A. PGE_2 gel
    B. $PGF_{2\alpha}$
    C. PGE_{1M} (misoprostol)
    D. PGE_2 suppository

72. During the labor of this patient with oligohydramnios and meconium, which of the following would *not* be an indication for use of an intrauterine pressure catheter (IUPC)?
    A. Amnioinfusion for recurrent variable decelerations
    B. Amnioinfusion for moderate meconium
    C. Amnioinfusion for recurrent late decelerations
    D. Difficulty measuring contractions because of maternal obesity
    E. To assess strength of contractions

ID/CC: 38-year-old G_1P_0 woman at 41 weeks GA in active labor with no cervical change in 2 hours.

HPI: A.D. presented to labor and delivery at 5-cm dilation, 100% effacement and –2 station. Her contractions were 3 minutes apart and painful. At the time of admission, she was ruled in for rupture of membranes and stated that she had been leaking fluid for about 2 days. She also stated that she had been having contractions every 10 to 15 minutes during the previous 24 hours. In the hospital, she progressed normally to 8-cm dilation and –1 station but remained there for 2 hours. During this time she developed a fever of 101.0°F and is diagnosed with chorioamnionitis. Ms. D is discouraged about the last two exams being the same and asks, "Doctor, am I going to need a C/S?"

PMHx: Moderate obesity　　**PSHx:** Appendectomy　　**Meds:** PNV　　**All:** NKDA

POb/GynHx: Gestational diabetes mellitus (GDM), class A2 (insulin controlled). The patient was found to be diabetic at 28 weeks gestation. She was poorly controlled on diet and was started on insulin at 34 weeks.

SHx: Lives with father of baby. Denies use of tobacco; occasional use of ethanol.

VS: Temp 101.4°F, BP 100/60, HR 100

PE: *Fingerstick blood sugar:* 78. *FHT:* 170s, moderate variability, no decelerations. *Toco:* contractions every 3 minutes. *Abdomen:* EFW by Leopold maneuvers is 3900 grams. *SVE:* 8-cm dilation, 100% effacement, –1 station. The position, left occiput transverse (LOT) based on the location of the sagittal suture and fontanelles, is depicted in Figure 19A.

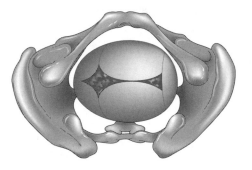

FIGURE 19A Left occiput transverse (LOT) position, with the posterior fontanelle to the left, anterior to the right. (Illustration by Electronic Illustrators Group.)

THOUGHT QUESTIONS

- What is "normal" labor for a nulliparous versus a multiparous patient?
- What are at least three reasons to explain this patient's lack of progress?
- How could you evaluate the origins of this patient's labor pattern?
- Does she need a cesarean delivery?

Labor is broken up into several stages: the first stage is from the onset of contractions until full dilation; the second stage is from full dilation until delivery of the fetus; and the third stage is from delivery of the fetus until delivery of the placenta. The first stage of labor is further broken down into latent and active phases, which are demarcated by an increase in the rate of dilation that usually occurs when the cervix is dilated between 3 and 4 cm.

Abnormal or protracted labor in a nulliparous patient without an epidural is defined as follows: Latent phase lasting longer than 20 hours duration, active phase with less than 1.2-cm dilation each hour or descent less than 1 cm per hour, or second stage greater than 2 hours (3 hours with an epidural). In a multiparous patient, prolonged latent phase is defined as greater than 14 hours duration, active phase with less than 1.5-cm dilation each hour or less than 2 cm descent per hour, or second stage greater than 1 hour (2 hours with an epidural). These are the values for the fifth percentile. Thus 95% of patients will have a labor course faster than these values. The Friedman curve describes this in graphical form (Figure 19B).

This patient's current protracted labor course may be explained by large fetal weight (her risk factors for this include maternal obesity and GDM), chorioamnionitis leading to inadequate forces, and malpresentation. To evaluate the etiology, an IUPC (intrauterine pressure catheter) should be placed to measure the force of the contractions. An external tocometer only indicates the timing and length of contractions; it does not quantify the strength. More than 70% of patients who stop making cervical change for 2 hours with inadequate forces measured by an IUPC and who are then started on Pitocin will go on to have a vaginal delivery.

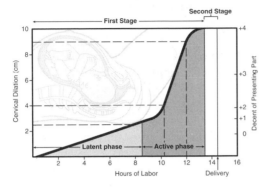

FIGURE 19B The Friedman Labor Curve (created in 1961) shows the progress of labor, plotting cervical dilation versus time. (Illustration by Electronic Illustrators Group.)

CASE CONTINUED

An IUPC is placed revealing uterine forces of 120 Montevideo (MV) units (the sum of the pressures due to contractions over 10 minutes). Because contractions generally need to be above 180–200 MV units to be considered adequate, the patient is started on Pitocin to help her achieve adequate forces. After 2 hours of adequate forces, she is rechecked and found to be completely dilated and +1 station. In addition, the fetal head is now in the occiput anterior position. She pushes for 2 hours and delivers a 4000-gram infant in the occiput anterior position.

QUESTIONS

73. What is the correct order of the cardinal movements of labor?
    A. Flexion, descent, engagement, internal rotation, extension, external rotation
    B. Descent, engagement, flexion, internal rotation, external rotation, extension
    C. Engagement, flexion, descent, external rotation, extension, internal rotation
    D. Engagement, flexion, descent, internal rotation, extension, external rotation

74. What is the diagnosis for this patient if she fails to dilate despite adequate forces?
    A. Arrest of dilation
    B. Arrest of descent
    C. Protracted labor
    D. Slow slope active

75. After pushing for 3 hours, the fetus does not descend beyond −1 station. What is the most appropriate next step? Note the fetal position is occiput anterior, and the patient has epidural anesthesia.
    A. Vacuum-assisted vaginal delivery
    B. Forceps-assisted vaginal delivery
    C. Forceps-assisted rotation to the occiput posterior position
    D. Cesarean delivery

76. After pushing for 3 hours, the fetus descends from +1 to +2 station but not beyond that. The estimated fetal weight is 4800 grams by Leopold's and ultrasound. The fetal position is left occiput anterior, and the patient has epidural anesthesia. What is the most appropriate next step?
    A. Vacuum-assisted vaginal delivery
    B. Forceps-assisted vaginal delivery
    C. Forceps-assisted rotation to the occiput posterior position
    D. Cesarean delivery

ID/CC: 23-year-old G_6P_2 woman at 36 weeks GA brought in by ambulance complains of vaginal bleeding and contractions.

HPI: P.A. began experiencing contractions about 4 hours ago. They increased in intensity over the ensuing 1 to 2 hours and at that time she noticed some bright red blood in the toilet that kept passing out of her vagina for the next 2 hours. At that point, she called the ambulance. She notes no leaking of clear fluid and notices that the fetus has been overly active. She has been to prenatal care appointments only occasionally. Her first appointment was at 22 weeks and she had normal lab results at that point. She has had one other appointment at 29 weeks and at that time had a normal 1-hour glucose loading test. She is an active user of crack-cocaine and upon further questioning, admits to doing so approximately 6 hours ago.

PMHx/PSHx: Substance abuse, primarily cocaine   **Meds:** PNVs   **All:** NKDA

POb/GynHx: Two prior term NSVDs, three prior TABs

SHx: Father of baby not involved; she lives on the streets and both of her children have been placed into foster care; she occasionally trades sex for money or drugs. Occasional ethanol and tobacco use; frequent crack-cocaine use (at least daily).

VS: Temp 98.0°F, BP 166/83, HR 92, RR 20

PE: *Gen:* NAD. *Lungs:* CTAB. *Abdomen:* soft, nontender, no distension with gravid uterus, size = dates, palpable contractions. *SSE:* old blood and clots in vault, no active bleeding from cervix. *SVE:* cervix 1-cm dilated, 50% effaced, −2 station. *FHT:* 140s, nonreactive, occasional decelerations after contractions. *Toco:* contractions every 1 to 2 minutes.

THOUGHT QUESTIONS

- What are the primary issues of concern in this patient?
- What unifying diagnosis encompasses all of the concerning issues?
- What laboratory tests should be ordered?

In this patient, the issues that are most concerning are 1) her vaginal bleeding, 2) fetal heart rate decelerations, 3) blood pressure of 166/83, and 4) history of crack-cocaine use. Each of the first three issues should bring several conditions to mind. For example, the vaginal bleeding in the third trimester can be related to a placenta previa, placental abruption, or labor. However, cocaine abuse leading to uterine contractions and placental abruption brings all of these findings into one etiology.

Although Ms. A's cocaine use is likely the cause of her elevated blood pressure, she should still be ruled out for preeclampsia by ordering lab tests that should include CBC, LFTs (AST, ALT), LDH (for hemolysis), and a creatinine level. Because of her vaginal bleeding and the concern for abruption, a set of coagulation factors in addition to the CBC should be ordered. Also, a Kleihauer-Betke, which tests for fetal blood in the maternal circulation, is a good idea. Her urine should be sent for protein and a toxicology screen.

CASE CONTINUED

The patient's initial lab results return.

Labs: Hct 32.1; WBC 9.7; Plts 189K; AST/ALT 18/22; LDH 476; PT/PTT/INR 12.3/33.6/1.1; Cr 0.5; Kleihauer-Betke: pending; urine dipstick: trace protein; tox: pending

The lab results do not suggest preeclampsia. However, because of the patient's elevated blood pressure, you begin a 24-hour urine collection to quantitate the proteinuria. Over the next hour, the patient's contractions become less frequent, every 2 to 3 minutes, but stronger in intensity. The patient asks for pain medicine and you check the cervix. It is now 3-cm dilated, 80% effaced, and –1 station, and you notice more vaginal bleeding. The fetal heart tracing is shown in Figure 20.

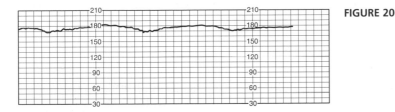

FIGURE 20

QUESTIONS

77. Describe the fetal heart tracing:
    A. Bradycardia with intermittent accelerations, moderate variability
    B. Bradycardia with intermittent accelerations, minimal variability
    C. Normal fetal heart rate with minimal variability and late decelerations
    D. Fetal tachycardia with minimal variability and late decelerations
    E. Fetal tachycardia with minimal variability and early decelerations

78. Which of the following is the best next step in management?
    A. Urgent cesarean section
    B. Elective cesarean section
    C. Forceps delivery
    D. Augmentation of labor
    E. Begin magnesium sulfate for seizure prophylaxis

79. When the fetus is delivered, what do you expect to see regarding the placenta?
    A. Placenta previa
    B. Vasa previa
    C. Adherent clot on the posterior placental surface
    D. Placenta adherent to the uterus
    E. Placenta accreta

80. Which of the following substances has not been associated with fetal abnormalities including developmental delay?
    A. Cocaine
    B. Alcohol
    C. Marijuana
    D. Benzodiazepines
    E. Phenobarbital

ID/CC: 29-year-old G_4P_1 woman at 38 weeks GA who presents with frequent contractions.

HPI: U.R. presents with complaints of contractions every 3 to 4 minutes that began 1 hour ago. She has not noticed any frank vaginal bleeding, but did pass a brown clump from her vagina yesterday. She has not had any clear fluid leak out and her fetus is very active. She has had an uncomplicated antepartum course and signed a consent form to undergo a trial of labor after cesarean (TOLAC) 2 weeks ago. She underwent a cesarean delivery in her last pregnancy because she failed to dilate past 7 cm.

PMHx/PSHx: C/S **Meds:** PNV **All:** NKDA

POb/GynHx: Term C/S for failure to progress (FTP) of 3800-gram infant (4 years ago), TAB (9 years ago), SAB (2 years ago)

SHx: Lives with husband and 4-year-old daughter; no domestic violence. No use of ethanol, tobacco, or recreational drugs.

VS: Temp 97.6°F, BP 114/68, HR 74, RR 16

PE: *Gen:* NAD. *Lungs:* CTAB. *Abdomen:* soft, nontender, no distension with gravid uterus, size = dates. *SVE:* cervix 4-cm dilated, 90% effaced, +1 station, *Leopold's:* cephalic, 3700 grams. *FHT:* 140s, reactive, occasional variable deceleration to the 110s. *Toco:* contractions on monitor every 3 to 4 minutes.

Labs: Hct 36

THOUGHT QUESTIONS

- What is the biggest risk faced by this patient with a history of prior cesarean section?
- What is her approximate chance for successful vaginal delivery?
- How are patients with a prior cesarean managed in labor?

The biggest risk Ms. R faces is that of a uterine rupture. Uterine rupture is reported to occur in 0.5% to 1% of patients undergoing a trial of labor after cesarean. It is increased in patients who are induced, receive prostaglandin agents, and have more than one uterine scar. The risk of uterine rupture is decreased in patients who have had a prior vaginal delivery, and who present in active labor.

On average, the overall probability for a patient to achieve a vaginal birth after cesarean (VBAC) is about 70%. This probability is increased in patients who have a nonrecurring indication for their first cesarean (e.g., breech, herpes, previa) as well as those patients who have had a vaginal birth either prior or subsequent to their cesarean delivery. Conversely, it is decreased in patients with a prior delivery for failure to progress as well as those patients who are being induced. Based on data from several recent case series associating prostaglandin agents with increased risk of uterine rupture, most clinicians will not use misoprostol as a cervical ripening agent in patients with a prior cesarean, and some clinicians will not use any prostaglandins at all. The use of oxytocin, although not conclusively associated with uterine rupture, is usually used gingerly in these patients.

CASE CONTINUED

While in labor and delivery, Ms. R makes reasonable progress, changing to 6 cm over the next 2 hours. At this point she requests an epidural, which is placed without complication. Two hours later, she is 8-cm dilated, +2 station, and her fetal heart tracing has recurrent variable decelerations. You place an intrauterine pressure catheter (IUPC) and begin an amnioinfusion. The fetal heart rate tracing improves and then, 30 minutes later, looks like Figure 21.

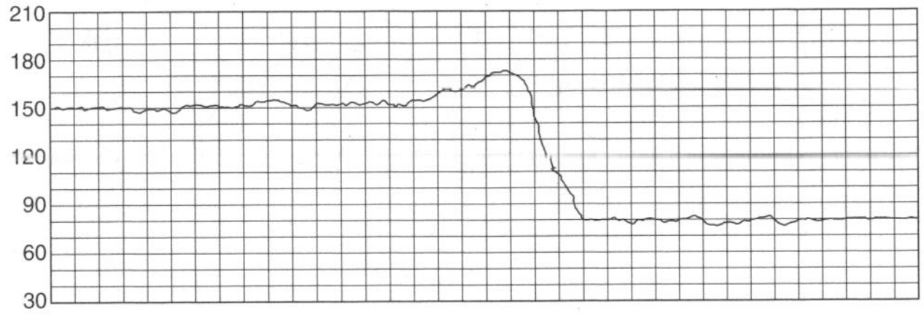

FIGURE 21

QUESTIONS

81. The next step in management is:
    A. Adjust the IUPC
    B. Immediate delivery
    C. Augment with Pitocin
    D. Give terbutaline
    E. Increase the O_2 by face mask

82. The most worrisome finding on physical exam at this point would be:
    A. Compound presentation
    B. Prolapsed umbilical cord
    C. Fetal head no longer palpable
    D. Contracted pelvis
    E. Breech presentation

83. Which of the following is *not* an indication for cesarean section?
    A. Previous cesarean section
    B. Breech
    C. No cervical change for 4 hours at 2-cm dilated
    D. Fetal bradycardia
    E. Placenta previa

84. The amnioinfusion was begun:
    A. To decrease the recurrent variable decelerations
    B. To dilute meconium
    C. To cool the fetus down
    D. To increase the strength of the contractions
    E. To help measure the strength of the contractions

ID/CC: 34-year-old G$_5$P$_5$ woman presents with vaginal bleeding 3 hours after a vaginal delivery.

HPI: P.H. delivered a 4000-gram baby over a third-degree perineal laceration (a tear into the anal sphincter) with a right vaginal sulcus tear (a tear high into the posterolateral vaginal wall). Both lacerations were repaired using local anesthesia. The labor was complicated by premature rupture of membranes and chorioamnionitis but with a normal labor course. Estimated blood loss (EBL) was 400 cc.

Ms. H was well until 3 hours after delivery when she noted passage of several large clots and was found to be sitting in a pool of blood. She is currently complaining of moderate pelvic cramping, and mild vaginal discomfort at the site of the repairs. She denies having rectal pain. She has been able to void 500 cc of urine since the delivery. You estimate that she has lost about 500 cc of blood in addition to the 400 cc she lost at the delivery.

PMHx/PSHx: None   **Meds:** Currently receiving IV Pitocin   **All:** NKDA

POb/GynHx: 4 prior term NSVDs

THOUGHT QUESTIONS
- What are the main causes of postpartum hemorrhage?
- How do you distinguish between each cause?
- For which conditions is this patient at particular risk?

Postpartum hemorrhage (PPH) is defined as blood loss of 500 cc or greater after a vaginal delivery and 1000 cc or greater after a cesarean delivery. Common causes of immediate (within minutes of delivery) postpartum hemorrhage include uterine atony, retained products of conception, vaginal laceration, and cervical laceration. Less common causes include placenta accreta, uterine inversion, uterine rupture, and coagulopathy. Postpartum hemorrhage that occurs more remote from delivery (1 hour to several weeks) may be caused by retained products of conception (POC), vaginal or retroperitoneal hematomas (though these result in concealed hemorrhage), and placental site subinvolution.

Distinguishing between each cause is done by careful examination and a consideration of the patient's risk factors. Feeling the uterine fundus abdominally or doing a bimanual exam will help identify uterine atony. Inspection of the placenta will reveal whether a lobe or pieces of the placenta are missing. Examination of the vaginal walls and cervix can be difficult, but is important. (Adequate exposure of the cervix requires appropriate retractors to retract the vaginal walls. A ring forceps is then used to grasp the anterior lip of the cervix. Using a second ring forceps, further cervical tissue is grasped and inspection of the cervix accomplished by "walking" along the cervix.) Inversion of the uterus occurs as the placenta delivers, dragging the attached uterus through the vagina. Placenta accreta is a diagnosis of exclusion with high-risk patients being women with a previous cesarean section scar and an anterior placenta. Risk factors for atony include grand multiparity, macrosomia, and chorioamnionitis. Chorioamnionitis places this patient at risk for both immediate and delayed PPH because it can complicate the delivery of an intact placenta, placing her at risk for retained POC.

CASE CONTINUED

VS: Temp 99.8°F, BP 100/60, HR 115, RR 16

PE: *Gen:* pale, anxious. *Abdomen:* soft. Fundus 3 cm above the umbilicus and moderately tender. *GU:* perineal laceration appears intact. Sulcus tear cannot be evaluated secondary to patient discomfort.

The patient is taken back to the operating room. Using conscious sedation, a careful examination is performed. The sulcus tear appears intact and hemostatic. The uterus is manually explored; 800 cc of clot and retained placental products are expressed. Under ultrasound guidance, gentle sharp curettage is performed to remove remaining placental products. Exam of the placenta expressed at delivery reveals a missing lobe.

QUESTIONS

85. Two hours after a NSVD a patient complains of rectal pain. This is a potential presentation of which of the following?
    A. Cervical laceration
    B. Vaginal hematoma
    C. Breakdown of a perineal laceration
    D. Infection of a perineal laceration

86. Immediately after a NSVD of a 4000-gram infant and delivery of an intact placenta, a patient is noted to have significant continued blood loss up to 700 cc. Her uterus is firm. What is the next source of bleeding to rule out?
    A. Retained POC
    B. Uterine inversion
    C. Cervical laceration
    D. Uterine atony

87. What is the most common cause of postpartum hemorrhage?
    A. Perineal laceration
    B. Uterine atony
    C. Cervical laceration
    D. Retained placental products

88. A preeclamptic (BP 168/102) patient delivers a 3800-gram infant. Immediately after delivery of the placenta, Pitocin is begun. Despite Pitocin and uterine massage, the uterus remains boggy and the patient continues to bleed. What medication should be given next?
    A. Magnesium sulfate
    B. Methylergonovine (Methergine)
    C. Prostaglandin F2α (Hemabate)
    D. IM Pitocin

ID/CC: 28-year-old G$_1$P$_1$ woman status post C/S presents with a fever of 101.4°F.

HPI: E.M. delivered a 3400-gram baby 5 days prior to presentation. Her labor course was significant for premature rupture of membranes that required induction of labor. She had a slow slope active course and developed chorioamnionitis. She underwent a primary low transverse C/S for arrest of descent at 0 station. She had a Foley catheter in place for the majority of her labor until 12 hours postpartum. After it was removed, she was unable to void and again had the Foley for an additional 24 hours. She received cefotetan for chorioamnionitis and was continued on the antibiotic until 48 hours postpartum. Her fever intrapartum declined and normalized within 6 hours after delivery.

Ms. M now presents with complaint of fever for 12 hours. She has lower abdominal cramps and back pain. She is breastfeeding and her breasts are mildly tender. She has some pain with voiding. Her lochia has been mild and appears light reddish-orange. She has noticed a foul smell.

PMHx: Frequent UTIs   **PSHx:** C/S only   **Meds:** PNV, ibuprofen, Vicodin   **All:** NKDA

POb/GynHx: As above. No STDs or PID.

SHx: Lives with father of baby. Denies use of EtOH, tobacco, or recreational drugs.

THOUGHT QUESTIONS
- What is your differential diagnosis?
- What risk factors does she have for each of these diagnoses?
- What is endomyometritis?

The differential diagnosis includes both complications from surgery as well as postpartum conditions. Her differential includes endomyometritis, pyelonephritis, breast engorgement, mastitis, wound infection, and septic pelvic thrombophlebitis.

Her risk factors for endomyometritis are stated below. Risk factors for pyelonephritis include history of frequent UTIs and need for catheterization. Surgery and the postpartum period put her at risk for wound infection and septic pelvic thrombophlebitis. She does not have any particular risk factors for engorgement or mastitis, but these should be included in the differential as both cause breast pain and a fever.

Endomyometritis or endometritis is an infection of the uterine lining and/or the wall of the uterus. It is a not uncommon complication of cesarean delivery. Other risk factors for endomyometritis include length of labor, duration of membrane rupture and chorioamnionitis, number of internal exams, retained placental products, internal fetal monitoring, and lower socioeconomic status. Presentation usually includes abdominal pain, fever, and foul-smelling lochia. Management includes a careful D&C if retained POC is suspected, in addition to antibiotic coverage. A mild case of endomyometritis after vaginal delivery may not require IV antibiotics, but generally infection after a cesarean section does. Intravenous antibiotics for 48 to 72 hours generally suffices.

CASE CONTINUED

VS: Temp 102.0°F, BP 112/52, HR 110, RR 14

PE: *Gen:* mild distress, shivering. *Breasts:* mildly erythematous nipples without cracks. Soft to palpation without tenderness or masses. No axillary lymphadenopathy noted. *Lungs:* CTAB. *Cor:* tachy, regular rate, no murmurs. *Abdomen:* +BS, soft. Fundus 6 cm below umbilicus and moderately tender to palpation. No CVAT appreciated. *GU:* Lochia noted to be tomato soup-like in appearance and foul smelling. *Extremities:* No calf pain or swelling noted.

Labs: Urine: SG 1.010, trace blood, negative nitrite/esterase, WBC 14.4

A diagnosis of endomyometritis is made based on the patient's fever, elevated WBC, tender uterus, and foul smelling lochia. The patient is started on ampicillin, gentamycin, and clindamycin for broad spectrum coverage of a likely mixed microbial infection (note that some hospitals would use a second-generation cephalosporin only). She responds within 24 hours with decreasing abdominal tenderness and defervesces. Once she has been afebrile for 48 hours and without abdominal tenderness, she is discharged to home.

QUESTIONS

89. What antibiotic regimen should she receive at home?
    A. Keflex, 500 PO QID for 10 days
    B. Keflex, 500 PO QID for 14 days
    C. Ofloxacin, 400 mg PO BID, and Flagyl, 500 mg PO BID for 14 days
    D. No antibiotics needed

90. The same patient does not respond within 48 hours to the antibiotic regimen. She is started on heparin and defervesces in 24 hours. What is her most likely diagnosis?
    A. Septic pelvic thrombophlebitis
    B. Deep venous thromboembolism
    C. Endomyometritis with retained placental products
    D. Pelvic abscess

91. Assume this patient presented instead with right breast pain and right axillary lymphadenopathy consistent with mastitis. What is the treatment?
    A. Avoid breastfeeding on the right. No antibiotics needed.
    B. Encourage continuation of breastfeeding from both breasts. No antibiotics needed.
    C. Avoid breastfeeding on the right and start oral antibiotics.
    D. Encourage continuation of breastfeeding from both breasts and start oral antibiotics.

92. What is the most common organism associated with mastitis?
    A. Group B *Streptococcus*
    B. *Staphylococcus aureus*
    C. *Streptococcus viridans*
    D. *Enterococcus*

CASE 24 / DESIRES CONTRACEPTION

ID/CC: 29-year-old G_4P_2 woman is 2 days postpartum after a normal vaginal delivery. She is due for discharge from the hospital today and would like to discuss options for contraception.

HPI: B.C. is breastfeeding without problems and intends to do so for a year. She and her husband have used condoms in the past. She briefly used the "minipill" many years ago, but stopped because she didn't like how "they made her feel." This pregnancy was unintended. She breastfed her older child, who is 18 months old now, for about a year. She and her husband have been married for 4 years and are both monogamous. He is 34 years old and healthy.

PMHx/PSHx: Migraines with visual, symptoms since childhood

Meds: Imitrex   **All:** NKDA

POb/GynHx: Regular cycles; 2 D&Cs; 2 NSVDs; history of *Chlamydia* infection, 10 years ago; normal Pap smears.

THOUGHT QUESTIONS

- What additional information would be useful in identifying appropriate contraception?
- Does this patient's history of migraines or the fact that she is breastfeeding affect your recommendations for contraception?

Desire for future fertility will help determine if she and her partner are candidates for permanent sterilization. If she is sure she wants no more children, she may consider a tubal ligation. This involves surgically occluding the fallopian tubes with bands, clips, suture, or coagulation. The failure rate is 0.2% to 0.4%. Vasectomy involves surgical ligation of the vas deferens. This procedure, because it is less invasive, is safer than tubal ligation. The failure rate is <0.5%, the majority of which is due to intercourse too soon after vasectomy when viable sperm are still present distal to the occlusion.

A history of severe migraine headaches are a relative contraindication for combined oral contraceptive use and should be considered on a case-by-case basis. Regarding this patient's plan to breastfeed, studies have demonstrated that milk production is decreased by the use of combination estrogen/progestin pills, whereas progestin-only contraceptive methods do not diminish milk production. Many patients believe that the amenorrhea related to breastfeeding is adequate birth control; they should be counseled against this as a primary form of contraception, as the actual failure rate is 15% to 55%.

CASE CONTINUED

PE: Her postpartum exam is normal. BP 116/72

After further discussion she states that her husband doesn't want more children, but she herself is not sure. She agrees that she would do better with a long-acting form of contraception. She has heard about the IUD and thinks she may want to try it.

THOUGHT QUESTIONS

- How does her history of *Chlamydia* infection effect your recommendation?
- In a postpartum patient such as this, when would be an appropriate time to insert an IUD?

Although a prior history of STIs is a relative contraindication to IUD use, the physician should weigh current risk for STIs more heavily in assessing whether a patient is a good candidate for an IUD. This patient is in a monogamous relationship and is therefore at a low risk for STIs.

In a postpartum patient, you should wait until 6 weeks after delivery to place an IUD. Before this point, the uterus and cervix may not have reverted to their prepregnancy size and the cervix may still be open, leading to high expulsion rates. There are three types of IUDs currently on the U.S. market: the copper IUD (no hormone reservoir) and the progesterone and levonorgestrel IUDs (both with progestin reservoirs).

QUESTIONS

93. Appropriate contraceptive options for this patient include all of the following *except*:
    A. Prescription for the progestin-only pill to start now
    B. Prescription for combined oral contraceptive pills (OCPs) to start now
    C. A 150-mg injection of medroxyprogesterone acetate (DMPA) to be given now
    D. Norplant, to be placed at a convenient time after her discharge from the hospital

94. A 30-year-old woman, G_1P_1, comes to your office requesting contraception. She is single and is currently sexually active with two partners. She was using the diaphragm without problems, but would now like to use OCPs. She denies a history of STIs or abnormal Pap smears. She smokes one pack of cigarettes per day. Her physical exam is normal. You *correctly* advise her that:
    A. Her smoking history is an absolute contraindication to OCP use.
    B. DMPA will induce amenorrhea in most women after the third injection.
    C. She is a good candidate for an IUD.
    D. OCPs do not decrease the risk of STDs.

95. A 22-year-old woman, G_0, calls your office stating that during intercourse 2 days ago, the condom broke. Her LMP began 10 days ago. She wants to know if there is anything she can do to prevent pregnancy. You *correctly* advise her that:
    A. You can prescribe low-dose combined OCPs that she should start immediately.
    B. You can prescribe two doses of combined OCPs with each dose containing 100 μg of ethinyl estradiol and either 1 mg of norgestrel or 0.5 mg of levonorgestrel. She should take the first dose immediately and the second dose in 12 hours.
    C. She is too late for the "morning-after" (Yuzpe) regimen because intercourse occurred 2 days ago.
    D. She is not likely to become pregnant because her last menses was only 8 days prior to intercourse.

96. A 29-year-old G_3P_3 would like to use long-acting contraception and asks you about the IUD. She is not using contraception now and is in a mutually monogamous relationship. Her gynecologic history is only notable for a history of persistent LGSIL for which she underwent cryotherapy. You *correctly* advise her that:
    A. The copper IUD needs to be changed every 2 years to maintain effectiveness.
    B. She is not a candidate for the IUD given her history of LGSIL and the fact that she had cryotherapy.
    C. The IUD increases her risk of ectopic pregnancy from her current baseline risk.
    D. Common side effects of the IUD are menorrhagia and dysmenorrhea.

ID/CC: A 24-year-old woman presents to the emergency room complaining of 3 hours of worsening right lower quadrant pain.

HPI: O.T. reports a dull pain in her right lower abdomen that started earlier in the day and has become so intense that she can barely move. She became nauseated shortly after the pain began and vomited twice before arriving at the emergency department. She had a similar episode of pain 2 days ago which was less intense and resolved after an hour. Otherwise, she has no prior episodes of similar pain. She denies fever or chills. On further review of systems she has no complaint of dysuria, back pain, diarrhea, or constipation and notes no change in vaginal discharge.

PMHx: Mild asthma   **PSHx:** None   **Meds:** Ventolin PRN   **All:** NKDA

POb/GynHx: G_0; LMP 4.5 weeks ago; irregular menses every 4 to 8 weeks; no STIs; sexually active, and uses condoms.

THOUGHT QUESTIONS

- What is included in the differential diagnosis?
- What single laboratory test would be most important to sort out possible Ob/Gyn diagnoses?

Based on the history, this patient's differential diagnosis is broad and includes appendicitis, ectopic pregnancy, ovarian torsion, ruptured ovarian cyst, and PID. Of these, ruptured ovarian cyst is less likely because the associated pain does not typically wax and wane. PID is also usually a constant pain. In patients with abdominal pain, bowel obstruction and gastroenteritis should also be considered. However in this patient, these are less likely because she has had no prior surgery or other cause for bowel obstruction, and gastroenteritis usually has associated nausea and vomiting followed by abdominal pain and then diarrhea. A urogynecologic origin for her pain is possible as well, but again, unlikely given the absence of urinary complaints, or back or flank pain. The most important test is a urine pregnancy test. If the patient is not pregnant, the most dangerous diagnosis, ectopic pregnancy, is effectively ruled out.

CASE CONTINUED

VS: Temp 37.5°C, BP 114/68, HR 96, RR 16

PE: *Gen:* uncomfortable appearing. *Abdomen:* soft, no distension. Diffusely tender, worse in right lower quadrant (RLQ). Moderate rebound in RLQ. *Pelvic/BME:* uterus normal size AV/AF. Tenderness in RLQ with manipulation of cervix and uterus. Right adnexal mass, 7 to 8 cm and tender to palpation.

Labs: WBC 8.1; Hct 38.6; urine pregnancy negative; UA negative; stool guaiac negative.

THOUGHT QUESTIONS

- Now what is your most likely diagnosis?
- What imaging study (if any) would be most helpful now?
- What is your treatment plan?

After the physical exam, with her history, ovarian torsion is most likely, given the finding of a tender adnexal mass. We can exclude ectopic pregnancy on the basis of the negative pregnancy test. PID is unlikely in the setting of no fever and a normal WBC. A large adnexal mass would also be unlikely for a ruptured ovarian cyst. Although early appendicitis may have a normal WBC count and temperature, appendicitis of several days duration is usually associated with an elevated WBC count and fever.

A pelvic ultrasound would be the most helpful study at this time. For the most likely diagnoses, the findings would be as follows:

- Ovarian torsion: Ovarian mass, typically neoplasm or a large functional cyst. There may be no ovarian artery flow seen if the ovarian blood supply is compromised.
- Ruptured cyst: Usually free fluid in the cul-de-sac. An ovarian cyst may or may not be seen.
- PID: Normal ultrasound exam (unless a pelvic abscess is present).

The treatment for ovarian torsion is surgery (laparoscopy or laparotomy). The cyst must be removed and the torsion relieved before the ovary itself is compromised.

CASE CONTINUED

A pelvic ultrasound is obtained (Figure 25).

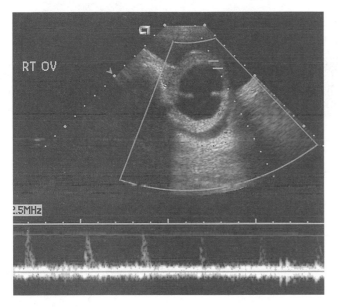

FIGURE 25 There is a large simple cyst in the ovary. Note the Doppler signal from the ovarian artery is diminished, as only brief arterial flow is allowed during systole. (Image provided by Departments of Radiology and Obstetrics & Gynecology, University of California, San Francisco.)

QUESTIONS

97. What type of ovarian cyst is this patient most likely to have?
    A. Corpus lutein cyst
    B. Cystic teratoma
    C. Follicular cyst
    D. Theca lutein cyst

98. On routine physical exam of a 28-year-old woman, you palpate a 5-cm left ovary. After obtaining an ultrasound that reveals a 4.2-cm simple cyst, which of the following is the best management?
    A. Obtain a CA-125
    B. Observe for 6 weeks and repeat the ultra-sound
    C. Obtain a CT scan
    D. Exploratory surgery and removal of the ovary and/or cyst

99. The most common ovarian neoplasm to undergo torsion is:
    A. Endometrioid tumor
    B. Benign cystic teratoma
    C. Cystadenocarcinoma
    D. Granulosa cell tumor

100. A woman presents with sudden acute pelvic pain and signs of hypovolemia. The most likely cause is:
    A. Ruptured endometrioma
    B. Ruptured cystic teratoma
    C. Ruptured corpus luteum cyst
    D. Ruptured ovarian follicle

ID/CC: A 28-year-old $G_3P_0S_2$ Hispanic woman who is at 8 weeks by LMP, presents with severe right-sided abdominal pain.

HPI: I.L. states the pain started gradually 2 days ago in her lower right abdomen. It is constant, dull, and not worsened by movement or eating. She reports mild fevers but denies N/V. Her bowel movements are normal. She denies vaginal bleeding or an abnormal vaginal discharge now, but she did have some spotting 4 days ago. This is a desired pregnancy.

PMHx: Anemia   **PSHx:** Appendectomy   **Meds:** PNV   **All:** NKDA

POb/GynHx: Regular cycles; heavy menses lasting 7 to 8 days; 2 first trimester losses. No STIs

---

THOUGHT QUESTION

- What would be the common causes of this patient's pain?

In a pregnant patient with acute pelvic pain, ruling out ectopic pregnancy should be the first thing on your mind. Ectopic pregnancy usually presents with unilateral pelvic pain and can be accompanied with vaginal bleeding or spotting. Other likely causes of this patient's pain include appendicitis, ovarian torsion, ruptured ovarian cyst, and a degenerating uterine fibroid. Given the history, gastroenteritis, bowel obstruction, and nephrolithiasis are less likely. A pelvic infection or PID is also possible, but also less likely because the pregnancy provides a barrier to ascending cervical infections.

CASE CONTINUED

VS: Temp 36.8°C, BP 116/78, HR 84, RR 16

PE: *Gen:* uncomfortable appearing. *Abdomen:* soft, no distension. Marked tenderness over palpable mass in right mid-quadrant. Mild rebound on right side. No guarding. Normal BS. *Pelvic:* normal appearing vagina, cervix, uterus 14-week size and irregular; tender to palpation, especially on right. Adnexae nontender and without masses.

THOUGHT QUESTION

- On physical exam, the uterus is larger than would be expected by the patient's last menstrual period. What two possibilities could account for this?

During early pregnancy, the most common cause of a size > dates (S > D) finding on physical exam is that the pregnancy is further along than the patient's recollection of her last menstrual period. This often happens because the patient has an episode of bleeding (likely due to implantation) that she perceives as her period. A uterus with fibroids (benign tumors of the smooth muscle cells of the myometrium) can also cause a S > D finding. A multiple gestation pregnancy is unlikely to cause S > D until at least the second trimester of pregnancy.

CASE CONTINUED

Labs: WBC 8.9; Hct 30.6; UA negative; β-hCG 26,769

US: Intrauterine pregnancy measuring 8 weeks and 5 days with cardiac motion. Diffusely myomatous uterus with 5-cm right fundal fibroid.

THOUGHT QUESTIONS

- How is this patient's pregnancy related to her acute pain?
- How can fibroids interact with a pregnancy?

Uterine leiomyomas or fibroids often grow in response to estrogen. They tend to enlarge during pregnancy and regress during menopause. When they enlarge rapidly, they can outgrow their blood supply, undergo degeneration, and consequently cause bouts of acute pain. Uterine fibroids can have an impact throughout pregnancy, causing pain (as in this patient), infertility, or spontaneous abortions when they affect the uterine cavity. In labor they can interfere with the ability of the uterus to contract; the mechanical obstruction can prevent the presentation and descent of the fetus. There are even case reports of uterine rupture during labor with myomatous uteri. Management is limited to treatment with pain medications.

QUESTIONS

101. In which ethnic group are fibroids most commonly found?
    A. Asian
    B. African-American
    C. Hispanic
    D. Caucasian

102. The cause of this patient's anemia is:
    A. Rupture of a degenerating fibroid
    B. Polymenorrhea
    C. Metrorrhagia
    D. Menorrhagia

103. Fibroids are associated with all of the following *except*:
    A. Hydronephrosis
    B. Recurrent pregnancy loss
    C. Anemia
    D. Endometritis

104. As this patient's pregnancy approaches term, she is at risk for all of the following *except*:
    A. Premature labor
    B. Polyhydramnios
    C. Cesarean section
    D. Malpresentation

ID/CC: 25-year-old G$_0$ woman presents with complaint of a new vaginal discharge.

HPI: T.V. states that she has recently become involved with a new sexual partner. They have been sexually active for the past month using oral contraceptive pills (OCPs) for birth control. She noticed a whitish-gray vaginal discharge about a week ago and now has significant pruritus as well. She was recently treated for bronchitis but does not recall the antibiotic she completed. She has had yeast infections before and wonders whether this could be another one. Ms. V denies a history of sexually transmitted infections or PID but does not know her partner's sexual history. She denies having fever or chills, or abdominal or pelvic pain. She denies having dysuria, dyspareunia, or abnormal bleeding.

PMHx/PSHx: Tonsillectomy as a child   **Meds:** OCPs   **All:** NKDA

POb/GynHx: Last Pap smear 6 months ago. No history of abnormal Pap smears. Menarche at age 13; regular 28-day cycles when not on OCPs, bleeds for 4 days. Her LMP was 2 weeks ago. She first became sexually active at age 17 and has had two partners in the past 6 months.

SHx: Lives alone. No use of tobacco; occasional use of marijuana; and social use of ethanol.

> *THOUGHT QUESTIONS*
> - What is your differential diagnosis?
> - What will you look for in the physical examination to distinguish between these diagnoses?
> - How can you distinguish between a vaginal infection versus a pelvic infection, and why is it important to do so?

Your differential diagnosis should include both sexually transmitted and nonsexually transmitted infections: gonorrhea, chlamydia, trichomonas vaginalis, vaginal candidiasis, and bacterial vaginosis. On examination, any evidence of pruritus, the type of vaginal discharge, and the appearance of the cervix are helpful to the diagnosis. On bimanual examination, the presence of cervical, uterine, or adnexal tenderness can help clarify whether a pelvic infection is present. You should have a good idea of the diagnosis after your history and physical examination, with the wet mount and KOH confirming your diagnosis.

Distinguishing between a vaginal versus pelvic infection is very important as pelvic infections can lead to infertility and, if left untreated, significant morbidity. PID can present in many ways but its three cardinal symptoms are pelvic pain, uterine tenderness, and adnexal tenderness.

CASE CONTINUED

VS: Temp 98.6°F, BP 98/64, HR 72

PE: *Gen:* thin female, NAD. *Lungs:* CTAB. *Cor:* RR&R. *Abdomen:* soft, nontender, no distension with normal BS. *EGBUS:* Normal female genitalia with mild erythema on labia minora. *SSE:* white-gray thin discharge, foul smelling. Normal appearing cervix. Cervical cultures obtained. *BME:* Small anteverted uterus, nontender. No adnexal masses. No CMT.

Labs: Wet prep: no clue cells; motile protozoa seen, many WBCs seen. KOH: no pseudohyphae seen. Vaginal pH 6.0. Urine dipstick: SG 1.020, negative nitrates/negative leukocyte esterase, negative RBC/WBCs

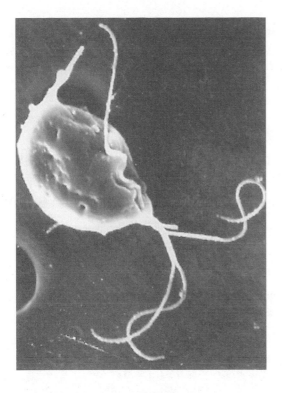

FIGURE 27 Trichomonad at high resolution. (Cox FEG. Modern Parasitology: A Textbook of Parasitology. 2nd ed. Oxford: Blackwell Science, 1993:9.)

You diagnose Ms. V with *Trichomonas* vaginalis (Figure 27). You discuss this diagnosis with her, explaining how it is transmitted and the need to treat her partner as well. As part of a full discussion of sexually transmitted infections (STIs), you instruct the patient to follow up on the results of her cervical cultures taken today and also discuss whether the patient wishes to be tested for hepatitis C, hepatitis B, and HIV. Lastly, you discuss the need for the use of condoms to help prevent STIs.

QUESTIONS

105. What is the medication and dosage you prescribe for this patient and her partner?
    A. Metronidazole, 2 grams orally only
    B. Metronidazole, 5 grams of 0.75% gel intra-vaginally, every night for 5 days
    C. Azithromycin, 1 gram orally only
    D. Fluconazole, 150 mg orally only

106. If this patient had presented with increased malodorous discharge without pruritus, what diagnosis would be more likely and what would you see on wet mount/KOH?
    A. *Chlamydia*—clue cells
    B. *Chlamydia*—white blood cells
    C. Bacterial vaginosis—clue cells
    D. Bacterial vaginosis—white blood cells

107. Use of broad spectrum antibiotics can contribute to the development of which infection?
    A. Bacterial vaginosis
    B. *Chlamydia*
    C. Vaginal candidiasis
    D. Gonorrhea

108. If this patient had also presented with dysuria, what three infections listed below could cause urethritis?
    A. Gonorrhea, *Chlamydia*, and *Trichomonas*
    B. Gonorrhea, *Chlamydia*, and candidiasis
    C. Gonorrhea, *Trichomonas*, and bacterial vaginosis
    D. *Chlamydia, Trichomonas*, and candidiasis

ID/CC: 21-year-old G_0 woman presents to the emergency room after being sexually assaulted.

HPI: E.C. was on her way home from a campus library at approximately 11:00 PM. Just a few hundred feet from the library, she was grabbed by an unidentified man and raped at knifepoint. At first she had struggled and was struck several times in the face and abdomen. After the assailant left, Ms. C was able to make her way back to the library where campus security was called, and she was brought to the local university hospital.

PMHx/PSHx: Appendectomy, age 7   **Meds:** None   **All:** Penicillin, anaphylaxis

POb/GynHx: G_0; menarche age 13; regular menses. Sexually active, currently monogamous with male partner; using OCPs.

SHx: College senior; lives with two other women three blocks from campus. Denies use of tobacco, ethanol, or recreational drugs.

THOUGHT QUESTIONS

- What further history should be obtained from this patient?
- What do you need to consider during the physical examination?

While it may feel intrusive, there is additional information that will help guide your medical management of this patient. In addition, as you may be called as a witness to this crime, it is important to get a clear, detailed story as soon as possible. Additional history regarding the event itself should include any information regarding identification of the assailant, particularly if he or she was known to the victim; how long ago the attack occurred; what specific physical and sexual assault took place, specifically whether oral, vaginal, or anal penetration occurred; whether the victim believes there was ejaculation; whether the victim has any history of STIs; and what the victim's physical complaints are. Often, the police will be involved before the physician. However, if they have not yet been involved, they need to be called to report the crime.

The physical examination of a victim of sexual assault needs to be performed in a systematic manner. Often there will be a "rape kit," a collection of instructions of how to proceed with evidence collection, which includes shaking out the victim's clothing, collecting tissue from under her fingernails, and combing her pubic hair to collect foreign hair. In addition to evidence collection, cultures of any possible exposure should be collected. If the patient has been physically assaulted, photographic evidence should be collected as well.

CASE CONTINUED

Upon further review with the patient, she reports that the attack was an hour ago. Currently what hurts the most is the left side of her face. There was vaginal penetration, and she is unsure about ejaculation. She did not recognize the perpetrator and cannot describe him as it was quite dark. She has no history of STIs, but is concerned about her risk of contracting one from this assault.

VS: Temp 97.2°F, BP 118/66, HR 98, RR 24

PE: *Gen:* in moderate emotional distress, tear-stained face, dirt on lower extremities (LEs), bruises and scrapes on face and LEs. *HEENT:* ecchymoses on left side of face and around left eye. *Back:* nontender, no CVAT. *Chest:* RR&R, tender beneath the left breast, ecchymoses. *Abdomen:* soft, nontender, no distension. *Pelvic:* normal external genitalia, no obvious bruising or evidence of trauma. Pubic hair combed out to collect samples. *SSE:* swabs of vagina and cervix are taken for cultures and for the rape kit. *BME:* patient is apprehensive about exam, but no evidence of CMT, no adnexal masses or tenderness; uterus is midline, normal in size.

> *THOUGHT QUESTION*
> • At this point what laboratory tests should be sent in addition to the cultures collected?

In this patient who has been exposed to an unknown assailant, there is no test that can be performed immediately to determine whether she has been exposed to or infected with an STI. It is common to offer baseline testing on the off-chance that she is infected in order to establish causality. Thus, baseline serum testing for hepatitis B, hepatitis C, HIV, and RPR are commonly performed. A serum pregnancy test is also sent to establish a baseline.

CASE CONTINUED

You offer the patient the testing mentioned above and she agrees. She also wants to know whether she is at risk for getting pregnant. She has been using OCPs for 2 years and rarely misses a pill. The last time she missed a pill was 3 months ago. You reassure her that the possibility is remote, given that she is so compliant with her OCP use. You then offer her prophylactic treatment for her possible exposure to STIs.

QUESTIONS

109. If this patient had not been on OCPs, which of the following would be an appropriate form of emergency contraception?
    A. IUD placement
    B. Lo Ovral, two-pill dose, given twice
    C. IM Depo-Provera
    D. Vaginal misoprostol
    E. Alesse, five-pill dose, given twice

110. Your offered treatment could include all of the following except:
    A. Ceftriaxone, 250 mg IM × 1
    B. Azithromycin, 1 gram PO × 1
    C. Azithromycin, 2 gram PO × 1
    D. Ofloxacin, 400 mg PO × 1
    E. Ciprofloxacin, 500 mg PO × 1

111. Which of the following is *least* necessary at this point in her management?
    A. X-rays of the face
    B. Social services consultation
    C. Prophylaxis for HIV
    D. Psychiatry consultation
    E. Chest x-ray

112. No prophylaxis can be given to prevent which of the following?
    A. *Chlamydia trachomatis* infection
    B. *Neisseria gonorrhoeae* infection
    C. HIV infection
    D. HPV infection
    E. Hepatitis B infection

ID/CC: 25-year-old G_0 woman presents with a mass on her perineum.

HPI: B.C. reports that she had a very tender mass in the same region 6 weeks ago that was treated with drainage and a course of antibiotics. The mass initially rose over 2 to 3 days, causing significant discomfort when sitting and walking. The pain resolved quickly with treatment at that time, but she still feels a mass in the area, which is noticeably uncomfortable when she is physically and sexually active. Now she feels that over the past 2 days it has become larger and more painful.

PMHx: None   **PSHx:** Appendectomy age 7   **Meds:** None   **All:** None

POb/GynHx: Sexually active and usually uses condoms. Genital HSV, last outbreak 1 year ago.

SHx: Single, graduate student in psychology. Occasional tobacco and ethanol use.

VS: Temp 97.2°F, BP 120/70, HR 85, RR 14

PE: *Abdomen:* soft, nontender, no distension, no palpable masses. *Pelvic:* normal except for a 5 × 4 cm cystic mass in the inferior aspect of the right. Labium majora, moderately tender, with minimal surrounding erythema.

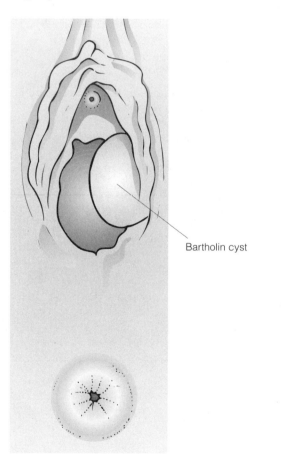

FIGURE 29 Bartholin gland cyst. These cysts can become enlarged or infected. (Champion RH. Textbook of Dermatology. 5th ed. Oxford: Blackwell Science, 1992:2852.)

Bartholin cyst

Labs: GC and *Chlamydia* negative by DNA probe 6 weeks ago

THOUGHT QUESTIONS

- What is the differential diagnosis for vulvar masses?
- What kinds of cysts arise on the vulva?
- When do you treat them?

A differential diagnosis for benign growths on the vulva includes Bartholin gland cyst, epidermal inclusion cyst, lipoma, fibroma, hidradenoma, hydrocele, leiomyoma, nevus, and supernumerary mammary tissue. Malignant growths would include squamous cell carcinoma, melanoma, adenocarcinoma, and sarcoma. The majority of vulvar masses are benign, fortunately. Generally, three types of cysts arise in the vulva: Bartholin gland cysts, epidermal inclusion cysts, and hydroceles. Treatment is rendered for pain, infection, or recurrent cyst formation, and usually involves a simple surgical procedure for release of the accumulated secretions.

CASE CONTINUED

The patient notices the mass when sitting down and is unable to engage in sexual intercourse secondary to the pain. As the pain has increased over the past couple of days, walking is becoming more uncomfortable. She also denies a prior history of other STIs such as gonorrhea or chlamydia. She is worried about a persistent infection.

QUESTIONS

113. What is the most common cystic mass in the vulvovaginal region?
  A. Fibroma
  B. Epidermal inclusion cyst
  C. Hidradenoma
  D. Nevus
  E. Bartholin cyst

114. What is the best treatment plan, given your diagnosis?
  A. Insertion of a Word catheter
  B. Marsupialization
  C. Needle aspiration and antibiotic treatment
  D. Incision and drainage of the cyst via the labium majora
  E. Warm sitz baths and follow-up in 1 week

115. This same presentation occurs in a 56-year-old postmenopausal woman. What is the most appropriate management?
  A. Insertion of a Word catheter
  B. Insertion of a Word catheter and biopsy of the cyst wall
  C. Marsupialization
  D. Incision and drainage of the cyst
  E. Excision of the cyst

116. What is the most common cause of Bartholin gland enlargement?
  A. Trauma
  B. Physiologic secretions
  C. Infection
  D. Unknown
  E. *Neisseria gonorrhoeae*

ID/CC: 38-year-old G₂P₂ woman complains of persistent vulvar burning and pain.

HPI: V.V. reports acute onset of vulvar discomfort 9 months ago. She initially noticed the pain with penetration during intercourse but now the discomfort is constant. She describes the pain as a "burning" sensation. She has also had increased vaginal discharge. Use of over-the-counter antifungal creams worsened the pain. A doctor then examined her and prescribed fluconazole orally. She saw this physician several times with the same complaints and he continued prescribing antifungals, which offered no relief. At this point she is concerned that the pain is a sign of some underlying disease that hasn't been diagnosed. She notes no pruritus, and no vaginal irritation or discharge.

PMHx: Migraine headaches   **PSHx:** Umbilical hernia repair

Meds: Antifungals PRN, NSAIDs, sumatriptan   **All:** NKDA

POb/GynHx: 2 forceps-assisted vaginal deliveries, 10 and 8 years ago. History of *Chlamydia* infection 12 years ago. Normal Pap smears, has had annually for past 3 years. Regular menses every 28 days. She uses condoms for birth control.

SHx: Married. Drinks 2 cups of coffee per day; social ethanol use; denies tobacco use.

VS: Temp 97.5°F, BP 102/60, HR 84, RR 14

PE: *Gen:* slightly anxious, thin woman. *Pelvic:* external genitalia—symmetric labia, no obvious lesions. *SSE:* vagina—physiologic discharge, mild erythema in the posterior vestibule which is tender to touch; cervix—multiparous os, no lesions. *BME:* uterus—small, AV/AF, nontender. No palpable adnexal masses.

THOUGHT QUESTIONS

- What is vulvodynia?
- What are the causes of vulvodynia?
- What physical findings support this clinical diagnosis?

Vulvodynia is a complex clinical syndrome of unexplained vulvar pain—burning and/or stinging, often accompanied by sexual dysfunction, physical disability, and psychological distress. The pain usually has an acute onset, which unfortunately can evolve into a chronic problem lasting months to years. Vulvodynia may have multiple causes such as vulvar vestibulitis, cyclic vulvovaginitis, dysesthetic vulvodynia, and vulvar dermatoses. Given symptomatology overlap, the same differential diagnosis for vulvar pruritus needs to be considered in vulvodynia as well. Physical findings are often normal, limited to pain on palpation of the vestibule, and/or present as inflammation in the vestibule or vagina. Because vulvodynia can be the initial presentation of both vulvar infections such as candidiasis and vulvar cancer, these need to be ruled out with culture, KOH prepared slides, colposcopy of the vulva, and biopsy.

CASE CONTINUED

Ms. V does not recall any particular event preceding the onset of her symptoms. The patient denies history of physical or sexual abuse. You perform a thorough examination including a Pap smear, KOH/wet mount, and gonorrhea and chlamydia cultures. Upon colposcopic examination of the vulva, you note no particular acetowhite areas. You perform an unguided biopsy of the vulvar vestibule.

QUESTIONS

117. If on clinical examination you see multiple pits and scars on the vulva as well as areas with draining sinuses, what do you need to include in the differential diagnosis?
    A. Psoriasis
    B. Acanthosis nigricans
    C. Behçet syndrome
    D. Hidradenitis suppurativa
    E. Squamous cell carcinoma

118. The Pap smear is normal. The KOH/wet mount preparation is normal. The biopsy returns as moderate to marked inflammation, with an abundance of plasma cells, most prominent in the stroma beneath the vestibular epithelium. What is her diagnosis?
    A. Contact dermatitis
    B. Cyclic vulvovaginitis
    C. HPV infection
    D. Lichen planus
    E. Vestibulitis

119. What is your first-line therapy for this diagnosis?
    A. Amitriptyline
    B. Topical corticosteroid ointment
    C. Oral fluconazole followed by topical antifungal medication
    D. Topical estrogen
    E. Sitz baths with Burow solution compresses

120. 18 months later despite topical steroid therapy she is distraught and complaining of intractable burning and pain in the vulvar region. What can you offer her?
    A. Recombinant alpha-interferon injections into the vestibule
    B. CO_2 laser ablation of the vestibular glands
    C. Observation for spontaneous remission
    D. Perineoplasty and gland excision
    E. Empiric broad-spectrum antibiotics with concurrent topical steroid use

ID/CC: A 20-year-old $G_2P_1T_1$ woman presents to your office complaining of worsening pelvic pain.

HPI: T.A. began having pain approximately 5 days ago and it has gradually worsened. It is sharp, constant, bilateral, but worse in the lower left quadrant. She has had two episodes of diarrhea and mild nausea today. She denies fevers or chills and notes no urinary symptoms. She also denies vaginal discharge or bleeding, but has noted an abnormal vaginal odor.

PMHx: Hepatitis A 3 years ago. Pneumonia at age 12.

PSHx: None   **Meds:** None   **All:** NKDA

POb/GynHx: LMP 10 days ago; never pregnant; regular cycles; no STIs. Sexually active with new partner; uses OCPs.

THOUGHT QUESTION
- What is included in the differential diagnosis at this point?

This patient's history is most consistent with PID. Because GI symptoms are common complaints, it is sometimes difficult to distinguish PID from appendicitis. If the physical exam does not help rule out appendicitis, an imaging study (CT scan) may be necessary. As usual, with any female patient presenting with abdominal/pelvic pain, ectopic pregnancy needs to be ruled out with a negative pregnancy test.

CASE CONTINUED

VS: Temp 37.5°C, BP 107/68, HR 106, RR 16

PE: *Gen:* uncomfortable appearing. *Abdomen:* soft, no distension. Diffusely tender, worse in lower left quadrant. Mild diffuse rebound. No guarding. Normal BS. *SSE:* normal appearing vagina, cervix. *BME:* marked CMT tenderness. Uterus normal size, AV/AF, mildly tender to palpation. Tenderness in both adnexa (left > right), but no appreciable masses.

Labs: WBC 8.9; Hct 38.6; urine pregnancy test negative. Gonorrhea/chlamydia cultures pending.

THOUGHT QUESTIONS
- What is your diagnosis now?
- How would the culture results influence treatment for this patient?
- How would the finding of a pelvic mass affect your treatment?

Major and minor criteria are used for the diagnosis of PID. There are three major criteria: abdominal, adnexal, and cervical motion tenderness—all of which this patient has. If a patient has all three major criteria in the absence of another cause (such as appendicitis), she is diagnosed with PID. Minor criteria such as fever, an elevated WBC or erythrocyte sedimentation rate (ESR) are used to help establish the diagnosis of PID when all three major criteria are not met. PID is thought to be caused by an ascending cervical gonorrheal or chlamydial infection. However, once the infection reaches the upper genital tract, it is polymicrobial. Treatment is with a broad-spectrum cephalosporin and doxycycline. A stable patient who is compliant and able to tolerate oral medications can be treated as an outpatient. Otherwise, admission for IV antibiotics is necessary.

Persistent PID can lead to tubo-ovarian abscesses (TOAs) or tubo-ovarian complexes (TOCs). Unlike TOAs, TOCs are pelvic adnexal infections that are not walled off, and hence more responsive to antibiotic therapy. Finding an adnexal mass on exam should raise concern for a TOA, TOC, or ovarian torsion. Pelvic ultrasound can confirm the diagnosis. Treatment is hospitalization for broad-spectrum IV antibiotics, often ampicillin, gentamicin, and clindamycin. If antibiotic therapy fails, surgical removal of infected tissues is necessary.

QUESTIONS

121. A patient with a TOA fails IV cefotetan and doxy-cycline treatment. The next step in management would be:
    A. Expand antibiotic coverage with ampicillin, gentamicin, and clindamycin
    B. Laparoscopy for confirmation of the diagnosis
    C. Laparotomy with unilateral salpingo-oophorectomy
    D. Laparotomy with hysterectomy and bilateral salpingo-oophorectomy

122. Of the following, the most common sequelae of PID is:
    A. Fitz-Hugh-Curtis syndrome
    B. Infertility
    C. Toxic shock syndrome
    D. Bacterial vaginosis

123. A 17-year-old woman complains of an abnormal vaginal discharge. A mucopurulent discharge is seen and a first-stream urine test is positive for *Chlamydia*. Appropriate treatment for this patient is:
    A. A 10-day course of dicloxacillin
    B. A 7-day course of Keflex
    C. 2 grams of metronidazole once
    D. 1 gram of azithromycin once

124. Which of the following has been shown to be protective against PID?
    A. IUD use
    B. Oral contraceptive use
    C. Weekly douching with dilute vinegar solution
    D. Cigarette smoking

ID/CC: 45-year-old $G_4P_3S_1$ African-American woman presents complaining of heavy periods.

HPI: A.O. states that she is currently completing a menstrual period complicated by heavy bleeding requiring up to 30 pads a day for a 5-day period, and is now down to 5 pads a day. In total, she has been bleeding for 12 days. In general she has had regular 28- to 30-day cycles, bleeding for 5 to 6 days using 5 to 6 pads a day. During the past year her periods have become less frequent but occasionally quite excessive. Ms. O denies having spotting in between her menses. She has a history of significant cramping and breast tenderness with her menses, but states that these complaints have gotten better over the past year. She denies having any weakness or dizziness, but does complain of mild fatigue. She denies having any hot flashes, vaginal dryness, night sweats, or changes in weight over the past 6 months.

PMHx: Hypertension × 8 years, mild obesity

PSHx: Appendectomy as a child; 1 C/S with tubal ligation

Meds: Hydrochlorothiazide, 25 mg PO every day   **All:** NKDA

POb/GynHx: 2 NSVDs, 1 C/S for breech presentation. Menarche age 11; menstrual cycle as above. Normal Pap smears, last 6 months ago. Distant history of chlamydial infection; denies PID. Sexually active with husband; tubal ligation.

SocHx: Lives with husband, children grown; denies domestic violence. Quit smoking 5 years ago after 15 pack per year history; social ethanol use; denies other recreational drug use.

THOUGHT QUESTIONS

- What is the difference between menorrhagia, metrorrhagia, and menometrorrhagia?
- What is your differential diagnosis for this patient's complaint of menorrhagia?
- Should this patient be admitted to the hospital and/or receive a blood transfusion?

Menorrhagia is bleeding at the time of menses that is heavy or prolonged. Metrorrhagia is bleeding in between menses. Menometrorrhagia is a combination of the two (i.e., menses that are heavy or prolonged with occasional intermenstrual bleeding).

In general the differential diagnoses for menorrhagia include the following: endometrial hyperplasia, endometrial cancer, anatomical sources including fibroids or polyps, adenomyosis, hormonal sources including anovulation, and lastly bleeding disorders. The latter is usually a diagnosis made early in a patient's menstrual life and does not usually occur for the first time late in life unless that patient is acutely ill with a liver disorder and/or a coagulopathy. Polyps, cervical or endometrial, usually present as metrorrhagia, but should remain part of a differential diagnosis.

Acute bleeding from menorrhagia requiring a blood transfusion or hospitalization for hemodynamic stabilization can occur. It is important when evaluating a patient that you first determine whether the patient is hemodynamically stable. A patient who is not stable may present quite obviously (e.g., brought in by ambulance with tachycardia, low blood pressure, and mental obtundation). However, most patients will present with more subtle findings such as dizziness and fatigue with tachycardia, orthostatic hypotension, and a low hematocrit.

CASE CONTINUED

VS: Lying BP 135/88, HR 76; sitting BP 138/88, HR 80; standing BP 140/90, HR 84. Weight 160 lbs, Height 5'5"

PE: *Gen:* NAD. *Lungs:* CTA. *Cor:* RR&R, no murmurs. *Abdomen:* obese, soft, nontender, no HSM. *Extremities:* no clubbing, cyanosis, or edema. *Pelvic:* no vulvar lesions; pink, moist mucous membranes. *SSE:* thin, white vaginal discharge, scant blood in vault; cervix within normal limits. *BME:* small ante-verted nontender uterus, no adnexal masses noted.

Labs: Urine hCG negative; WBC 6.0; Hb 11.4; Hct 35.0; Plts 300. Endometrial biopsy sent.

Ten days later you receive the biopsy result, which shows no evidence of hyperplasia or carcinoma. You have Ms. O undergo a blood draw 21 days after the completion of her menses to see whether or not she ovulated. The findings above suggest that she did not ovulate during this cycle. You counsel her that her heavy menses is likely secondary to anovulation and you discuss therapies.

QUESTIONS

125. What hormone did you measure and what was the result that suggested anovulation?
    A. Progesterone—high
    B. Progesterone—low
    C. Estrogen—high
    D. Estrogen—low

126. What treatment options are available for this patient?
    A. Low-dose oral contraceptive pills
    B. Hormone replacement therapy
    C. Cyclical progesterone
    D. All of the above
    E. B and C only

127. If this patient had presented with a long history of heavy menses and an enlarged uterus, what would her most likely diagnosis be?
    A. Adenomyosis
    B. Fibroids
    C. Endometrial polyps
    D. Endometrial cancer

128. Which of the following patients should undergo an endometrial biopsy to rule out endometrial cancer?
    A. A 40-year-old female with a history of breast cancer on tamoxifen with vaginal bleeding
    B. A 40-year-old female with bleeding in between her menses for the last 6 months
    C. A 32-year-old female with 4 months of abnormal bleeding after starting OCPs
    D. All of the above
    E. A and B only

CASE 33 / METRORRHAGIA

ID/CC: 46-year-old G$_3$P$_3$ Caucasian woman presents complaining of vaginal spotting.

HPI: E.P. states that over the past 6 to 8 months she has noticed occasional vaginal spotting in between her menses. The bleeding lasts for 2 to 10 days and is quite light, not requiring a pad. Her periods remain regular, every 30 to 32 days, and she bleeds for 5 to 6 days using about four tampons each day. She is sexually active but is uncertain whether the spotting is related to sex. She denies having any pelvic pain. Her vaginal discharge is thick and white with some mild pruritus. She did have a yeast infection about 3 months before, which she treated with an over-the-counter yeast medication. Ms. P denies having any fever or chills, night sweats, or recent changes in weight. She is quite certain this is vaginal bleeding and denies having any rectal bleeding or changes in her bowel movements.

PMHx: Type II diabetes mellitus for 5 years; moderate obesity   **PSHx:** None

Meds: Glyburide, occasional Tylenol   **All:** Penicillin, causing rash

POb/GynHx: 3 NSVDs, uncomplicated. LMP 3 weeks prior. Menarche age 12; cycles as above. Distant history of chlamydial infection with PID. Sexually active, 2 partners in past 6 months, uses condoms. Last Pap 5 years ago, normal. Says she had an abnormal Pap many years ago, but on repeat "it was better" and she required no treatment.

SocHx: Lives alone. Smokes half-pack per day for 20 years; occasional ethanol use; denies recreational drug use.

FHx: Type II diabetes mellitus in multiple family members, Heart disease in an aunt and uncle.

THOUGHT QUESTIONS
- What is this patient's differential diagnosis?
- What tests would you like to perform on this patient and why?

The differential diagnosis for metrorrhagia includes cervical and endometrial polyps, cervical dysplasia and carcinoma, endometrial hyperplasia and carcinoma, cervicitis, and vaginal and vulvar lesions.

A KOH should be performed, as severe vaginal candidiasis when associated with excoriated areas can bleed. This patient is also overdue for a Pap smear and her vague history of an abnormal Pap in the past is worrisome. Cervicitis can cause spotting so gonorrhea and chlamydia tests should be done. In addition, an endometrial biopsy is warranted, given the patient's age and her risk factors for endometrial hyperplasia and carcinoma (i.e., diabetes mellitus, obesity).

CASE CONTINUED

VS: Temp 98.4°F, BP 138/86, HR 88, RR 16. Weight 174 lbs, Height 5'4"

PE: *Gen:* obese female, NAD. *Lungs:* CTAB. *Neck:* normal-size thyroid without nodules. *Cor:* RR&R, no murmurs. *Abdomen:* obese, soft, nontender. *EGBUS:* mild erythema of labia minora and majora, no lesions noted. *SSE:* thick white vaginal discharge; no cervical lesions or polyps noted. *BME:* limited secondary to habitus; midposition uterus noted, approximately 5 to 6 week size, nontender; no adnexal masses appreciated. *Rectal:* guaiac negative, no hemorrhoids noted. *Extremities:* no clubbing, cyanosis, or edema.

Labs: Urine pregnancy negative; Wet prep, normal, few WBCs; KOH: pseudohyphae noted. FSBG, 188. Pap smear, endometrial biopsy, gonorrhea and chlamydia cultures sent.

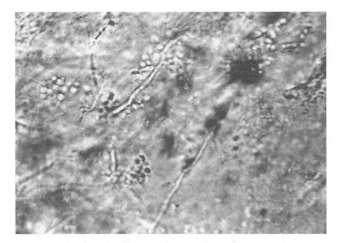

FIGURE 33 *Candida albicans.* Note the budding and pseudohyphae. (Crissey JT. Manual of Medical Mycology. Boston: Blackwell Science, 1995:90.)

The patient is told that she has a vaginal yeast infection. You prescribe Diflucan, one dose of 150 mg PO, and you refer her to her primary doctor for a reevaluation of her current oral hypoglycemic regimen. The gonorrhea and chlamydia cultures return as negative 5 days later. Ten days later, the endometrial biopsy result returns without evidence of hyperplasia or carcinoma. However, gland proliferation suggestive of an endometrial polyp is noted. The Pap smear is normal. You schedule the patient for a pelvic ultrasound, which reveals a thickened endometrial stripe, possibly secondary to a polyp, without other pathologic evidence.

QUESTIONS

129. In the face of this possible diagnosis, what is a potential next step?
    A. Operative hysteroscopy with possible polypectomy
    B. Laparoscopy
    C. No treatment needed
    D. Hysterectomy

130. Approximately what percentage of endometrial polyps are associated with cancer?
    A. Less than 1%
    B. 1% to 5%
    C. 5% to 10%
    D. 10% to 20%

131. Which hysteroscopic distension medium is incorrectly matched to its possible complication?
    A. Glycine—anaphylactic shock
    B. Sorbitol—hyponatremia
    C. Dextran—pulmonary edema
    D. Hyskon—bleeding diathesis

132. Assume that during your office examination you visualized a cervical polyp measuring 1.0 × 0.5 cm. What is the next step?
    A. Biopsy a piece of the polyp and send it to pathology.
    B. Remove the polyp with polyp forceps and send it to pathology.
    C. Remove the polyp with cryosurgery.
    D. Remove the polyp in the operating room in case of bleeding.

ID/CC: 32-year-old G_0 woman with severe, progressive dysmenorrhea.

HPI: For the past 4 years P.D. notes that her periods have become increasingly worse. She often has to miss work during the first and second days of her menses. The pain typically resolves 2 to 5 days after the end of her period. She finds only partial relief with ibuprofen. In addition, during the last 4 months she has experienced deep, sharp pain with intercourse. She has been in a monogamous relationship for the past 2 years.

PMHx: None   **PSHx:** None

POb/GynHx: Menarche age 14, LMP 3 weeks ago. Regular menses every 27 to 30 days, lasting 4 to 5 days, with moderate flow. No history of STI. Uses diaphragm.

Meds: Ibuprofen, 200–400 mg PRN   **All:** NKDA

SHx: No tobacco use, occasional ethanol use.

FHx: 35-year-old sister who has been unable to conceive for 5 years; otherwise noncontributory.

VS: Afebrile, stable.

PE: *Abdomen:* soft, nontender. No guarding. No palpable masses. Normal external genitalia, normal vagina and cervix. No discharge. *Pelvic:* small uterus, retroverted, slightly tender to palpation and mild CMT tenderness. No obvious adnexal masses or tenderness.

Labs: WBC 6.4; Hb 11.2; UA negative; negative urine hCG

THOUGHT QUESTIONS

- What is your differential diagnosis?
- What additional studies would you recommend to make a diagnosis?
- What first-line treatment option would you recommend?

This patient has progressive, severe dysmenorrhea. The differential diagnosis includes primary and secondary dysmenorrhea. Primary dysmenorrhea is a diagnosis of exclusion, when no organic cause can be identified. The age at presentation, the progressive nature of her complaint, the new onset dyspareunia, and the physical findings all suggest an organic lesion. Endometriosis, adenomyosis, uterine fibroids, pelvic infection, uterine polyps, intrauterine contraceptive device, cervical stenosis or obstruction in menstrual flow at any point in the genital tract, and pelvic adhesions can cause secondary dysmenorrhea. This patient's clinical presentation is suggestive of endometriosis, the classic symptoms of which are secondary dysmenorrhea, dyspareunia, and infertility. This patient has at least the first two symptoms. Additionally, a positive family history is present in about 20% of endometriosis patients, and this patient reports that her sister has infertility (but we do not know the cause). Endometriosis is formally diagnosed by direct visualization and tissue diagnosis, usually via laparoscopy.

Cultures (or a DNA based test) for *N. gonorrhoeae* and *C. trachomatis* should be sent to rule out acute or chronic PID. Pelvic ultrasound is helpful in evaluating for the presence of uterine fibroids, polyps or IUD, and ovarian cysts, the latter of which is consistent with endometriosis. Occasionally adenomyosis can be diagnosed with ultrasound, but often this diagnosis requires an MRI. Sonohysterogram and/or hysterosalpingogram to evaluate the uterine cavity and tubes are useful if submucosal fibroids or polyps are suspected, or if uterine synechiae are a possibility.

A trial of oral contraceptives for at least 3 months and/or NSAIDs at adequate dosing and schedule would be reasonable options as initial therapy, assuming the ultrasound was negative.

CASE CONTINUED

Chlamydia and gonococci cervical studies by PCR are negative. Pelvic ultrasound is normal. You start her on birth control pills (combined, monophasic OCP) and recommend that she keep a menstrual pain calendar. She is to come back and see you in 3 months.

QUESTIONS

133. On her next visit she reports that her menstrual pain has decreased significantly in the last menses. Which of the following would you recommend?
    A. Continue OCP use until conception is desired.
    B. Continue OCP for 6 months and then discontinue.
    C. Discontinue OCP at age 35 because of increased risk of thromboembolic events.
    D. Long-term OCP use is not a good choice because it increases the risk for ovarian cancer.

134. Six months later, she notes no improvement in her menstrual pain during the last 5 out of 6 periods. The next best step in management is:
    A. Begin antidepressant treatment with SSRIs
    B. Total abdominal hysterectomy, bilateral salpingo-oophorectomy, and appendectomy
    C. Laparoscopy
    D. GnRH agonist (Lupron)
    E. Vaginal hysterectomy

135. With regard to primary dysmenorrhea, which of the following is *false*?
    A. It is more common among women with irregular cycles and dysfunctional uterine bleeding.
    B. Response rates to NSAIDs and OCPs as first-line therapy are similar.
    C. Pelvic exam is usually normal.
    D. For best results, NSAIDs should be started prior to the onset of menses.
    E. Typically symptoms develop prior to age 20 years.

136. The following conditions are usually associated with the following signs or symptoms *except*:
    A. Cervical stenosis—hypomenorrhea
    B. Endometriosis—uterosacral nodularities
    C. Adenomyosis—diffusely enlarged uterus
    D. IUD—fixed, retroverted uterus
    E. Primary dysmenorrhea—nausea, vomiting, and diarrhea with menses

ID/CC: 14-year-old female presents with complaints of lower abdominal pain and fullness.

HPI: I.H. has had no prior medical complaints. She presents now to the emergency room with her mother complaining of low, midline abdominal pain. She notes that this pain began approximately 48 hours ago. It had increased slowly at first, but over the last 4 to 6 hours, it has dramatically worsened in severity. She reports prior episodes of this pain, though not as bad, for almost a year. The last episode of pain was approximately a month ago. She is slightly nauseous, but has not had any emesis. She also notes that she has had not had any fever or chills. She denies anorexia, but reports feeling a fullness in her abdomen for several months. She has no changes in bowel habits, but has noticed an increase in urinary frequency.

PMHx: Childhood illnesses   **PSHx:** None   **Meds:** Tylenol for pain   **All:** NKDA

POb/GynHx: Has not reached menarche yet.

SHx: On isolated history, no self-report of tobacco, ethanol, or recreational drug use. Has never been sexually active.

VS: Temp 98.4°F, BP 118/76, HR 92, RR 16

PE: *Gen:* appears uncomfortable, but in minimal distress. *Abdomen:* soft, no rebound or guarding, fullness consistent with mass in lower abdomen, slightly tender. *Pelvic:* normal external genitalia. Patient and parents refuse internal exam.

THOUGHT QUESTIONS

- What is in the differential diagnosis?
- What laboratory tests or studies would you order next?

Because of the question of an abdominal mass, the differential should include soft tissue tumors of the abdomen and pelvis. Benign adnexal tumors from the uterus and adnexa should also be considered. Two common ovarian tumors that will present as enlarged masses are the cystadenoma and benign teratoma. Either of these can undergo torsion, which can lead to increasing pain, though usually present with concomitant nausea, vomiting, and peritoneal signs.

At this time, the usual laboratory tests for abdominal pain are reasonable: a CBC to look for signs of infection, LFTs, and bilirubins, though the latter two are likely to be low yield in this patient. The most important study to get next is an imaging study of the abdomen and pelvis. If this is truly a pelvic mass, a pelvic ultrasound is the imaging modality of choice. However, this patient may decline a transvaginal ultrasound because of her virginal history. In that setting, an abdominal/pelvic CT is certainly reasonable to begin characterizing the mass.

CASE CONTINUED

Labs: WBC 7.6; Hct 36.7; Plts 269K

You discuss the possible imaging modalities with the patient and her mother, and they agree to try the ultrasound, though they would prefer that it be performed abdominally.

US: Pelvic, transabdominal—normal uterus, left ovary measures 3.2 × 3.4 × 3.1 cm, right ovary measures 2.6 × 3.2 × 3.6 cm. No evidence of adnexal mass. Moderate free fluid in the cul-de-sac, large amount of fluid below cervix in vagina, thickened endometrium in uterus along with heterogeneous material. Transvaginal approach failed secondary to patient discomfort.

THOUGHT QUESTION

• What is your differential diagnosis now?

With the new information provided by the transabdominal ultrasound, it is clear that there is an obstruction to the menstrual flow from the uterus. The multiple potential causes include abnormal fusion of the lower and upper genital tracts, transverse vaginal septum, imperforate hymen, and a variant of vaginal agenesis where there is just absence of distal vagina. The obstruction to flow has allowed a large collection of blood and menstrual tissue to collect in the upper vagina, and it has backflowed through the fallopian tubes into the pelvis. This has led to the patient's cyclic pelvic pain.

CASE CONTINUED

You explain this information to the patient and her mother and order an MRI to further detail the pelvic anatomy. You also perform a gentle speculum examination at this point to help with diagnosis and to plan treatment. There is about 1 cm of depth to the vagina beyond the external labia (Figure 35). There is no obvious evidence of a hymeneal ring and the obstruction to the upper vagina appears thin and fluctuant.

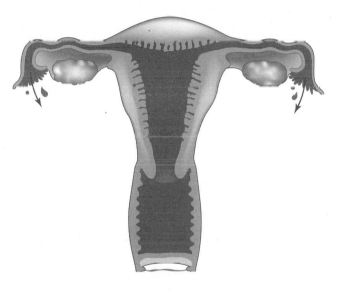

FIGURE 35 The uterus and adnexa are normal, but the outflow tract is occluded leading to a collection of menses that has filled the vagina and backed up into the uterus and pelvis. (Illustration by Electronic Illustrators Group.)

QUESTIONS

137. Based on the physical exam, what is the diagnosis?
    A. Imperforate hymen
    B. Transverse vaginal septum
    C. Vaginal agenesis
    D. Mayer-Rokitansky-Küster-Hauser syndrome
    E. Not enough evidence to diagnose

138. On MRI, what other structures should be characterized in addition to the pelvic organs?
    A. Adrenal glands
    B. Appendix
    C. Pancreas
    D. Kidneys
    E. Spine

139. Which treatment for recurrent miscarriages used from the 1950s to the 1970s was shown to be associated in müllerian abnormalities?
    A. Ethinyl estradiol
    B. Ethynodiol diacetate
    C. Diethylstilbestrol
    D. Desogestrel
    E. Norethindrone acetate

140. This agent was also associated with which unusual disease of the genital tract?
    A. Paget disease
    B. Vaginal adenocarcinoma
    C. Leiomyosarcoma
    D. Ovarian adenocarcinoma
    E. Squamous cell carcinoma of the cervix

ID/CC: 25-year-old G_0 woman with an 8-month history of pelvic pain.

HPI: S.E. presents with moderate dysmenorrhea that has progressively worsened over time and become periodically incapacitating. At the onset of symptoms 3 years ago, her previous gynecologist placed her on oral contraceptives (OCPs). This alleviated her symptoms for the subsequent year and a half, but the pain eventually returned and worsened. Over the last 8 months, Ms. E describes the pain as constant, dull pelvic pain radiating to her lower back, with occasional sharp exacerbations. She has had pain during intercourse (dyspareunia) for the last 4 to 5 months. The chronicity of her pain has gradually increased to the point that it occurs almost daily. Ibuprofen, which initially provided adequate relief for the dysmenorrhea, is no longer effective. In addition, she has experienced decreased appetite, libido, and energy as well as insomnia over the last 4 months. On review of systems, she notes increased urinary frequency and urgency. No hematuria. No GI symptoms.

PMHx: None

PSHx: Exploratory laparotomy at age 17 for suspected appendicitis, not confirmed. Diagnostic laparoscopy at age 22 for ruptured right ovarian cyst.

POb/GynHx: Menarche age 15, regular cycles every 27 to 30 days. LMP 3 weeks ago. No STIs.

Meds: Ibuprofen 600 mg PRN; with menses, OCPs   **All:** NKDA

SHx: Has lived with her boyfriend for over 2 years. No tobacco use, occasional ethanol use.

VS: Afebrile, stable.

PE: *Abdomen:* soft, mild suprapubic tenderness. No guarding. Normal external genitalia, normal vagina and cervix. *Pelvic:* smooth, regular 7 to 8 week size uterus, retroverted, fixed, and mildly tender to palpation. No CMT. Fullness consistent with an adnexal mass on the left, and mild to moderate adnexal tenderness, right > left. Rectovaginal exam reveals some nodularity in the cul-de-sac.

THOUGHT QUESTIONS

- What is the differential diagnosis?
- What studies would you recommend to help you in the diagnosis?

This patient has chronic pelvic pain (CPP) given the duration (greater than 6 months of pelvic pain) and the associated disturbances in both her mood as well as physical activity. The causes of CPP are multiple, and may be gynecologic and nongynecologic. Although not exclusive, the initial catamenial relationship of her pain and the presence of dyspareunia are suggestive of a gynecologic source. Furthermore, the abnormal findings on pelvic exam are highly indicative of a gynecologic source for her pain. The history of dysmenorrhea gradually progressing to constant pain, dyspareunia, and a fixed retroverted uterus makes endometriosis highly likely in the differential diagnosis. Adenomyosis is also a common cause of secondary dysmenorrhea that can be progressive and associated with dyspareunia. Pelvic adhesions, in this patient likely due to the two prior pelvic surgeries, are another important consideration. Primary dysmenorrhea is unlikely because the pain is intermenstrual now.

Laboratory studies have a limited role in the setting of CPP. Imaging studies such as pelvic ultrasonography have questionable value in the setting of a normal pelvic examination, but in this patient may be helpful given her physical examination findings. Laboratory studies should be tailored to the patient's history. A urinalysis (UA) with micro and possible culture is indicated in this patient due to her history. Cervical cultures for gonorrhea and *Chlamydia trachomatis* should also be obtained. CBC with a sedimentation rate may be helpful in detecting a chronic inflammatory response.

CASE CONTINUED

CBC, sedimentation rate, urinalysis, gonorrhea, and chlamydia studies are all within normal limits. Her urine pregnancy test was negative. Pelvic ultrasound revealed a slightly enlarged, homogeneous uterus and a 4-cm left adnexal mass (Figure 36).

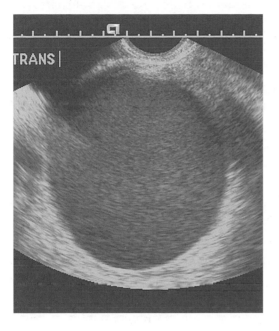

FIGURE 36 Large endometrioma in the ovary. It is filled with heterogeneous material, mostly old blood. (Image provided by Departments of Radiology and Obstetrics & Gynecology, University of California, San Francisco.)

QUESTIONS

141. The next best step in management is:
    A. Exploratory laparotomy
    B. Repeat ultrasound in 6 to 8 weeks
    C. Obtain CA-125 level
    D. Laparoscopy

142. Appropriate surgical management in this patient would include which of the following?
    A. Copious irrigation and IV antibiotics
    B. Total abdominal hysterectomy and bilateral salpingo-oophorectomy
    C. Right salpingo-oophorectomy
    D. Ovarian cystectomy and fulguration or excision of peritoneal implants
    E. No intervention is necessary

143. After her surgery, the patient is begun on the following to help keep her pain free:
    A. Cyclic oral contraceptives
    B. Continuous oral contraceptives
    C. A GnRH analog (Lupron)
    D. Fentanyl patches

144. Common side effects of GnRH analogs (Lupron) include all of the following *except*:
    A. Hot flashes and vaginal dryness
    B. Reversible bone loss with short-term treatment (6 months or less)
    C. Adverse impact on serum lipid levels
    D. Osteoporosis with long-term therapy (more than 6 months)

ID/CC: A 28-year-old $G_2P_1T_1$ woman presents with an 8-month history of amenorrhea.

HPI: S.A. had a normal vaginal delivery 2 years ago and breastfed for 1 year. She was amenorrheic until about 9 months ago when she had two menses spaced 6 weeks apart. Since then she has not menstruated. She was on Depo-Provera (DMPA) for 6 months immediately after delivery, but stopped because she felt she didn't need it. On review of systems, she denies headache or visual changes but reports that she is still able to express milk from both breasts.

PMHx: None   **PSHx:** D&C 8 years ago. Cone biopsy 6 years ago.

Meds: None   **All:** NKDA

POb/GynHx: History of high-grade squamous intraepithelial lesion (HGSIL) treated with cone biopsy; menarche at age 12. Irregular cycles for last 4 years. Denies STDs.

THOUGHT QUESTIONS

- What are the two types of amenorrhea and how are they defined?
- What are the causes of amenorrhea?
- Why are the possible anatomic causes for this patient's amenorrhea unlikely?
- What serum and urine tests should be checked first in this patient?

There are two types of amenorrhea and they are defined by the patient's menstrual history. Primary amenorrhea is defined as the absence of menses in women who have not undergone menarche by age 16 (or age 14 with the concurrent absence of normal growth and development and secondary sexual characteristics). Secondary amenorrhea is the absence of menses for 3 cycles or at maximum 6 months in women who have had a history of menstruation. Within these two types, possible causes for amenorrhea fall into three broad categories: anatomic/outflow abnormalities, end-organ (ovarian) disorders, and central disorders. Some causes of amenorrhea are listed in Table 37.

TABLE 37. Causes of Primary and Secondary Amenorrhea		
	PRIMARY AMENORRHEA	**SECONDARY AMENORRHEA**
Anatomic/outflow abnormality	Imperforate hymen Transverse vaginal septum Vaginal atresia Müllerian agenesis Testicular feminization	Asherman syndrome Cervical stenosis
End-organ disorder	Primary ovarian failure (hypergonadotropic hypogonadism) Savage syndrome Turner syndrome (45,XO) Gonadal agenesis (46,XY) Swyer syndrome 17α-hydroxylase deficiency	Premature ovarian failure Polycystic ovary syndrome
Central disorder	Kallman syndrome (absent GnRH) Pituitary stalk compression Pituitary tumors	Hypothyroidism Pituitary tumors Chest wall and nipple stimulation Drug induced CNS disease

Possible anatomic causes for secondary amenorrhea in this patient include uterine adhesions or scarring (Asherman syndrome) caused by her prior D&C, and cervical stenosis, a consequence of surgical or obstetric trauma. Neither is likely as she has menstruated after her surgical procedures and twice since her vaginal delivery.

A pregnancy test should be performed for all patients with secondary amenorrhea. If this is negative, prolactin (PRL) and thyroid-stimulating hormone (TSH) will help exclude common causes for secondary amenorrhea. Hypothyroidism leads to elevated TRH, which in turn stimulates pituitary cells to secrete PRL. In this case, both TSH and PRL are elevated. An isolated elevation in PRL should trigger an evaluation for drug-induced hyperprolactinemia; an MRI can help rule out a hypothalamic or pituitary lesion.

CASE CONTINUED

VS: Weight 172 lbs, Height 5'4"

PE: *Neck:* supple, without masses. *Breasts:* normal, able to express milky fluid from both. *Pelvic:* well-estrogenized pelvic tissues. Cervix consistent with prior surgery. Uterus normal, anteverted, and mobile. No adnexal masses.

Labs: TSH 9.7 mU/L (normal: 0.5–4.5 mU/L); PRL 37 ng/mL (normal: 2–15 ng/mL)

THOUGHT QUESTION

• How would you treat this patient's amenorrhea?

Because both TSH and prolactin levels are elevated, this patient has hypothyroidism-induced hyperprolactinemia. A low free T_4 level will confirm the diagnosis. In addition, an MRI of the head may reveal hypertrophy or hyperplasia of the pituitary. This, along with the patient's amenorrhea and galactorrhea, should resolve quickly with treatment of her hypothyroidism with thyroid hormone replacement (Synthroid).

QUESTIONS

145. You are evaluating a patient who has a 3-year history of secondary amenorrhea. Her TSH is normal, but her prolactin level is elevated. You review her medications. Which of the following could be the cause of the hyperprolactinemia?
    A. The ibuprofen she takes for chronic pain.
    B. The fluoxetine she takes for depression.
    C. The clozapine she takes for agitation.
    D. The famotidine she takes for GERD.

146. If the patient you have just seen in the case above had complained of visual changes, the most likely visual or ocular defect found on physical examination would be:
    A. bitemporal hemianopsia
    B. retinal hemorrhages
    C. lateral nystagmus
    D. amaurosis fugax

147. A 34-year-old G_2P_1 woman has not had a menstrual cycle for 9 months. Prior to this her cycles were irregular. Her TSH and PRL levels are normal. The next step in management is:
    A. Measure serum FSH
    B. Perform a progestin challenge test
    C. Begin treatment with oral contraceptives
    D. Ultrasound to evaluate for ovarian neoplasm

148. A 22-year-old professional dancer (G_0) presents with absence of menses for 6 months. Prior to this her cycles had been irregular. Physical examination finds that she is 5'6", weighs 98 lbs, and is healthy appearing. The cause of her amenorrhea is most likely:
    A. Premature ovarian failure
    B. Hypogonadotropic hypogonadism
    C. Sheehan syndrome
    D. Pregnancy

ID/CC: 32-year-old G_0 woman presents complaining of an inability to conceive.

HPI: M.F. reports regular menstrual cycles every 28 days since stopping birth control pills 3.5 years ago. For the last 2.5 years she and her husband have had unprotected intercourse on a regular basis. She reports mild cramping with her cycles that is relieved with ibuprofen. She denies prior pelvic surgery or IUD use. She was diagnosed with PID 9 years ago and was treated with antibiotics. Ms. F's husband is 38 and has not fathered any children before.

PMHx: Unremarkable   **PSHx:** Knee surgery   **Meds:** None

POb/GynHx: LMP 2 weeks ago; menarche at age 13.   **All:** NKDA

THOUGHT QUESTIONS

- Based on her history, what are the likely causes for this couple's infertility?
- What laboratory tests for her would be most helpful?
- Which single laboratory test for him would be most helpful?

Infertility is the inability to conceive after 1 year of unprotected intercourse. The causes are grouped into three categories: male factor (accounts for 40%), female factor (also 40%), and unknown etiology (20%). Causes of male factor infertility include endocrine disorders, abnormal spermatogenesis, abnormal sperm motility, and sexual dysfunction. Causes of female factor infertility include endocrine abnormalities (anywhere along the hypothalamic-pituitary-ovarian axis) that result in anovulation, and anatomic abnormalities that result in barriers to conception. Because this patient menstruates regularly, she is having ovulatory cycles. She may have peritoneal factors such as endometriosis or pelvic adhesions or tubal factors affecting fertility. Her history of PID puts her at risk for tubal occlusion. Her husband has not fathered children before, so male factor may also be the cause. A hysterosalpingogram, x-rays of the uterus and fallopian tubes taken while a radio-opaque dye is being injected into the uterus, would help establish tubal patency. A semen analysis would identify any abnormalities in sperm count, volume, morphology, and motility.

CASE CONTINUED

PE: *Gen:* normal appearing, Tanner V. Normal breasts without nipple discharge. Well estrogenized pelvic tissues. Normal cervix. Uterus normal, anteverted, and mobile. No adnexal masses.

Labs: Semen analysis: low volume and concentration with normal morphology and motility. HSG: bilateral patent fallopian tubes.

THOUGHT QUESTIONS

- What further evaluation of the husband is necessary?
- What initial fertility treatment would be appropriate for this couple?

The semen analysis is abnormal. A physical examination and an endocrine evaluation are warranted. The endocrine evaluation should include thyroid function tests, and serum testosterone, prolactin, and FSH levels. In addition, a postejaculatory urine analysis may identify retrograde ejaculation.

Treatment is directed toward overcoming the particular cause of the couple's infertility. For example, oligo-ovulation can be treated with gonadotropic medications that stimulate the ovaries. In this case, a low sperm quantity is the only abnormality, as both the sperm morphology and motility were normal. Intrauterine insemination (IUI), a procedure in which washed sperm are directly placed in the uterus (bypassing the cervical mucus barrier), can be attempted in these cases.

QUESTIONS

149. If IUI is unsuccessful, which of the following would be the next best treatment for this couple?
    A. Ovulation induction with clomiphene citrate
    B. Ovulation induction with gonadotropin treatment
    C. In vitro fertilization (IVF)
    D. Donor ovum IVF

150. The semen analysis of the male partner of an infertile couple reveals normal sperm volume and count, but abnormal morphology and low motility. Possible causes for this include all of the following *except*:
    A. Mumps orchitis
    B. Radiation exposure
    C. Varicocele
    D. Retrograde ejaculation

151. A young couple, both aged <30 years, comes to your office concerned that they have not conceived after attempting for the last 6 months. Your next step in management is:
    A. Reassure them that they do not have a diagnosis of infertility
    B. Complete history and physical for both partners
    C. Semen analysis and hysterosalpingogram (HSG)
    D. Perform a postcoital test

152. Clomiphene citrate acts by:
    A. Binding to the FSH receptor on the ovary and stimulating follicle development
    B. Binding to the estrogen receptor in the hypothalamus and stimulating pulsatile GnRH
    C. Binding to the progesterone receptor in the uterus and providing luteal phase support
    D. Blocking the GnRH receptor in the pituitary

ID/CC: 21-year-old G_1P_0 woman complains of increasing hair on her face, upper back, and abdomen.

HPI: A.H. has noticed an increase in the hair on her face over the last 6 months. During that time, she has developed acne, noticed some hair on her upper back as well as hair that extends above her underwear and bathing suit on her abdomen. This has led her to shave and use depilatory creams, but she has only mild success with these strategies and is quite upset. On review of systems, she denies changes in energy level, bowel or bladder habits, appetite, or diet. However, she has gained 10 lbs over the past year and her menses have become increasingly irregular.

PMHx: Asthma, no hospitalizations   **PSHx:** None

POb/GynHx: Menarche at age 12 with regular cycles until 2 years ago; first trimester pregnancy termination (3 years ago), which she associates with the change in her cycles. No STIs; not currently sexually active.

Meds: Ventolin inhaler   **All:** NKDA

SHx: Junior in college majoring in economics; social ethanol and tobacco use; no recreational drug use.

VS: Temp 98.0°F, BP 132/84, HR 88, RR 16. Weight: 144 lbs, Height 5'4"

PE: *Gen:* healthy young woman, NAD, appears stated age. *HEENT:* no obvious moon facies. *Neck:* no LAD, no thyromegaly, acanthosis nigricans. *Back:* normal spine, no hump. *Chest:* RR&R/CTA. *Abdomen:* soft, nontender, no masses. *SSE:* normal vaginal mucosa, cervix normal without lesions, Pap smear done. *BME:* uterus AV/AF, adnexae not palpated secondary to habitus

---

THOUGHT QUESTIONS
- What additional history and physical information would you like?
- What laboratory tests should be performed?

This patient, who has concerns about her hirsutism, should be questioned regarding the timing of symptoms (chronic versus acute), whether she has any signs of virilism (the presence or development of male secondary sexual characteristics in a woman, including deepening of voice, male-pattern baldness, clitoral enlargement, irregular menses, and increased facial and body hair), and whether there is any evidence of this in her family history. If the patient had signs/symptoms of virilism, the differential diagnosis would include testosterone-secreting tumors, adrenal tumors, and congenital adrenal hyperplasia.

To help sort out the differential, the following laboratory tests should be performed: DHEAS, testosterone, and 17-hydroxyprogesterone. If the DHEAS level is elevated, an adrenal source of androgens would be likely. Elevation of testosterone is suggestive of germ cell tumors of the ovary. Congenital adrenal hyperplasia, a deficiency in the 21-hydroxylase enzyme, leads to an elevation of 17-hydroxyprogesterone because there is accumulation of cortisol precursors. In addition, the mineralocorticoids cannot be processed without the deficient enzyme (Figure 39). Without any lab abnormalities, a diagnosis of polycystic ovary syndrome should be entertained. In addition to her presenting complaint of hirsutism, she has also had recent weight gain and irregular menses. Standard workup for these would include a pregnancy test, prolactin and TSH levels, and a test for ovulation.

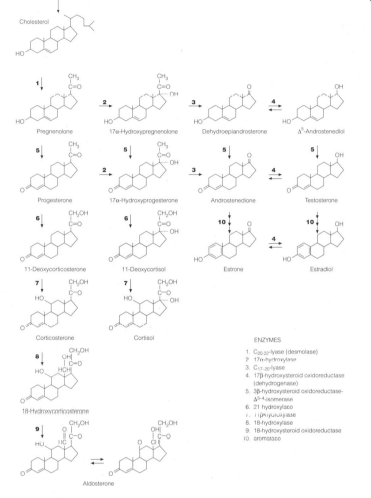

FIGURE 39 Steroid biosynthesis. Note key enzymes that will lead to a precursor accumulation. (Mishell DR, et al. Infertility, Contraception, and Reproductive Endocrinology. 3rd ed. Cambridge, MA: Blackwell Science, 1991.)

ENZYMES

1. C_{20-22}-lyase (desmolase)
2. 17α-hydroxylase
3. C_{17-20}-lyase
4. 17β-hydroxysteroid oxidoreductase (dehydrogenase)
5. 3β-hydroxysteroid oxidoreductase-Δ^{5-4}-isomerase
6. 21 hydroxylase
7. 11β-hydroxylase
8. 18-hydroxylase
9. 18-hydroxysteroid oxidoreductase
10. aromatase

CASE CONTINUED

Labs: LH, FSH, TSH, DHEAS, prolactin, and testosterone are all within normal limits. Her 17-hydroxy-progesterone is mildly elevated at 350 ng/dL.

QUESTIONS

153. The next step in her diagnosis should be:
    A. ACTH stimulation test
    B. Check a cortisol level
    C. Check a GnRH level
    D. No further tests necessary; she has Cushing disease
    E. No further tests necessary; she has congenital adrenal hyperplasia (CAH)

154. If her only test abnormalities were an elevated LH/FSH ratio, her diagnosis would be:
    A. Polycystic ovary syndrome (PCOS)
    B. Congenital adrenal hyperplasia
    C. Gonadoblastoma of the ovary
    D. Adrenal tumor
    E. Idiopathic hirsutism

155. In addition to managing her primary diagnosis, which of the following would *not be* used to treat her hirsutism?
    A. Spironolactone
    B. Dexamethasone
    C. Finasteride
    D. Bromocriptine
    E. Oral contraceptive pills

156. In addition to her primary diagnosis, what other tests are indicated in this patient?
    A. 24-hour urinary catecholamines
    B. Head MRI
    C. CT of the adrenal glands
    D. Glucose loading test
    E. Creatinine clearance

ID/CC: 17-year-old woman is concerned because she has not yet begun to menstruate.

HPI: T.F. comes into the office with her mother. They feel her development has been normal to date. She has no medical illnesses. She denies cyclic abdominal pain. She has not yet engaged in sexual intercourse. She is the youngest of three children. Her older sister had menarche at age 13. Her review of symptoms is negative.

PMHx: None   **PSHx:** None   **Meds:** None   **All:** Penicillin, rash

POb/GynHx: No prior gynecologic exam; no gynecologic infections.

THOUGHT QUESTIONS

- How would a history of cyclic abdominal pain narrow your differential diagnosis?
- In addition to the pelvic exam, what aspects of the physical examination will help with the differential diagnosis?

Cyclic abdominal pain suggests that this patient is having menstrual cycles but that there is an obstruction leading to retrograde menstrual flow into the abdomen and causing peritoneal irritation. A vaginal septum, imperforate hymen, cervical atresia, or an isolated rudimentary uterine horn can cause primary amenorrhea in this manner.

An important component of the physical exam for primary amenorrhea is evaluation of secondary sex characteristics. The absence of breasts suggests gonadal agenesis or failure, deficiencies in steroid synthesis or disruptions in the hypothalamic-pituitary axis. Lagging breast development may be due to varying degrees of gonadal dysgenesis.

TABLE 40. Diagnosis of Cause of Primary Amenorrhea

	UTERUS ABSENT	UTERUS PRESENT
Breasts absent	Gonadal agenesis in 46,XY Enzyme deficiencies in testosterone synthesis	Gonadal failure/agenesis in 46,XY Disruption of hypothalamic-pituitary axis
Breasts present	Testicular feminization Müllerian agenesis or MRKH	Hypothalamic, pituitary, or ovarian pathogenesis similar to that of secondary amenorrhea Congenital abnormalities of the genital tract

Callahan T, Caughey A, Heffner L. Blueprints in Obstetrics and Gynecology. 2nd ed. Malden, MA: Blackwell Science, 2001:155.

PE: *Gen:* normal appearing young woman. Normal breasts, Tanner V. *Pelvic/SSE:* normal external genitalia, no cervix seen, short vault. *BME:* short vagina ends blindly at 3 cm. Uterus not palpable.

THOUGHT QUESTION

- What would be the most useful test to obtain at this point?

This patient is phenotypically female, but with absent uterus and cervix. Breast development indicates the presence of estrogen. The differential diagnosis includes müllerian agenesis (normal ovaries, hence estrogen present) and testicular feminization (defect in the testosterone receptor, hence testosterone peripherally converted to estrogen). You can distinguish the two by obtaining a karyotype.

CASE CONTINUED

Labs: An ultrasound confirms an absent uterus and cervix. No pelvic masses are seen. Karyotype analysis reveals 46,XY.

THOUGHT QUESTION

• What treatments should you pursue?

Individuals with testicular feminization have functioning testes, which usually are not completely descended. They have almost a 50% lifetime risk of developing testicular cancer, hence the testes should be removed surgically. After the procedure, estrogen replacement is given to maintain secondary sex characteristics and prevent osteoporosis. Historically, these patients would also undergo surgical reconstruction to enhance the vagina, which is a foreshortened blind pouch. However, this can also be accomplished by serial dilation with vaginal dilators over a period of 6 to 9 months, allowing patients to avoid the risks of surgery. Because the vagina must be kept open either with dilators or intercourse once it is created (either surgically or via serial dilation), these procedures are not performed until the patient is interested in becoming sexually active.

QUESTIONS

157. You see an 18-year-old woman with primary amenorrhea. On exam she has a uterus, but no breast development. A karyotype reveals 46,XY. Her amenorrhea and exam are consistent with:
    A. Gonadal agenesis
    B. Müllerian agenesis
    C. Absent GnRH secretion
    D. 17α-hydroxylase deficiency

158. A 16-year-old woman with primary amenorrhea has a normally developed vagina and uterus but no breast development. Karyotype is 46,XX. The next step in diagnosis is to obtain a:
    A. Urine pregnancy test
    B. Serum FSH
    C. Serum free testosterone
    D. 24-hour urine cortisol collection

159. A 15-year-old woman presents to your office because she has not started menstruating. She underwent telarche 3 years ago. She denies sexual activity and is otherwise healthy. Her physical examination is normal. Your next step is to:
    A. Advise her that some females do not start menstruating until age 16. She should come back if she has not started menstruating by then.
    B. Obtain a pregnancy test, as she should have started menstruating by age 14
    C. Obtain a karyotype analysis.
    D. Check a serum FSH.

160. An individual with Kallmann syndrome will have which of the following characteristics?
    A. Phenotypic female without uterus, but with normal breast development, 46,XX.
    B. Phenotypic female with uterus but no breast development, 46,XY.
    C. Phenotypic female without uterus or breast development, 46,XY.
    D. Phenotypic female with uterus but no breast development, 46,XX.

ID/CC: A 27-year-old $G_1P_0T_1$ woman presents to your clinic complaining of inability to conceive.

HPI: F.F. reports irregular menstrual cycles for the last 6 years. Her cycles occur every 28 to 42 days and are heavy at times. For the last 1.5 years, she and her husband have had regular, unprotected intercourse. She denies prior PID or pelvic surgery. Her husband is also 27 years old and has not fathered any children. On review of systems, she denies galactorrhea and has noted a 20-lb weight gain and a slight increase in facial hair over the last 3 years.

PMHx: Unremarkable   **PSHx:** Appendectomy   **Meds:** None   **All:** NKDA

POb/GynHx: LMP 3 weeks ago; first trimester termination at age 19; normal Pap smears; menarche at age 12.

THOUGHT QUESTIONS

- Based on the history what are the likely causes for this couple's infertility?
- What laboratory tests for her would be most helpful?
- Which laboratory test for him would be most helpful?

Given this patient's irregular menses, anovulation is the likely cause of infertility. Common causes for anovulation include polycystic ovary syndrome, premature ovarian failure, thyroid disorders, hyperprolactinemia, and medications. A semen analysis is useful to exclude male factor infertility. An endocrine evaluation of this patient will help identify causes of anovulation. At minimum, this should include FSH, thyroid studies, and prolactin.

CASE CONTINUED

PE: *Gen:* moderate central obesity, moderate facial hair on upper lip and chin, Tanner V. *Breasts:* symmetric with no masses or nipple discharge. *Abdomen:* diamond-shaped escutcheon. *Pelvic:* well estrogenized pelvic tissues. Normal cervix. Uterus normal, anteverted, and mobile. No adnexal masses.

Labs: FSH: 8 mIU/mL (normal: 5–20); LH: 19 mIU/mL (normal: 5–20); Testosterone: 13 nmol/L (normal: 0.7–2.8); 17-OH Progesterone: 8 nmol/L (normal: 3–9); PRL: 14 ng/mL (normal: 1–20); TSH: 2.9 μU/mL (normal: 0.35–5.0). HSG: bilateral patent fallopian tubes. Semen analysis: normal.

THOUGHT QUESTIONS

- What is your most likely diagnosis now?
- What is the best first treatment for this couple?

In polycystic ovary syndrome (PCOS), excess LH stimulates cystic changes in the ovary, which in turn causes increased androgen secretion from the ovarian stroma. An LH/FSH ratio greater than 2:1 suggests PCOS, but because it is not particularly sensitive, the diagnosis is made by excluding other causes of anovulation such as premature ovarian failure, hyper- or hypothyroidism, and prolactine-mia. Ms. F's elevated testosterone levels are also consistent with PCOS, but not high enough to suggest an androgen-secreting tumor. Because this patient has a functioning hypothalamic-pituitary-ovarian axis, she may ovulate with clomiphene citrate treatment. Clomiphene citrate acts as an antiestrogen at the estrogen receptor in the hypothalamus. This leads to increased GnRH, then FSH and LH, and subsequent follicle growth and ovulation.

QUESTIONS

161. The most common complication of clomiphene citrate is:
    A. Ovarian torsion
    B. Multiple gestation
    C. Ovarian hyperstimulation
    D. Premature ovarian failure

162. This patient should be screened regularly for:
    A. Insulin-resistant (type II) diabetes
    B. Pituitary microadenoma
    C. Thyroid dysfunction
    D. Ovarian cancer

163. All of the following are associated with increased risk of ectopic pregnancy *except*:
    A. Pelvic surgery
    B. In vitro fertilization
    C. Gonadotropin ovulation induction
    D. Salpingitis

164. An appropriate candidate for clomiphene citrate treatment is:
    A. A 41-year-old woman who failed gonadotropin ovulation induction
    B. A 27-year-old woman with Asherman syndrome
    C. A 28-year-old woman with mild hypothalamic amenorrhea
    D. A 29-year-old woman with cervical stenosis

ID/CC: 48-year-old G$_2$P$_2$ woman complains of frequent hot flashes and irregular menstrual cycles.

HPI: M.P. reports an 8-month history of hot flashes and irregular menstrual cycles varying from 25 to 45 days. Previously she had had regular 30-day cycles without any intermenstrual bleeding. She sheepishly adds that her family has noted that her moods have been quite labile, which she has noticed as well.

PMHx/PSHx: None   **Meds:** Vitamins   **All:** NKDA

POb/GynHx: No STIs. 2 NSVDs. No contraception.

FHx: Cardiac disease and hypertension in parents, no cancers.

SHx: No tobacco use. Occasional wine.

VS: Temp 36.0°C, BP 142/82, HR 80, RR14. Weight: 160 lbs

PE: *Breasts:* symmetrical, no masses, no nipple discharge. *Abdomen:* soft, nontender, no distension, no palpable masses. *Pelvic:* external genitalia within normal limits; vagina—with rugae and physiologic discharge; cervix—multiparous os, no lesions. *BME:* uterus—small, AV/AF, nontender. No palpable adnexal masses.

Labs: Hb 11.2

THOUGHT QUESTIONS

- What physiologic state classically encompasses her complaints?
- What diagnostic tests would you be interested in obtaining?
- How would you manage her symptoms?

This patient's complaints of irregular menstrual cycles, vasomotor instability, and mood changes are characteristic of the perimenopausal period (the transition period to the menopause). The average age of menopause in the United States is 50 to 51 years, with menopausal symptoms beginning typically any time after age 40. The decreasing estrogen production and response to stimulatory hormones of the ovaries leads to a breakdown in the feedback cycle of the hypothalamic-pituitary-ovarian axis and ultimately to an increase in circulating FSH levels. The diagnosis of menopause is thus usually made clinically with symptoms of diminished estrogen and confirmed by an elevated FSH level.

In this patient, an endometrial biopsy is warranted, given the history of new onset metrorrhagia in an older woman. Results of the biopsy will evaluate the endometrium for endometrial polyps, hyperplasia, or cancer, and additionally will help confirm her perimenopausal status. In the absence of other pathologic abnormalities and medical contraindications, it would be appropriate to place her on hormone replacement therapy (HRT).

CASE CONTINUED

She denies passage of heavy clots, postcoital bleeding, dyspareunia, or dysuria. In fact her bleeding has been light to normal. Nevertheless, you recommend an endometrial biopsy. The results reveal disordered proliferation of the endometrium without evidence of hyperplasia or cancer. An FSH level was 35.

QUESTIONS

165. Which of the following treatment regimens is most appropriate for her at this point?
    A. Combination oral contraceptives
    B. Continuous combined Premarin (0.625 mg) and Provera (2.5 mg) every day
    C. Unopposed continuous low-dose estrogen therapy
    D. Placement of progestin-releasing IUD
    E. Transdermal estrogen therapy

166. At the age of 50 she is switched to a continuous combined estrogen and progestin menopausal regimen. She has no bleeding during the first 15 months of this regimen but now complains of three episodes of vaginal bleeding over the last 6 months. What do you now do in light of these complaints?
    A. Perform a Pap smear
    B. Observation only
    C. Perform an endometrial biopsy
    D. Order a pelvic ultrasound
    E. Do a hysteroscopy, and dilation and curettage

167. What if you perform an endometrial biopsy and the results return as atrophic endometrium, with no evidence of hyperplasia? How would you manage her complaints of unpredictable bleeding now?
    A. Continue the current regimen
    B. Change to a cyclic sequential HRT regimen
    C. Hysterectomy followed by estrogen replacement
    D. Start transdermal clonidine
    E. Increase the dose of the progestin to 5 mg every day

168. She returns to the clinic the following year with a DEXA (dual x-ray absorptiometry) T-score of 2.5 standard deviations below the mean and a lower extremity deep venous thrombosis. She wants to know if she should stop HRT, and if so, what options she has for alternative therapy. What do you recommend?
    A. Stop HRT with no other treatment initiated
    B. Stop HRT and start raloxifene with micronized progesterone
    C. Continue HRT
    D. Stop HRT and continue with calcium supplementation and initiate alendronate
    E. Stop HRT and supplement with ginseng

ID/CC: A 62-year-old G$_2$P$_1$ woman presents with complaints of urinary incontinence.

> *THOUGHT QUESTION*
> • What are the types of incontinence and how can they be differentiated?

Continence involves several factors: 1) structural integrity (no holes/fistulae) of the bladder and urethra, 2) ability of the urethral sphincters to withstand increases in intra-abdominal and intravesicular pressure, and 3) the ability to inhibit bladder contractions. There are four general categories of incontinence:

1. Stress incontinence—urine loss with exertion or straining, associated with pelvic relaxation and displacement of the urethrovesical junction. Patients describe leaking small quantities of urine when coughing, laughing, or exercising.

2. Urge incontinence—patients can't suppress the urge to void, and often large quantities of urine are lost secondary to involuntary and uninhibited contraction of the detrusor muscle.

3. Overflow incontinence—poor bladder tone leads to urinary retention, increasing distension, and eventual overflow of the urine out the urethra. Patients present with frequent or constant dribbling and with symptoms of stress or urge incontinence.

4. Total incontinence—a rare form that is typically the result of a urinary fistula formed between the bladder and vagina. Patients present with a painless continuous loss of urine. In the United States, the most common risk factors for such a fistula are pelvic surgery and pelvic radiation. Worldwide, childbirth is the primary cause.

The type of incontinence can usually be diagnosed by history and physical exam. Sometimes, the patient's history is consistent with a mixed type of incontinence (both stress and urge components). In this setting, urodynamic testing, which measures bladder and urethral pressures as the bladder is filled and emptied, is necessary for diagnosis.

CASE CONTINUED

U.I. reports that she leaks large amounts of urine 1 to 3 times a day. It occurs when she has the urge to void but she can't make it to the bathroom in time. Sometimes, when she is almost home and thinks about voiding, it will suddenly happen. She denies leakage when she coughs, laughs, or exercises. Ms. I has taken to wearing adult diapers because she can't predict when the leakage will happen.

PMHx: Diabetes (type II)   **PSHx:** Appendectomy, C/S   **Meds:** None

POb/GynHx: No STDs. Normal pap smears. Menopause at age 51. SAB. C/S at age 30 with neonatal death.

All: NKDA

PE: *Gen:* healthy appearing woman. *Pelvic:* normal external genitalia and vaginal mucosa. Cervix normal, no descent with strain. Uterus small. No apparent rectocele or cystocele.

THOUGHT QUESTIONS

- Based on her history and physical, what type of incontinence do you think this patient has?
- What diagnostic tests would be helpful at this juncture?

This patient's history is consistent with urge incontinence, which is usually caused by involuntary detrusor contractions during the filling phase of bladder function. The urge to urinate or the thought of urination can prompt the detrusor to contract. Because of this, the quantity of urine leaked can be large. The treatment for urge incontinence involves the use of medications to inhibit or relax the detrusor muscle. Anticholinergics inhibit the cholinergic enervation of the detrusor muscle. Beta-adrenergic agonists and smooth muscle relaxants both relax the detrusor muscle and constrict the urethral sphincter. There is no effective surgical treatment for urge incontinence.

A urinalysis and urine cultures should always be obtained to rule out infection as a cause of incontinence. A cystometrogram uses pressure sensors to measure bladder and sphincter tone as the bladder is filled. An early detrusor reflex and the patient's inability to inhibit the desire to void suggest detrusor instability.

CASE CONTINUED

Labs: Urinalysis and urine cultures are both normal. The cystometrogram reveals involuntary detrusor contractions starting at 150 cc of bladder filling.

QUESTIONS

169. You are seeing a patient with detrusor instability. All of the following treatment options would be appropriate *except*:
    A. Tolterodine (Detrol)
    B. Oxybutynin (Ditropan)
    C. Metaproterenol (Alupent)
    D. Prazosin

170. A 68-year-old woman complains of frequent urinary dribbling. A measured void is 150 cc and the postvoid residual is 400 cc. Causes for her symptoms could include all of the following *except*:
    A. Diabetes mellitus
    B. Use of anticholinergic medications
    C. Bladder neck hypermobility
    D. Pelvic masses

171. A 54-year-old woman who just finished a course of pelvic radiation for treatment of endometrial cancer reports a continuous loss of small amounts of urine. She denies any pain. The likely cause of her urine leak is:
    A. Overflow incontinence
    B. A vesicovaginal fistula
    C. Detrusor hyperreflexia
    D. Pelvic relaxation

172. All the following statements regarding the events leading to micturition are true *except*:
    A. Stretch receptors in the bladder wall send a signal to the CNS to begin voiding.
    B. Activation of the sympathetic nerves via the hypogastric nerve allows for micturition by relaxing the bladder neck and internal sphincter.
    C. Parasympathetic control of the bladder is derived from S2–4 of the spinal cord.
    D. Activation of the parasympathetic pelvic nerves results in contraction of the detrusor muscle and micturition begins.

ID/CC: A 64-year-old G$_3$P$_3$ woman complains of pressure in her vagina and occasionally feeling "something down there" when she strains.

HPI: C.C. denies pain or vaginal bleeding. Review of systems reveals that she often has dysuria and that she occasionally leaks small amounts of urine when she coughs, laughs, or exercises. Ms. C tries to limit her physical activity so as to minimize urine leakage.

PMHx: Hypothyroidism, chronic bronchitis **PSHx:** None

Meds: Synthroid, Ventolin **All:** NKDA

POb/GynHx: No STDs. Normal Pap smears. Forceps delivery for first child, then 2 NSVDs. Menopause at age 48; no hormone replacement.

SHx: Denies use of ethanol and recreational drugs. Had 30 pack per year history of tobacco use; quit 5 years ago.

THOUGHT QUESTIONS

• What causes could lead to this patient's symptoms?

• What risk factors does this patient have for each of the possible diagnoses?

The sensation of a mass in the vagina can be due to the following:

1. Pelvic organ prolapse (POP). This occurs when the pelvic ligaments weaken to the point where the pelvic organs sag into the vagina. This includes bladder prolapse (cystocele), uterine prolapse and rectal prolapse (rectocele). Risk factors for POP include factors that chronically increase intra-abdominal pressure (chronic cough, ascites, pelvic tumors, and straining due to chronic constipation) and those that weaken the pelvic supporting ligaments (history of traumatic vaginal delivery).

2. Neoplasm. Both benign and malignant neoplasms can cause the sensation of a vaginal mass. Malignant neoplasms include vaginal and cervical cancer, although these patients more commonly present with bleeding, pain, and pruritus. Possible benign neoplasms include a cervical polyp or a prolapsing uterine fibroid.

3. Hemorrhoids. These are dilated hemorrhoidal veins in the anal canal. External hemorrhoids can protrude (or protrude farther than baseline) upon straining, giving the sensation of a mass.

This patient has multiple risk factors for pelvic relaxation, including chronic cough (chronically increased intra-abdominal pressure), history of obstructed labor or traumatic delivery (forceps delivery), aging, and menopause.

CASE CONTINUED

PE: *Gen:* appears older than stated age. *Pelvic:* external genitalia and vaginal mucosa moderately atrophied. Moderate bulge in the anterior vaginal wall (Figure 44). Cervix normal appearing, descends to halfway down vagina with straining. Uterus small, anteverted.

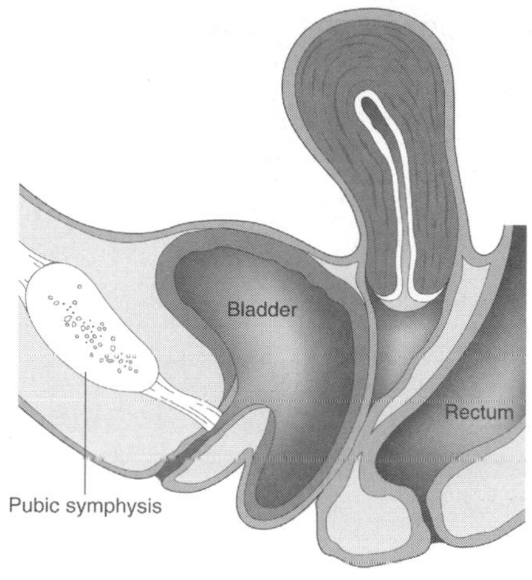

FIGURE 44 A defect in the anterior vaginal wall leads to the bladder herniating into the vagina down to the introitus and beyond. (Illustration by Electronic Illustrators Group.)

Bladder

Rectum

Pubic symphysis

Cystocele

THOUGHT QUESTIONS

- What could account for the bulge at the anterior vaginal wall on this patient's exam?
- How does this relate to her incontinence?
- What initial therapies can you try in this patient?

The vaginal bulge is most likely a cystocele. Cystoceles occur when the bladder herniates into the vaginal vault. Other possibilities include a urethral diverticulum or a Skene gland abscess, but these are rare. The prolapsing bladder is probably accompanied by bladder neck relaxation. This leads to stress urinary incontinence. Kegel exercises (tightening and relaxing of the pubococcygeus muscle throughout the day) can strengthen the pelvic musculature and thereby reduce pelvic organ prolapse. It also works to increase the external urethral sphincter tone and reduce stress incontinence. Estrogen replacement can also help by reversing atrophy of the vaginal mucosa and improving tissue tone.

QUESTIONS

173. If Kegel exercises and estrogen replacement fail in this patient, what other therapy can you try?
    A. Treatment with prazosin
    B. Placing a vaginal pessary
    C. Placing a cervical cap
    D. Improving management of her chronic bronchitis

174. Surgical treatment of stress urinary incontinence includes:
    A. A urethral dilation procedure
    B. A urethral sling procedure
    C. A hysteroscopic myomectomy procedure
    D. No effective surgical procedures can treat stress urinary incontinence

175. A 36-year-old woman, G_3P_3, comes to your office reporting loss of urine when she coughs or goes jogging. This started shortly after her third NSVD 2 years ago. You diagnose mild stress urinary incontinence. The first step in treatment for this patient is:
    A. Begin Kegel exercises
    B. Begin hormone replacement therapy
    C. Begin a course of Ditropan
    D. Fit the patient for a pessary

176. A 78-year-old woman presents to your office for an annual examination. You find uterine prolapse to 2 cm above the introitus and a moderate cystocele. She denies any symptoms consistent with pelvic organ prolapse or urinary incontinence. The best management for this patient is to:
    A. Do nothing now and monitor for symptoms
    B. Perform a vaginal hysterectomy
    C. Start her on hormone replacement therapy
    D. Perform a vaginal vault suspension

ID/CC: 57-year-old G$_3$P$_3$ postmenopausal woman complains of vaginal and vulvar itching.

HPI: V.D. reports that she has been in good health except for worsening vulvovaginal pruritus over the last few years. She noticed the onset of itching soon after menopause. She had some relief initially with estrogen cream prescribed by her doctor. Then she tried over-the-counter antifungal creams but to no avail. Her symptoms are particularly bad in the nighttime. Ms. D denies any postmenopausal vaginal bleeding but notes that sexual intercourse is painful.

PMHx: Basal cell CA (BCC) on face   **PSHx:** Excision procedures for BCC

Meds: Vitamins, calcium   **All:** NKDA

POb/GynHx: 3 vaginal deliveries. Menarche at age 15, menopause at 55. No HRT. No history of STIs or abnormal Pap smears.

SHx: Lives with husband. Remote history of tobacco use.

VS: Temp 97.6°F, BP 135/80, HR 76, RR 18

PE: *Gen:* well-developed, well-nourished slightly overweight woman. *External genitalia:* fused labia minora and majora with focal areas of raised, shiny white plaques around the posterior fourchette and at 4 o'clock. *Pelvic:* cervix flush with vagina—no lesions; atrophic vagina; uterus—small; no palpable adnexal masses.

Labs: Pap smear (1 year ago): atrophy. Mammogram (last year): negative.

THOUGHT QUESTIONS

- What have her symptoms been attributed to?
- What other possible causes of vulvar pruritus and vulvodynia need to be investigated?
- How would you manage her?

Her report of symptomatic relief with local estrogen cream suggests an atrophic component to her symptoms. Overgrowth of organisms such as *Candida, Trichomonas,* and *Gardnerella* are common causes of vulvar pruritus. Yeast dermatitis is usually diagnosed by a KOH preparation, although its sensitivity is variable (25% to 80%). One could also perform a gram stain examination, which is almost 100% sensitive for a yeast infection. Besides infection, dysplasia, cancer, and vulvar dystrophy are other causes of chronic vulvar pruritus. This patient needs a complete workup with a KOH/wet mount and gram stain to evaluate for infection. Colposcopic-directed biopsies to evaluate for disease processes such as vulvar dysplasia, vulvar cancer, or vulvar dystrophy are also warranted.

CASE CONTINUED

The KOH/wet mount was normal and gram stain revealed no evidence of a yeast infection. You perform a colposcopic examination using topical acetic acid to isolate suspicious areas of the vulva. You identify several areas of acetowhite epithelium and take biopsies of these areas of the vulva. Ms. D is very anxious for some alleviation of her itching.

QUESTIONS

177. What is the most common cause of vulvar pruritus?
     A. Estrogen deficiency
     B. Yeast dermatitis
     C. Contact dermatitis
     D. Bacterial vaginosis
     E. Trichomoniasis

178. What would you recommend the patient do for symptomatic relief while awaiting the biopsy results?
     A. Testosterone gel
     B. Nothing
     C. Topical clotrimazole cream
     D. Hydrocortisone cream
     E. 5% imiquimod topical cream

179. The colposcopic examination revealed areas of acetowhite epithelium at the posterior fourchette and at the 4 o'clock position. Punch biopsies were performed without difficulty. What would you expect the final pathologic report to show?
     A. Chronic inflammation
     B. Vulvar intraepithelial neoplasia (VIN) II–III
     C. Condyloma
     D. Superficial spreading melanoma
     E. Lichen sclerosus et atrophicus

180. What is the best management for a patient with VIN III?
     A. Continue treatment with a topical steroid cream
     B. Perform a wide local excision
     C. Treat with TCA (trichloroacetic acid application)
     D. Perform a vulvectomy
     E. Apply topical steroid/testosterone creams

ID/CC: 26-year-old G_0 woman presents for an annual gynecologic exam.

HPI: C.D. states that overall she is doing well. Her last exam and Pap smear, she believes, was 3 years ago and was normal. She is currently sexually active with one male partner for the past 5 months and uses oral contraceptive pills. She has been on the OCPs for 3 months and has had some episodes of spotting, which are bothersome to her. She notes no change in her vaginal discharge, which she says is generally white and thin. Her last clinical breast exam was 3 years ago. She examines her own breasts at home every couple of months.

PMHx: Asthma, well-controlled by medication. No hospitalizations.

PSHx: Tonsillectomy as a child. Appendectomy at age 18.

Meds: Albuterol MDI PRN; Loestrin   **All:** NKDA

POb/GynHx: Menarche age 13, 28 to 30 day cycles, 5 days of moderate bleeding. Last Pap smear 3 years ago. No history of abnormal Pap smears. History of chlamydia in college. Denies history of PID.

SHx: Works as a paralegal. Lives with a roommate. Has smoked 1 pack per day of tobacco for 8 years; social ethanol use; denies recreational drug use.

FHx: Significant for heart disease in her father at age 60, history of ovarian cancer in a maternal aunt at age 64.

THOUGHT QUESTIONS

- What is part of a routine gynecologic exam in this patient? How about a patient at age 40? 50?
- What high-risk behaviors and risk factors does this patient have and how do they relate to a routine gynecologic exam?
- Why might this patient have episodes of spotting?

A routine gynecologic examination can differ, depending on the individual needs and risk factors. In general, all patients should receive a thorough discussion of their gynecologic history with a focus on current issues: menstrual history, sexual history, obstetric history, a discussion of birth control if pertinent, infection history, and general gynecologic history (i.e., ovarian cysts, fibroids). A full examination concentrates on the breasts, abdomen, external genitalia, and pelvic organs. Thus, speculum, bimanual, and rectal examinations are required for all patients. Any sexually active patient should be offered a screen for STIs. Pap smears are performed annually in the younger population and in any patient with a history of dysplasia. Mammograms are currently recommended every 2 years in patients older than 40 and annually in patients older than 50.

Most notably, Ms. D's smoking history is worrisome not only because of her asthma but also as a significant risk factor for cervical cancer. Her family history of ovarian cancer should be further explored. Patients with a family history of ovarian cancer may benefit from the use of oral contraceptive pills. Thus, discussing this with her may encourage her to continue their use despite the episodes of spotting.

Spotting on OCPs in young women is very common during the first 3 to 6 months of use. If the spotting continues, she may benefit from using a different OCP. A change from a monophasic to a multiphasic with an increased amount of estrogen may help to prevent breakthrough bleeding. Other diagnoses associated with spotting in a patient on OCPs include cervicitis (especially with a chlamydial infection), cervical polyp, endometrial polyp, and cervical cancer. In older patients, spotting can be associated with endometrial hyperplasia, endometrial cancer, polyps, anovulation, or atrophy.

CASE CONTINUED

VS: Temp 98.3°F, BP 104/68, HR 74, RR 14. Weight 140 lbs, Height 5'5"

PE: *Gen:* NAD. *HEENT:* unremarkable. *Neck:* no thyroid nodules or enlargement. *Breasts:* no masses or axillary LAD. *Lungs:* CTAB. *Cor:* RR&R without murmurs. *Abdomen:* soft, nontender, no distension. *Extremities:* no clubbing, cyanosis, or edema. *Pelvic:* normal female genitalia, otherwise unremarkable. *SSE:* thin white discharge; no cervical lesions. *BME:* small anteverted uterus, no adnexal masses.

Labs: Wet prep: no clue cells or trichomonads, few WBCs. KOH: no pseudohyphae

As part of the routine exam you collect a Pap smear and send it off. You discuss with Ms. D that the episodes of vaginal bleeding may be related to her OCP. She decides to continue the current OCP but will return in 3 months if she continues to have spotting. You discuss with her the need to quit smoking, and she agrees to try with the assistance of the nicotine patch.

Two weeks later, the patient's Pap smear returns with the following result: "low grade squamous intraepithelial lesion (LGSIL), endocervical cells present."

QUESTIONS

181. Given the Pap result of LGSIL, what is your recommendation to this patient?
    A. Repeat the Pap smear immediately
    B. Repeat the Pap smear in 6 to 8 months
    C. Colposcopic exam of the cervix with directed biopsies
    D. Loop electrosurgical excision procedure (LEEP)

182. If instead the Pap smear result was "atypical squamous cells of unknown significance (ASCUS)," what might be your recommendation?
    A. Repeat the Pap smear immediately
    B. Repeat the Pap smear in 3 to 6 months or colposcopic exam now
    C. Colposcopic exam now
    D. LEEP

183. If instead the Pap smear result was "atypical glandular cells of undetermined significance (AGUS)," what would be your recommendation?
    A. Repeat the Pap smear immediately
    B. Repeat the Pap smear in 3 to 6 months
    C. Colposcopic exam now
    D. LEEP or cone biopsy

184. Which serotypes of human papillomavirus (HPV) are associated with cervical cancer?
    A. 6, 11
    B. 16, 18, 31
    C. all of the above
    D. none of the above

ID/CC: 65-year-old G_0 woman presents with irregular vaginal bleeding over the last 6 months.

HPI: E.C. notes that she has not had any vaginal bleeding or abnormal discharge since menopause at age 53. She first noticed a watery discharge and scant irregular vaginal bleeding 6 months ago. Her gynecologic exam last year was normal. Occasionally Ms. C has had mild abdominal cramps but denies any weight loss or anorexia.

PMHx: Type II diabetes, hypertension   **Meds:** Glyburide, HCTZ, Prinvil (ACE inhibitor)

All: NKDA   **PSHx:** Breast biopsy for benign cyst.

POb/GynHx: G_0. Polycystic ovary syndrome (PCOS)—chronic anovulation. No STIs, no abnormal Pap smears.

SHx: Unmarried, lives with sister. No use of ethanol or tobacco.

VS: Temp 97.8°F, standing BP 150/80, HR 80; sitting BP 140/72, HR 78; RR 14. Weight: 65 kg, Height: 156 cm

PE: *Oral mucosa:* moist and pink. *Abdomen:* soft, nontender, no distension, no palpable masses. *Pelvic:* atrophic external genitalia and vagina; cervix—nulliparous os, no lesions. *BME:* uterus—approx 8-week size, AV/AF, nontender. No palpable adnexal masses.

THOUGHT QUESTIONS

- What is in the differential diagnosis for this patient?
- What is the most common finding in women with postmeno-pausal bleeding?
- What is the diagnosis of most concern and how would you work it up?

The differential diagnosis for postmenopausal uterine bleeding includes bleeding from adjustment to hormone replacement therapy, endometrial atrophy, atrophic vaginitis, endometrial or cervical polyps, endometrial hyperplasia, fibroids, and endometrial carcinoma. The most common cause of postmenopausal bleeding is endometrial atrophy (Table 47). Only 10% of patients with postmenopausal bleeding have endometrial cancer, but over 90% of women with endometrial carcinoma complain only of abnormal uterine bleeding. A thorough physical examination including a Pap smear, endometrial biopsy, and CBC needs to be performed. You could consider transvaginal ultrasonography as an adjunctive study to the endometrial biopsy.

TABLE 47. Common Causes of Postmenopausal Bleeding

CAUSE	PERCENTAGE
Atrophic endometrium	65–75
Hormone replacement therapy	15–25
Cancer of the endometrium	9–12
Endometrial hyperplasia	5–10
Endometrial or cervical polyps	2–12

CASE CONTINUED

You send off a Pap smear, an endometrial biopsy, and a CBC. The Pap smear shows atypical glandular cells of undetermined significance (AGUS). The pathology report from the endometrial biopsy reveals endometrial complex atypical hyperplasia and a focus of well-differentiated adenocarcinoma. The CBC is normal with a Hb of 12/Hct of 37.

Ms. C returns to your clinic for a discussion of the diagnosis and potential management options. You explain to her that her risk factors for endometrial cancer include diabetes, hypertension, and nulliparity. In addition, you discuss that the overall 5-year survival rate for endometrial cancer is about 65%, and 75% or greater in stage I disease.

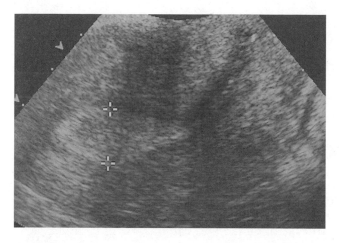

FIGURE 47 The 12-mm thickness of the endometrium here is worrisome for hyperplasia or polyp. A typical postmenopausal endometrium should be <5 mm in thickness. (Image provided by Departments of Radiology and Obstetrics & Gynecology, University of California, San Francisco.)

QUESTIONS

185. Upon initial presentation to the office, the diagnostic test with the best sensitivity and specificity for endometrial cancer is:
    A. Endometrial biopsy
    B. Ultrasonography
    C. Abdominal and pelvic CT
    D. Wet mount
    E. Pap smear

186. What percentage of complex atypical hyperplasia progresses to carcinoma?
    A. 1%
    B. 3%
    C. 8%
    D. 15%
    E. 29%

187. Given the finding of complex atypical hyperplasia with a focus of well-differentiated adenocarcinoma, the most appropriate management is:
    A. Observation and rebiopsy in 3 months
    B. Treatment with progestins and careful follow-up
    C. Dilation and curettage (D&C)
    D. Hysterectomy and bilateral salpingo-oophorectomy (BSO)
    E. Pelvic irradiation

188. The surgical pathology report notes the presence of a well-differentiated endometrioid adenocarcinoma with 30% invasion of the myometrium. What is her FIGO stage?
    A. Stage IA, Grade 1
    B. Stage IB, Grade 1
    C. Stage IB, Grade 3
    D. Stage IC, Grade 1
    E. Stage IIA, Grade 3

ID/CC: 72-year-old G_3P_2 woman complains of abdominal distension and anorexia.

HPI: O.C. had been in her usual state of good health until approximately 4 months ago when she noticed increasing abdominal girth and worsening abdominal discomfort. She also reports anorexia and mild fatigue. She denies any alteration in her bowel movements but has had a few episodes of urinary incontinence. She also denies any postmenopausal uterine bleeding.

PMHx: Ductal CIS of breast, age 53

PSHx: Wide local excision on right breast

Meds: Calcium, multivitamin, vitamin D, alendronate

All: NKDA

POb/GynHx: 2 NSVDs, 1 SAB. Menarche at age 13, menopause at 51. No history of abnormal Pap smears. No STIs.

SHx: Lives alone, widowed. Has one drink per night ethanol; no use of tobacco.

VS: Temp 97.2°F, BP 130/74, HR 90, RR 20; O_2 saturation 93%

PE: *Chest:* CTAB except decreased breath sounds at the bases. *Breasts:* well-healed scar on right breast, no masses, no discharge, symmetrical. *Abdomen:* moderate distension with fluid wave, mild tenderness, firm 12-cm midabdominal mass. *Pelvic:* atrophic genitalia and vaginal mucosa; cervix within normal limits, stenotic os. *BME:* cervix immobile, large pelvic mass.

THOUGHT QUESTIONS

- What is the differential diagnosis?
- Will tumor markers such as CA-125 be helpful?
- How would you manage this patient's care at this point?

The differential diagnosis for abdominal distension in this patient includes ovarian carcinomatosis, ascites from hepatic disease, pancreatic cancer, and metastatic carcinoma. CA-125 levels can be elevated in nongynecologic and gynecologic conditions such as epithelial ovarian cancer, endometrial cancer, endometriosis, adenomyosis, uterine leiomyomata, cirrhosis, peritonitis, pancreatitis, pancreatic cancer, and colon cancer (Table 48).

Studies to assess the ascites and rule out metastatic disease are necessary. Imaging studies of the abdomen/pelvis, a mammogram, and a chest x-ray are in order. These studies will assist in evaluating the site of origin of the mass (for example, pancreas versus ovary) and help define the extent of disease. An ultrasound would be most helpful in assessing for adnexal masses; a CT scan of the abdomen and pelvis would yield more information about the involvement of the disease process in the abdominal organs, intestines, and lymph nodes.

TABLE 48. Gynecologic and Nongynecologic Conditions Associated with Elevated CA-125 Levels

GYNECOLOGIC CANCERS	NONGYNECOLOGIC CANCERS	BENIGN GYNECOLOGIC CONDITIONS	BENIGN NONGYNECOLOGIC CONDITIONS
Epithelial ovarian cancer	Pancreatic cancer	Normal and ectopic pregnancy	Pancreatitis
Fallopian tube cancer	Lung cancer	Endometriosis	Cirrhosis
Endometrial cancer	Breast cancer	Fibroids	Peritonitis
Endocervical cancer	Colon cancer	Pelvic inflammatory disease	Recent laparotomy

Callahan T, Caughey A, Heffner L. Blueprints in Obstetrics and Gynecology. 2nd ed. Malden: Blackwell Science, 2001:222.

CASE CONTINUED

In taking her family history, you learn that her mother died of ovarian cancer in her 60s and a maternal aunt developed ovarian cancer and died at age 50. You perform a Pap smear and order an abdominal-pelvic ultrasound and CT, a screening mammogram, and a chest x-ray. The ultrasound findings of significant ascites, probable omental caking, and bilateral solid, cystic adnexal masses with septations and nodularity are confirmed on CT as well. The Pap smear and mammogram are normal. Her chest x-ray is normal.

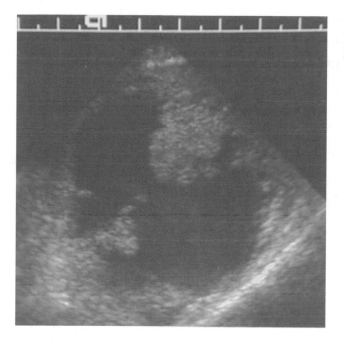

FIGURE 48 Large complex mass in the ovary. Particularly worrisome are the excrescences in the interior of the cyst. (Image provided by Departments of Radiology and Obstetrics & Gynecology, University of California, San Francisco.)

QUESTIONS

189. You explain to her that she probably has ovarian cancer. She asks you how the disease spreads and you inform her that the cancer *most* commonly spreads by:
    A. Direct exfoliation from the ovaries
    B. Hematogenous spread
    C. Lymph node metastases
    D. Transperitoneal dissemination
    E. Parenchymal involvement of the brain and lung

190. The next step in her management is:
    A. Diagnostic laparoscopy
    B. Chemotherapy with a platinum-based regimen
    C. Total abdominal hysterectomy, bilateral salpingo-oophorectomy, lymph node dissection, omentectomy
    D. Laparoscopically-assisted vaginal hysterectomy, bilateral salpingo-oophorectomy, lymph node sampling
    E. Bilateral salpingo-oophorectomy, lymph node dissection, omentectomy

191. Findings at time of surgery included 6 liters of ascites, diffuse tumor implants over the abdominal peritoneal surfaces and omentum measuring up to 4 cm in diameter, enlarged para-aortic lymph nodes, and bilateral solid-cystic ovarian masses. All the above sites were histologically confirmed to contain adenocarcinoma. What stage of ovarian cancer did she present with?
    A. Stage IIIa
    B. Stage IIIb　·
    C. Stage IIIc
    D. Stage IV
    E. Stage IIc

192. Given this patient's family history, you should inform the patient's two daughters that:
    A. They are not at increased risk for ovarian or breast cancer.
    B. They should be screened with annual pelvic examinations only.
    C. They should be screened with CA-125 levels to decrease mortality.
    D. They should be screened with ultrasonography to decrease mortality.
    E. Prophylactic oophorectomy decreases the risk of ovarian cancer.

ID/CC: 39-year-old G$_4$P$_1$T$_3$ woman presents to the emergency department with complaint of vaginal bleeding and profuse vaginal discharge over the past 6 months.

HPI: C.C. denies any abdominal pain but reports at least a 6-month period of irregular vaginal bleeding, periodically with large clots. She has also noticed increased foul-smelling watery vaginal discharge. Ms. C reports occasional chills. She denies any nausea or vomiting, changes in bowel and bladder habits, and has had no recent change in weight.

PMHx/PSHx: 3 D&Cs   **Meds:** None   **All:** NKDA

POb/GynHx: 3 TABs, SUD 20 years ago. Last Pap smear 5 years ago, within normal limits. History of gonorrhea, chlamydia 2 to 3 years ago.

SHx: Lives in a homeless shelter. Smokes 1.5 packs per day of cigarettes; uses EtOH, heroin, and cocaine.

VS: Temp 96.7°F, BP 110/62, HR 76; Weight 95 lbs, Height 5'3"

PE: *Gen:* cachectic-appearing woman in mild distress. *HEENT:* poor dentition, pale mucosa, neck without masses. *Abdomen:* soft, nontender, no distension, bilateral shoddy inguinal lymph nodes. *Pelvic:* cervix with a polypoid, friable, fungating mass protruding through the os. Vagina without lesions. *BME:* cervix is firm and nodular, enlarged to approximately 4 to 5 cm; parametria and pelvic sidewalls appear free; positive CMT. *RV:* confirms the above findings, thin rectovaginal septum.

Labs: Urine pregnancy test, negative; WBC 1.1; Hb 9.0; Cr 1.2.

THOUGHT QUESTIONS
- What is the differential diagnosis for this woman with painless vaginal bleeding?
- Should the laboratory finding of leukopenia be of concern in her workup?
- What further diagnostic tests would help focus the differential diagnosis?

The differential diagnosis would have to include cervical carcinoma, a prolapsing cervical polyp, condyloma, a myoma, and an infected degenerating/necrotic polyp or myoma. A WBC of 1.1 is worrisome in this patient with cachexia, anemia, a painless cervical mass, and a history of polysubstance use, all of which suggest a possibly immunocompromised state. If she is clinically stable, a Pap examination, endocervical curettage, and biopsy of this mass need to be performed.

CASE CONTINUED

She confides that her partner died of *Pneumocystis* pneumonia. You obtain her consent for hepatitis, HIV, CD4, and viral load testing. You also perform biopsies of the cervical mass and obtain a social work consultation. These tests eventually return, confirming your suspicions that she is HIV-positive and has adenocarcinoma of the cervix.

THOUGHT QUESTIONS
- What is the staging work-up for cervical cancer?
- What is the management of cervical cancer?

Cervical cancer is clinically staged via an examination under anesthesia, as well as cystoscopy and proctoscopy to assess for local spread of disease. CT scans of the abdomen, pelvis, and chest should be obtained. Although cervical cancer is clinically staged, these imaging studies help evaluate for metastatic disease (Table 49; Figure 49). A radical hysterectomy would benefit a patient with invasive cervical cancer confined to the cervix, uterine corpus, and vagina (stage IIA or less). More advanced disease, stage IIB and beyond, is treated with combined radiation therapy and adjuvant cisplatin-based chemotherapy. In fact, radiation therapy and radical hysterectomy have been found to be equally effective in treating stage IB disease.

TABLE 49. Staging Cervical Cancer			
Stage I.	Confined to the cervix	**Stage III.**	Extension to the pelvic wall or distal vagina
	IA. Microscopic disease		**IIIA.** Not to the pelvic wall
	IB. Clinically identifiable lesions		**IIIB.** To the pelvic wall
Stage II.	Extracervical, but not to the pelvic walls or distal third of the vagina	**Stage IV.**	Beyond the true pelvis
	IIA. No parametrial involvement		**IVA.** To the bladder or rectum
	IIB. Parametrial involvement		**IVB.** Distant metastases

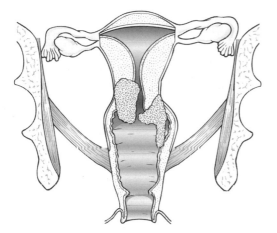

FIGURE 49 The cervical cancer is bulky, larger than 4 cm, but confined to the cervical corpus. (Callahan T, Caughey A, Heffner L. Blueprints in Obstetrics and Gynecology. 2nd ed. Malden: Blackwell Science, 2001:212.)

QUESTIONS

193. The hospital resident who consulted you about this patient wants to know the true relationship between cervical neoplasia and human papillomavirus (HPV). You briefly tell him that:
   A. HPV serotypes 6 and 11 are correlated with cervical cancer whereas serotypes 16 and 8 predispose to condyloma.
   B. Sexual-behavioral risk factors are not surrogates for cervical cancer.
   C. HPV DNA is frequently found to be integrated into the DNA of cervical cancer cells.
   D. There is no relationship between cigarette smoking and HPV-associated dysplasia of the cervix.
   E. HPV prevalence is lowest in a population of young sexually active individuals.

194. Her presentation is most concerning for an occult cervical carcinoma. The CT scan of her abdomen and pelvis does not show hydronephrosis or ureteral obstruction. What stage cervical carcinoma does this patient have?
   A. Stage IA
   B. Stage IB1
   C. Stage IB2
   D. Stage IIA
   E. Stage III

195. Which of the following would be appropriate if she was clinically unstable secondary to cervical bleeding?
   A. Transfuse with blood products and perform a total abdominal hysterectomy and bilateral salpingo-oophorectomy
   B. Transfuse and perform a trachelectomy (amputation of the cervix)
   C. Transfuse and treat with high-dose progestins
   D. Transfuse and pack the vagina
   E. Transfuse, pack the vagina, and consult interventional radiology for possible embolization of the hypogastric vessels

196. The Centers for Disease Control and Surveillance (CDC) revised the definition and surveillance criteria for HIV and AIDS in 1993 to include certain gynecologic diseases as markers for progression from HIV infection to full-blown AIDS in women. Which of the following was included as an AIDS-defining illness?
   A. Recurrent vulvovaginal candidiasis
   B. Multiple episodes of PID
   C. Invasive cervical cancer
   D. Abnormal cervical cytology
   E. Genital ulcer disease

ID/CC: 29-year-old G$_0$ woman presents with a painful lump in her right breast.

HPI: S.C. noticed the onset of breast pain approximately 4 weeks ago. She initially thought that she had strained a muscle but then felt a small tender area on the outer part of her right breast in the shower. She denies any abnormal nipple discharge.

PMHx/PSHx: None   **Meds:** Medroxyprogesterone acetate (DMPA)   **All:** NKDA

POb/GynHx: Menarche at age 13, regular cycles until amenorrhea due to DMPA. No STIs

SHx: Recently married. 2 cups of coffee per day.

VS: Temp 97.6°F, BP 110/60, HR 76, RR 16

PE: *Chest:* CTAB. *Breasts:* symmetrical, nontender, no skin changes, no galactorrhea or other discharge. Right breast—palpable 2.5 cm smooth, round, mobile mass, minimally tender at 10 o'clock 3 cm from the nipple; Left breast—within normal limits.

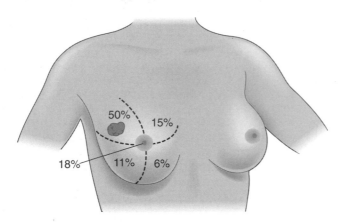

FIGURE 50 Diagram of common locations for breast masses. In this case, the location is at 10:00. (Illustration by Electronic Illustrators Group.)

THOUGHT QUESTIONS

- What is the differential diagnosis for a painful lump in the breast of a premenopausal woman? Of an older woman?
- What characteristics are associated with benign versus malignant masses?
- What other pertinent facts in her history would you like to know?

In a premenopausal woman the differential diagnosis includes cysts, fibrocystic change, fat necrosis, or an abscess. Fat necrosis typically results from trauma to the breast. Although an abscess usually occurs in the postpartum period from progression of mastitis, subareolar abscesses have also been seen in older, nonlactating women. Sclerosing adenosis can sometimes present as a hard, fixed, tender mass, as can cystosarcoma phyllodes, a rare and potentially aggressive tumor. Malignancy should always be considered in an older woman, even though the majority of invasive tumors tend to be painless (unless it is an advanced stage invasive cancer).

When attempting to differentiate between malignant and benign tumors on physical examination, benign tumors tend to be smooth, regular, and mobile, whereas malignant masses are typically irregular and fixed to adjacent tissue. There can be associated skin or nipple retraction if an underlying malignant mass is present. One should elicit a more detailed history about fluctuations in either the size of the lesion or the nature of the discomfort, history of injury to the breast, prior similar episodes, and a family history of breast disease.

CASE CONTINUED

She does not recall trauma to the breast and she has not noticed any change in pain or size of the lump over the last few weeks. Notable in her family history is fibrocystic disease in her mother and sister. Her other sister, maternal grandmother, and two maternal aunts have had no breast disease. Her paternal grandmother had breast cancer in her 70s and is alive and well after therapy.

QUESTIONS

197. What is the most likely diagnosis for her breast lump?
    A. Fibroadenoma
    B. Fibrocystic disease
    C. Cyst
    D. Cystosarcoma phyllodes
    E. Fat necrosis

198. You recommend:
    A. Excisional biopsies of both masses
    B. Mammography
    C. Ductogram
    D. Aspiration of the cyst
    E. MRI study

199. The cyst on the left breast was aspirated with resolution of pain and no residual mass. Fluid cytology report was benign but within 6 weeks the patient returns to your office with pain and a larger mass at the same site. What has occurred and what do you recommend now?
    A. She has a cellulitis and you start dicloxacillin.
    B. She has a breast abscess and needs an incision and drainage procedure.
    C. She has a breast abscess, and you start oral antibiotic therapy.
    D. She has a breast abscess, and you recommend follow-up with an ultrasound.
    E. She has reaccumulation of fluid in the same cyst, and you recommend cyst excision.

200. Rank the following risk factors for breast cancer in descending order:
    A. First-degree relative with bilateral premenopausal breast cancer > first-degree relative with bilateral postmenopausal breast cancer > nulliparity > menarche before age 12
    B. Nulliparity > menarche before age 12 > first-degree relative with bilateral premenopausal breast cancer > first-degree relative with bilateral postmenopausal breast cancer
    C. Menarche before age 12 > nulliparity > first-degree relative with bilateral premenopausal breast cancer > first-degree relative with bilateral postmenopausal breast cancer
    D. First-degree relative with bilateral premenopausal breast cancer > nulliparity > first-degree relative with bilateral postmenopausal breast cancer > menarche before age 12
    E. First-degree relative with bilateral premenopausal breast cancer > menarche before age 12 > first-degree relative with bilateral postmenopausal breast cancer > nulliparity

ANSWERS

ANSWERS

1–C

This couple's ethnic background places them at risk for β thalassemia. The anemia should therefore be evaluated in both parents. "Physiologic anemia" of pregnancy occurs because of the relatively greater expansion of plasma volume compared to the increase in total RBC mass. As a result, the hematocrit decreases and reaches a nadir at approximately 32 weeks GA. However, this anemia is not associated with hypochromia and microcytosis. Although iron deficiency anemia is the most common anemia seen in pregnancy, empiric treatment for iron deficiency anemia without simultaneous diagnostic workup is inappropriate. As amniocentesis is an invasive procedure with associated risks, direct testing on the fetus for β thalassemia is not indicated unless the parents are known carriers.

2–E

Optimal assessment of a potentially heritable disorder in a family is best achieved by evaluation of the known affected individual. In this case, because chromosomal analysis was done 20 years prior and the resolution of karyotypes is far greater today, it is reasonable to repeat an analysis in addition to investigating the possibility of fragile X, which should be ruled out in any male with mental retardation of unknown cause, particularly if they have traits associated with this syndrome, such as autistic behavior. In cases where evaluation of the affected family member is not possible, or a rapid diagnosis is necessary, amniocentesis may be performed. However, a normal ultrasound and a normal triple screen test, while reassuring, do not invalidate the need for the workup outlined above. Usually both these tests are normal in fragile X as well as in unspecified mental retardation.

3–C

Transvaginal ultrasound can detect an intrauterine gestational sac as early as 4.5 weeks gestational age (GA), and an embryo by 6 weeks GA. Fetal movements can be felt on average at approximately 18 weeks GA, and typically 1 or 2 weeks sooner in multiparous women. Between approximately 18 weeks until 36 weeks GA, the fundal height in centimeters is roughly equal to weeks of GA. Hence, the uterine fundus should be palpable at the umbilicus by 20 weeks GA. Prior to this at 12 weeks GA, the uterine fundus should be palpable transabdominally at the symphysis pubis. With the aid of Doppler, fetal heart tones can be heard as early as 11 weeks, if not sooner with more modern equipment. Failure to detect fetal heart tones at 12 weeks GA or greater should warrant further investigation with ultrasound.

4–D

Cystic fibrosis, Canavan disease, and Tay-Sachs disease are autosomal recessive disorders that can affect individuals from any ethnic background. However, their incidence is higher among Ashkenazi Jews. In addition, Ashkenazi Jews are good candidates for genetic screening because of the Founder effect; that is, common gene mutations existing within the group. There is debate whether universal screening should be offered for cystic fibrosis (CF). The detection rate of mutations is different for each ethnic group. With current mutation panels, less than 60% of CF mutations can be detected among Latinos, who have a low prevalence of CF. Among African-Americans, the carrier rate for sickle cell anemia (SCA) is 8%. SCA prenatal screening via hemoglobin electrophoresis is routinely offered to individuals of African-American descent.

5–A, 6–D

The diagnosis of spontaneous abortion is any pregnancy that terminates itself prior to 20 weeks GA. The subcategories based on the clinical situation are as follows: 1) *threatened abortion*, intrauterine pregnancy with vaginal bleeding; 2) *missed abortion*, closed cervix, but a nonviable gestation based on absent fetal heart motion or absent fetal pole when one should be present based on GA or β-hCG; 3) *inevitable abortion*, intrauterine pregnancy, but dilated cervix; 4) *incomplete abortion*, a portion of the pregnancy has already passed, but often the trophoblastic tissue is still in situ; and 5) *complete abortion*, the entire pregnancy has passed through the cervix.

7–E

Patients who are diagnosed with a missed abortion can be managed in a variety of ways. Expectant management is commonly practiced and will lead to 60% to 70% of patients passing the pregnancy on their own. However, this can be uncomfortable and can take several days to several weeks to occur. Thus, many patients would prefer an intervention. This can range from an immediate

D&C or a D&C scheduled the next day or several days later, to a less invasive approach of giving vaginal misoprostol to help induce uterine contractions and the expulsion of the pregnancy. If the patient opts for expectant management, this is usually done at home. The only reason for a patient to be observed in the hospital is if they are worrisome for an ectopic pregnancy.

8–A

A patient who has had one SAB does not have much of an increased risk of SAB over the general population. Thus, the risk remains between 15% and 20%. In patients with two consecutive SABs, 25% to 30% risk of SAB is quoted for the next pregnancy. In patients with three consecutive SABs, 35% to 45% risk of SAB has been quoted, though it would depend enormously on the cause of the SABs and the patient's age.

9–C

The most common presenting symptom is vaginal bleeding, occurring in over 84% of cases. Patients complain of prune juice-like fluid leaking from the vagina. Hyperemesis is less frequent of a complaint, occurring in 8% of patients. Tachycardia as part of the manifestation of hyperthyroidism or thyroid storm is quite uncommon. However, patients with untreated or poorly controlled hyperthyroidism can develop thyroid storm at the time of anesthesia induction and evacuation, and may require β-adrenergic blockade. Excessive uterine size as compared with gestational age occurs in 30% to 50% of patients with a complete mole because of retained blood and excessive trophoblastic proliferation. Also, infrequently, patients complain of pelvic or abdominal pain from ovarian hyperstimulation by high levels of hCG, and development of theca lutein cysts.

β-blocker

10–A

Following suction evacuation of a molar pregnancy, serial hCG titers need to be monitored initially weekly and then biweekly and then monthly until normal for at least 1 year. The patient needs to receive concurrent reliable contraception to prevent pregnancy during this time period in order to follow the hCG titers. Persistently elevated hCG titers suggest malignant GTD, and a distinguishing feature of GTD is its sensitivity to chemotherapy. Repeat suction evacuation or ultrasonographic examination is of little use or benefit in the treatment of a molar pregnancy in the immediate period after an evacuation.

11–D

The risk of subsequent GTD associated with a complete mole is 15% to 25%, compared with the risk of subsequent GTD following a partial mole of approximately 5%. Malignant GTD can be classified as nonmetastatic or metastatic for the purposes of treatment planning and prognosis. A metastatic workup would include evaluation of liver, brain, or lung metastases. As this patient had no evidence of metastatic disease 6 weeks ago, it is reasonable to begin single-agent chemotherapy at this point. Nevertheless, some practitioners will do a complete workup to rule out metastatic disease prior to initiating chemotherapy. Transvaginal ultrasound could be performed to evaluate for retained placental products. Surgery does not have a role in the management of her disease at this point, particularly because GTD is extremely chemosensitive.

12–A

Approximately 8% of patients with molar pregnancies present with hyperemesis requiring antiemetic therapy. It is usually associated with markedly elevated hCG values from trophoblastic proliferation and growth, and an excessively enlarged uterus. Nevertheless, it is the high circulating levels of estrogen that are thought to be the cause of hyperemesis. There are conflicting data on whether hCG is a thyroid stimulator in these patients, but it is relatively uncommon today for women with molar pregnancies to have clinical evidence of hyperthyroidism.

13–C

Trisomy 21 as well as trisomy 13 can be associated with growth retardation and omphalocele but not as commonly as with trisomy 18. However, although maternal serum AFP and estriol are low in fetuses with Down syndrome, the hCG is usually elevated. Trisomy 13 is generally not detected by maternal serum screening. The pattern of the maternal serum screen shown with all three values decreased is typical for trisomy 18, which can detect up to 50% of affected fetuses. The malformations listed are typical of trisomy 18. X-linked ichthyosis is caused by a deletion of the steroid sulfatase (STS) gene, leading to almost undetectable levels of estriol and dry, scaly skin. However maternal serum hCG and AFP are usually normal, and this condition is usually not associated with malformations. Beckwith-Wiedemann syndrome is characterized by exomphalos, gigantism, and macroglossia.

14–D

An Rh-negative woman can become sensitized at the time of amniocentesis. Therefore, RhoGAM is indicated at the time of the procedure in these patients. Pregnancy loss, premature rupture of membranes, prematurity, and fetal injury are the more common risks associated with amniocentesis.

15–C

On ultrasound, 50% of Down syndrome fetuses are "normal"; the other half have major malformations and/or ultrasound markers that are associated with, but not diagnostic of, Down syndrome. A nuchal translucency greater than 3 mm as a single marker has a sensitivity comparable to that of maternal serum triple screen for the detection of Down syndrome. A number of morphologic variants or "ultrasound markers" have been proposed for the detection of Down syndrome, including the ones mentioned.

16–B

Trisomy 21, trisomy 13 (Patau syndrome), and trisomy X are all correlated with advanced maternal rather than paternal age. Neurofibromatosis I (NF I), like other autosomal dominant disorders, increases exponentially with increasing paternal age. Cystic fibrosis is an autosomal recessive condition and is not associated with increasing paternal age.

17–A, 18–E

The value of the β-hCG should increase by at least 65% every 48 hours in a normal gestation. This has led to the "rule of doubling." Thus, hemodynamically stable patients with a diagnosis of "rule out ectopic pregnancy" are followed with laboratory tests and clinical exams every 48 hours, and the β-hCG is expected to approximately double. In case of lab error and a less than 48-hour time lapse, in a desired pregnancy of a stable patient, if the increase in β-hCG is 30% to 60%, the β-hCG is followed for an additional 48 hours to see if the rise normalizes. However, with an increase of only 25% in this patient with left lower quadrant pain, an abnormal pregnancy is presumed and the uterus should be evacuated either with a manual vacuum aspirator or via D&E to determine whether this is an intrauterine pregnancy

(IUP). If the pathology report is negative for IUP, then she would be diagnosed with ectopic pregnancy. If she remained stable and without evidence of fetal cardiac activity, she would be a candidate for pregnancy termination with IM methotrexate. If the patient was unstable, had a large adnexal mass, or a large amount of blood in the pelvis, she would be considered a poor candidate for medical management and would undergo laparoscopic surgery for the presumed ectopic pregnancy.

If the β-hCG was actually falling, then the diagnosis of spontaneous abortion is more likely. However, because ectopic is still possible, the β-hCG levels should be followed serially until negative. If the patient is diagnosed with spontaneous abortion and is bleeding or has an intrauterine sac on ultrasound, she is often offered expectant management versus D&C. In this case, as the patient had nothing on ultrasound and has only been spotting, expectant management is the preferred management.

19–B

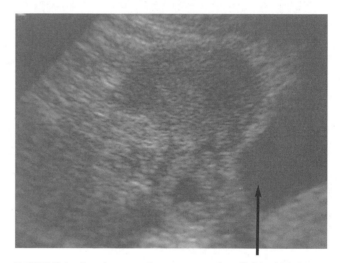

FIGURE 5 In the ultrasound you can see free fluid which is consistent with blood in the pelvis. (Image provided by Departments of Radiology and Obstetrics & Gynecology, University of California, San Francisco.)

In a patient with moderate to large free fluid in the pelvis, a cause should be determined. This is even more important in a patient with peritoneal signs, which include rebound tenderness, tenderness to shaking, and cervical motion tenderness on rectal exam. Laparoscopy is adequate because this patient may simply have a collection of fluid or blood from a hemorrhagic corpus luteum that has stabilized or an ectopic pregnancy that can be resected via laparoscope. Because the pregnancy is desired, it is probably best to determine the cause of the moderate free fluid before performing a D&C of what might be a normal pregnancy.

20–C

The patient in this question most likely has an ectopic pregnancy with a small adnexal mass and an empty uterus. Because she is stable and there is no evidence of fetal cardiac activity in the adnexal mass, it is reasonable to treat her ectopic pregnancy medically with methotrexate. Contraindications for the use of methotrexate include moderate or large free fluid, baseline liver disease, adnexal mass greater than 3 cm, positive fetal heart rate in the adnexa, or β-hCG greater than 5000 (occasionally up to 10,000 is used). The latter three findings are suggestive of a gestation that is likely beyond the age where methotrexate would be successful.

21–A

The use of valproic acid in pregnancy has been associated with a 6% risk of NTDs. Lithium during pregnancy is associated with an increased risk for Epstein's anomaly, a rare heart defect, not NTDs. Fluoxetine is not associated with an increased risk of major malformations. Prednisone does not cross the placenta and is not associated with an increased risk of major anomalies, but rather increases the risk of PPROM and prematurity. There are no known teratogenic risks associated with the use of Tylenol during pregnancy.

22–B

Studies have shown that the recurrence of NTDs can be reduced from 3.5% to 1.0% by the administration of 4 mg of folic acid from at least 1 month prior to conception through the end of the first trimester; 0.4 mg of folic acid has been shown to be effective in reducing the occurrence of NTDs in women without a prior affected pregnancy. It is unclear whether levels of folic acid adequate for NTD prevention can be attained by dietary supplementation.

23–D

Unexplained elevated MSAFP is likely related to the way the placenta acts to transport molecules between the fetal and maternal circulation. These patients are at an increased risk for developing intrauterine growth retardation, abruptio placentae, and preeclampsia later in the pregnancy. Increased surveillance is recommended in these pregnancies. Gestational diabetes is not correlated with unexplained elevated MSAFP, and unlike pregestational diabetes, is not associated with an increased risk of congenital anomalies.

24–C

Because fetuses with Down syndrome are at an increased risk for miscarriage, the likelihood of identifying a fetus with Down syndrome at 16 to 18 weeks is higher than having a live born with Down syndrome. The risk of recurrence of trisomy 21 is increased, and approximately 1% for those women who have had an affected fetus/live-born conceived at age 30 or younger, which is thought to be due to germ line mosaicism. Although not currently used for routine screening, there are several ultrasound findings associated with Down syndrome, including thickened nuchal fold, mild hydronephrosis, echogenic bowel, and slightly shortened long bones. A normal ultrasound does not rule out Down syndrome because midtrimester ultrasound is normal in at least 50% of Down syndrome fetuses. Obtaining a karyotype in affected fetuses can yield valuable genetic information that can be used to predict recurrence in future pregnancies. Down syndrome is due to trisomy 21 in 96% of the cases, mosaicism in 1%, and unbalanced translocations in 2% to 3%, with the risk of recurrence being much higher in cases of unbalanced translocation in which one of the parents is a balanced translocation carrier.

25–C

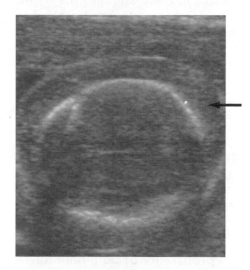

FIGURE A25 In this fetus with hydrops note the scalp edema (Image provided by Departments of Radiology and Obstetrics & Gynecology, University of California, San Francisco.)

ANSWERS

In this case, the fetus has now begun to show signs of hydrops. In this setting, without another cause for fetal hydrops, it can be assumed to be secondary to fetal anemia from hemolysis. Thus, the fetus needs an intrauterine transfusion (IUT) with Rh D-negative blood that has been cross-matched against the mother's serum. At the initial entry of the needle into the umbilical cord, a sample should be taken to assess fetal hematocrit; this can help guide the volume of transfusion, but is not the primary purpose of the PUBS. In the setting of a fetus at 34 weeks and beyond, immediate delivery would be an option, but at 25 weeks gestation, the best option is to attempt IUT.

26–E

Fetal hydrops, in the setting of alloimmunization, is the result of high output cardiac failure secondary to fetal anemia. The anti-D IgG antibodies cross the placenta and cause hemolysis of the fetal red blood cells carrying the D antigen. Signs of fetal hydrops seen on ultrasound include edema, ascites, and pericardial and pleural effusions. A cystic hygroma, which is collection of fluid at the base of the skull in the neck, is associated with fetal aneuploidy as well as with fetal hydrops. However, its association is more of a precursor to fetal hydrops in a fetus with anomalies rather than an association with fetal anemia and cardiac failure.

27–C

Assuming this patient is telling the truth regarding prior paternity, her husband has fathered one Rh D-positive child and one Rh D-negative child. Thus, he must be heterozygous. If he had fathered only Rh D-positive or only Rh D-negative children, his zygosity would be uncertain.

28–B

The probability can be calculated in two ways, long and short. The long method involves calculating the probabilities of each of the parents using the Hardy-Weinberg formula

$$p^2 + 2pq + q^2 = 1$$

where p = probability of dominant allele, and q = probability of recessive allele. Keeping in mind that there is no "d" allele and that being Rh D-negative means the absence of the "D" allele (written as "−"), p = 0.6 and q = 0.4; thus the parents can each be:

$$DD = p^2 = 0.36, D- = 2pq = 0.48,$$
$$and -- = q^2 = 0.16$$

For them to have an Rh-negative child, the following possibilities must occur:

$$D- \times D-\ ;\ D- \times --;\ or\ -- \times --$$

This can occur with the following probability:

D− × D− leading to −− = (0.48) * (0.48) * (0.25)
$$= 0.0576$$

D− × −− leading to −− = (0.48) * (0.16) * 2 * (0.5)
$$= 0.0768$$

−− × −− leading to −− = (0.16) * (0.16) = 0.0256

$$0.0576 + 0.0768 + 0.0256 = 0.16$$

The short way is to realize that in a population, the probability of any of the members of that population being homozygous recessive is equal to q^2, in this case 0.16.

29–D

If noncompliance is suspected, further diabetic teaching and counseling is reasonable. Hospitalization is not indicated unless glucose levels are extremely poorly controlled. One week of dietary therapy is generally sufficient to evaluate metabolic control, and to make the decision of whether to start insulin. Oral hypoglycemics are not routinely recommended during pregnancy because of concerns about teratogenicity and neonatal hypoglycemia. For a GDM patient who has inadequate metabolic control, a starting regimen of NPH insulin, 0.5–0.7 U/kg/day divided in 2/3 AM and 1/3 PM doses, is a reasonable approach. In addition, a patient who has elevated postprandial values at breakfast and dinner may require regular insulin prior to meals. More recently, providers have begun using fast-acting Lispro or Humalog insulin prior to meals. Home monitoring of FSBG and frequent visits and/or telephone calls by a diabetic nurse specialist have largely avoided the need for routine hospitalization for these patients.

30–E

The complications of GDM are related to the large weight and bodily proportions of the fetus (e.g., increased risk of cesarean section, operative delivery, shoulder dystocia, brachial plexus injury) and metabolic complications of the neonate (e.g., hypoglycemia, hypocalcemia, polycythemia, hyperbilirubinemia). Both of these types of complications can be avoided by adequate glucose control during pregnancy. Preexisting diabetes mellitus is associated with an increased risk of major malformations, which is related to the degree of metabolic control during the time of organogenesis. Unless a patient had preexisting diabetes that was detected for the first time during pregnancy, GDM is not associated with an increased risk of congenital malformations.

31–A

Antenatal testing should be started between 32 to 34 weeks GA in diabetic patients on insulin to evaluate fetal growth and well-being. Given that NPH insulin is long-acting, it should be stopped once the patient is in active labor or on the morning of a planned induction/elective C/S. Pregnant women, irrespective of GDM status, spill glucose in their urine. Therefore, glucosuria should not be used as an indicator of metabolic control. One-hour postprandial FSBG levels provide the best criteria to establish glucose control in pregnancy. Perinatal mortality is higher among diabetic patients with poor metabolic control. Therefore, GDM patients with poor glycemic control should be delivered after 37 to 38 weeks GA with confirmed fetal lung maturity. Ideally, they should be under adequate metabolic control at least 2 days before delivery to avoid metabolic complications of the neonate.

32–C

After delivery there is a dramatic reduction in insulin requirements due to the clearance of placental hormones with anti-insulin action, specifically human placental lactogen (hPL). As a result, GDM patients can be allowed to resume a regular diet after birth. There is a 20% to 30% chance that a GDM patient will develop type II diabetes after a long-term follow-up period. Therefore, screening for early detection should occur at 6 weeks postpartum and on an annual basis thereafter.

33–D

Approximately 15% of women are asymptomatic carriers of Group B *Streptococcus*, which has historically been the leading organism causing neonatal sepsis. At the time of admission, most preterm patients have a vaginal and anal culture obtained to test for this organism. However, the culture takes a few days to grow, so all preterm labor patients are given antibiotic prophylaxis. The antibiotic of choice is penicillin. Many institutions use ampicillin, a practice that can increase antibiotic resistance. Clindamycin is given to patients with an allergy to penicillin. Group B *Streptococcus* is one of many organisms that can cause chorioamnionitis. However, it is particularly virulent, with an associated 25% to 50% mortality rate in preterm neonates with sepsis.

34–C

Betamethasone is a corticosteroid that is given to help reduce the incidence of respiratory distress syndrome in preterm neonates between 24 and 34 weeks of gestation. It differs from prednisone in that it crosses the placenta into the fetal circulation. Once there, it is thought to work by increasing the production of surfactant in type 2 pneumocytes in the fetal lung. The neonate benefits optimally from this steroid shot if delivery is delayed at least 48 hours from the first dose. The second dose is given 24 hours after the first.

35–A

In addition to being a membrane stabilizer by increasing baseline resting potential, magnesium sulfate acts as an antagonist at calcium channels.

36–B

Fetal fibronectin detection is one of the latest tests to help determine who is at greatest risk of preterm delivery. Fetal fibronectin is a glycoprotein associated with the fetus; its presence on a cervical or vaginal swab is thus abnormal. The test has a 90% negative predictive value. Therefore, a negative test result indicates the likelihood is very low that a patient will deliver in the following week. The test has a poor positive predictive value, of approximately 30%; therefore, a positive test does not necessarily mean that a patient is at risk for delivery.

37–B

The patient has a surgical abdomen and requires exploration. Laparoscopy is not recommended in pregnancy after 20 weeks GA due to difficult access given the size of the uterus. Although IV antibiotics are indicated, they should not be the primary therapy. Surgery should not be delayed

ANSWERS

in a patient with worsening status and a surgical abdomen.

38–B

Often patients with an acute abdominal process have associated uterine contractions but they seldom lead to premature delivery. Prophylactic use of tocolytics is not considered standard practice, particularly in this patient who has no cervical change. If uterine contractions are persistent, with a regular pattern, tocolysis may be appropriate. Beta mimetics are not a good choice in this already tachycardic patient because of the associated tachycardia.

39–C

Steroids are recommended for enhancement of fetal lung maturity between 24 and 34 weeks GA whenever premature delivery is a possibility, as is the case here. A single course is not associated with adverse effects on the fetus. Although there can be maternal side effects with the use of steroids in this context, it is unlikely that an acute infectious process may be worsened by its use. A transient elevation of WBC is frequently seen due to steroid-induced demargination of leukocytes. However, this should not have a significant impact in assessing her overall clinical response.

40–A

Contraindications to vaginal delivery include placenta previa, active genital herpes simplex infection, and history of prior classic cesarean section, but do not include recent abdominal laparotomy. Therefore, this patient should be allowed to deliver vaginally if cephalic presentation is confirmed. The risk of abdominal wall defect associated with significant maternal effort such as pushing in the second stage of labor is small. In general, breech vaginal deliveries are not attempted for fetuses weighing less than 1500 grams. The risk of wound infection is likely increased but this is not a reason to withhold an indicated procedure. The patient should receive anesthesia as she and the provider feel it is necessary.

41–B

A course of ampicillin and erythromycin has been shown to increase the latency period, the time between rupture of membranes to the onset of labor. Without antibiotics, approximately 50% of patients will go into labor within 24 hours and 75% within 48 hours. In general, the younger the

gestational age, the longer the latency period unless complicated by chorioamnionitis.

42–C

Abdominal trauma, procedures such as amniocentesis, preterm labor, and infection are all associated with PPROM; however, in most cases, the cause is unknown. Studies suggest that ascending subclinical infection may be the main culprit.

43–B

This question exemplifies the difficult and controversial management of PPROM. On initial presentation, this patient lacked any symptoms of chorioamnionitis, such as fever, abdominal tenderness, elevated WBC, maternal tachycardia, fetal tachycardia, or uterine contractions. However, the main cause of PPROM is likely subclinical infection, so she is still at great risk for the development of an overt infection. Pitocin is thus given as the patient has already developed chorioamnionitis and rapid delivery may help prevent neonatal sepsis.

44–D

This is a controversial topic. However, most practitioners would agree that at 35 weeks gestation or beyond, the risks of prematurity are low as compared to the risk of infection. Some practitioners would consider doing an amniocentesis at this gestational age for fetal lung maturity and giving betamethasone first if the lungs are immature. On the other hand, some practitioners feel comfortable at 33 to 35 weeks GA inducing delivery immediately after PPROM. The reason for these different management styles is in part based on the decreasing risk of respiratory distress syndrome (RDS) with increasing gestational age. At 28 weeks GA, the risk of RDS is 60% to 75%. By 30 weeks GA, the risk is decreased to 40% to 50%. Between 33 to 35 weeks GA, the rate of RDS declines from 20% to 30% to only 6%. And finally, the risk at 36 weeks GA is about 3% to 5%.

45–A

See answer to question 46.

46–C

No interval growth is an indication for delivery in a viable pregnancy. Induction of fetal lung maturity with steroids is useful when delivery is anticipated between 24 and 34 weeks of gestation.

Due to the oligohydramnios and IUGR, this fetus is at risk for fetal death and should therefore be monitored closely until delivery. Amnioinfusion may be used in the setting of repetitive variable decelerations during labor or thick meconium, but is contraindicated if fetal distress is suspected, as it is in this case. A fetal bradycardia in this already compromised fetus warrants immediate delivery by cesarean section.

47–D

Fetal growth restriction is a heterogeneous group of disorders that can be subdivided into two groups of disorders. Decreased growth potential is associated with constitutionally small/small maternal stature, genetic chromosomal abnormalities, intrauterine infections, and teratogenic exposure. Intrauterine growth restriction is related to maternal factors such as chronic hypertension, severe anemia, autoimmune disease, severe malnutrition, diabetes with vascular disease, and placental factors such as chronic abruption and multiple gestations. Gestational diabetes is associated with large for gestational age (LGA) not SGA.

48–C

Reverse diastolic flow on umbilical cord Doppler is the best predictor of adverse perinatal outcome, with a perinatal mortality of 25% to 50% (a BPP of 0/10 also has a perinatal mortality of about 50%). NST is a better predictor when reactive or normal (perinatal mortality of 5/1000 within 1 week of the test). In a high-risk population, only 25% of initially nonreactive NSTs have a positive OCT. OCT is also a better predictor when normal or negative (perinatal death of 0.4/1000). A positive OCT (late deceleration in at least 50% of uterine contractions) is associated with fetal compromise but has a false-positive rate of at least 30% to 50%. A normal BPP (10/10) is again an excellent predictor of good perinatal outcome (perinatal mortality of 0.8/1000). At 31 weeks, a score of 4/10 should be repeated within less than 24 hours. Decreased fetal movement warrants antenatal testing but is a poor predictor of adverse perinatal outcome.

49–A

Management of preterm labor involves use of steroids for the prevention of RDS and intraventricular hemorrhage (IVH), tocolysis until the desired effect on fetal lung maturity is obtained, and antibiotics for the prevention of Group B *Streptococcus* (GBS) sepsis in the neonate. Delivery is not considered imminent in the case presented, and even in cases of advanced cervical dilation, steroids may still have some value if delivery is deferred for just a few hours. The use of tocolysis and antibiotics in the absence of corticosteroid administration is not considered adequate management of preterm labor, as the maximal gain from medical intervention is obtained from the latter. Trendelenburg position and emergent cerclage is indicated in cases of incompetent cervix (painless cervical dilation, usually in the midtrimester), not preterm labor.

50–C

The combination of twin gestation, corticosteroids, aggressive IV hydration, and IV tocolysis with either magnesium sulfate or β-adrenergic agonists has been associated with pulmonary edema. Physical examination and chest x-ray should confirm the diagnosis. Pulmonary embolism and amniotic fluid embolism typically present with sudden onset of shortness of breath and low O₂ saturations. Chest x-ray, electrocardiogram (ECG), arterial blood gas (ABG), spiral CT, or V/Q scan are useful when this diagnosis is suspected.

51–B

For dizygotic twin gestations, the risk of aneuploidy in at least one fetus is equal to 1 in 200 at maternal age 32, which is 3 years earlier than in singleton gestations (risk of 1 in 200 at age 35). Although the rate of malformation in twins is higher than for singletons, prematurity is the number one cause of perinatal mortality in twins. Serial ultrasounds are recommended to assess fetal growth because the fundal height measurements are not well correlated with fetal growth. Furthermore, one fetus may be growing, while the other is experiencing intrauterine growth restriction (IUGR). Preeclampsia is more frequent in multiple gestations.

52–D

Fetal causes of polyhydramnios include gastrointestinal obstructions, and neurologic or mechanical conditions (tracheoesophageal fistulas) that interfere with swallowing. Placental causes include twin-to-twin transfusion syndrome (polyhydramnios in the recipient twin, and oligohydramnios in the donor), and placental tumors.

ANSWERS

Diabetes mellitus with poor glycemic control is a well-known maternal cause of polyhydramnios. Polyhydramnios can be severe enough to lead to maternal respiratory distress, in which case reduction amniocentesis is indicated.

53–C, 54–E

The biophysical profile is an evaluation completed over approximately 30 minutes by ultrasound. The following variables are evaluated for a total of 10 points possible: 2 points for a reactive FHR tracing; 2 points for at least one episode of fetal breathing movements (or hiccoughs) lasting at least 30 seconds; 2 points for at least three discrete body or limb movements; 2 points for at least one episode of active extension with return to flexion of a limb, hand, or trunk; and 2 points for an amniotic fluid index greater than 5 or at least one pocket measuring 2 × 2 cm or greater. Variables that are not met completely are given 0 points rather than 1, as there is no partial scoring in this test. Based on these criteria, this patient's BPP score is 8/10, with 2 points off for a nonreactive FHR tracing. A score of 8/10 or 10/10 is considered "reassuring," and therefore, the patient can be followed expectantly but should return with further episodes of decreased fetal movement. Depending on the clinical situation and gestational age, a score of 6 or less (or a score of 8/10 with oligohydramnios) warrants a contraction stress test and observation on continuous monitoring (repeat NST). At term, delivery should be considered in such patients.

55–C

The interpretation of a fetal heart rate tracing involves the evaluation of four factors. The first is the baseline heart rate which is normally between 110 and 160 bpm. A second factor is a determination of the heart rate variability, which is represented by the fluctuations in the amplitude of the baseline heart rate. Put more simply, it is the appearance of the heart rate (i.e., does it look like a straight line and lack variability, or is it jagged?). A third factor is the absence or presence of decelerations and their relationship, if present, to a contraction. A fourth factor is the presence of accelerations in the baseline heart rate. A "reactive" tracing for a fetus greater than 32 weeks EGA by definition is a 20-minute continuous tracing that has two accelerations of greater than 15 beats above baseline heart rate lasting at least 15 seconds. A "reactive" tracing for a fetus less than 32 weeks EGA is a 20-minute continuous

tracing that has two accelerations of greater than 10 beats above baseline lasting at least 10 seconds. A reactive tracing is a term used for a tracing that is considered normal or reassuring.

56–B

A CST or OCT is defined as three contractions within a 10-minute period. A CST can occur spontaneously, if the patient is contracting on her own, or can be achieved via Pitocin or nipple stimulation. A negative or reassuring CST is a tracing without decelerations; a positive or abnormal CST is one with decelerations. Although there is some disagreement between obstetricians, a CST with decelerations associated with less than half of the contractions is generally considered "indeterminate." Again, a CST is used as another measure of fetal well-being. A positive CST warrants consideration of immediate delivery or continuous observation. A negative CST is reassuring and the patient can be scheduled for outpatient testing in the future depending on the situation for which the test was performed.

57–D

Test result abnormalities in preeclampsia will not improve until delivery and often not for hours to days after delivery. One exception to this is that there is often a transient improvement in lab abnormalities when steroids are given, particularly in the setting of betamethasone given for probable preterm delivery (antenatal corticosteroid). Choices A, B, and C all show some lab improvement. However, this is not expected in this patient who did not receive ACS. The values in choice E are possible, but lab values tend to follow a trend and thus one would expect the next set of results to be closer to those in choice D. Lab tests should be followed closely postpartum, watching for the nadir of the platelets.

58–B

In patients with preeclampsia, magnesium sulfate is often given for seizure prophylaxis. This is continued for 24 hours after birth. The basis for this treatment is that the bulk of eclamptic seizures occur antepartum, intrapartum, and in the first 24 hours postpartum. Thus, with this therapy most eclamptic seizures will be prevented. Some physicians will treat with magnesium sulfate beyond 24 hours if the lab values are still worsening, blood pressures are poorly controlled, or severe headache continues. However, this management style has never been studied and is based on risk aversion rather than clinical evidence.

59–E

Patients with systemic lupus erythematosus (SLE) can have symptoms and lab test abnormalities very similar to patients with severe preeclampsia. Furthermore, all of the diagnostic criteria for severe preeclampsia, including pulmonary edema, oliguria, and even seizures, can be seen in these patients. To determine which is the more likely cause, two lab tests have been used. Patients having a lupus flare will usually have a decreased total complement level, and patients with severe preeclampsia usually have an elevated uric acid. Other than these values, careful discussion with the patient and her rheumatologist is important and may help in this differential. Class RF diabetics (refer to White's classification of gestational diabetics) have the elevated blood pressures and proteinuria of preeclampsia, but they do not usually get the lab test abnormalities and symptoms of preeclampsia.

60–C

Even with postpartum seizures, magnesium sulfate has been shown to be as efficacious or more so than other commonly used anti-seizure medications in patients with eclampsia. In patients who are admitted with postpartum eclampsia, a set of lab tests including electrolytes, Ca^{2+} and the preeclamptic tests (LFTs, Cr, LDH, and CBC) should be ordered. Usually these patients warrant a neurology consultation, as well as a head CT. The usual finding in eclampsia is some cerebral edema in the occipital cortex. As long as the lab results and blood pressures are stable, the magnesium is continued IV for 24 to 48 hours and then stopped. The patient is usually watched for an additional 24 hours and then discharged home without further anti-seizure medications unless they are recommended by the neurologist.

61–B

See answer to question 62.

62–A

IHCP is associated with an increase in perinatal mortality and prematurity, but is not associated with congenital malformations. The recurrence risk is 1/3 in subsequent pregnancies and about

50% of the patients have a positive family history, suggesting a genetic basis. Treatment of pruritus is important for comfort care, but it does not improve perinatal outcome. Recommended practice is to deliver between 35 to 38 weeks GA in an attempt to prevent late intrauterine demise. Many clinicians will also check fetal lung maturity to ensure that they are not causing morbidity of prematurity related to RDS. Antenatal testing is generally started at 32 to 34 weeks gestation although its benefit has not been proven. Liver biopsy is almost never indicated, as IHCP is typically a benign maternal condition that resolves postpartum. S-adenosyl-L-methionine is among one of many therapies used in the treatment of itching in IHCP with doubtful symptomatic relief and no change in the perinatal outcome. Few cases of IHCP are complicated by a prolonged PT, which can be reverted by the administration of vitamin K. Women with prior history of IHCP should be alerted that cholestasis might develop when taking OCPs, which resolves after discontinuation of its use.

63–B

The clinical scenario described strongly suggests acute fatty liver of pregnancy (AFLP), a rare complication of pregnancy that carries a high mortality if unrecognized. The management includes supportive care and delivery without delay. Plasmapheresis has been proposed in the treatment of AFLP, but has not been shown to make a difference in outcomes. Fifty percent of AFLP cases are associated with severe preeclampsia or the HELLP syndrome, neither of which is evident in this patient. Steroids may be helpful for the treatment of HELLP syndrome, particularly when it occurs postpartum. IHCP can cause mild jaundice and mild elevations of liver enzymes and rarely elevations of PT, but has an otherwise benign maternal course. Ursodeoxycholic acid has been used in the treatment of ICHP but has no role in AFLP.

64–D

PUPPP is a common, benign dermatitis of pregnancy that typically presents in the third trimesters with 1- to 2-mm erythematous papules that quickly coalesce to form urticarial plaques that first arise on the abdomen. The face is uniformly spared, and pruritus is the major complaint. High-dose topical steroids are usually effective, with oral steroids being reserved for only the more severe cases. PUPPP is not

ANSWERS

associated with poor pregnancy outcome and resolves spontaneously during the pregnancy or postpartum. Recurrence in subsequent pregnancies is rare. Histologic examination shows a mild nonspecific lymphohistiocytic perivasculitis. The cause is unknown.

65–A

In any preterm patient between 24 and 34 weeks of gestation who presents at risk for imminent delivery, a course of betamethasone should be given. In a patient with a placenta previa who is contracting and bleeding, a tocolytic is also indicated. The tocolytic of choice in this setting is usually magnesium sulfate because both terbutaline and nifedipine can cause maternal tachycardia, which could potentially mask a sign of further bleeding. If the well-being of either the patient or the fetus becomes worrisome, cesarean delivery may be necessary. At this gestational age, however, the judicious use of tocolytics to delay delivery long enough to achieve fetal benefit from a course of betamethasone is important to decrease the rate of respiratory distress syndrome. Finally, although the glucose loading test (GLT) is usually done at the beginning of the third trimester to screen for gestational diabetes and is an important part of prenatal screening, appropriate management of this patient requires stabilization of her bleeding and contractions prior to performing routine prenatal labs. In addition, the GLT would be inaccurate in the setting of antenatal corticosteroid administration and should not be performed until at least 96 hours after the patient has received betamethasone.

66–D

Risk factors for placenta previa include history of prior placenta previa, uterine anomalies (e.g., bicornuate uterus), uterine scarring (e.g., prior cesarean delivery), multiple gestation, multiparity, increasing maternal age, and smoking. Fetal macrosomia, which occurs from growth in the second half of pregnancy is not related to placentation.

67–B

The abnormal placentation of placenta previa is associated with placenta accreta in about 5% of cases. In patients with a prior cesarean, this rate increases to 25%; with three or more cesareans, the rate is 50% and above. Placenta accreta is the invasion of the placenta beyond the uterine endometrium and even into the myometrium or beyond. There is no association of placenta previa with uterine rupture, placental abruption, or a female fetus. There is no association with a successful trial of labor after cesarean, because all patients with placenta previa deliver via cesarean section.

68–D

A routine aspect of any obstetric ultrasound is placentation. If the lower aspect of the placenta is difficult to see transabdominally, it can be more closely examined using a translabial or transvaginal probe. The placenta implants early in pregnancy and does not grow to cover more surface of the uterine cavity. However, it is possible for portions of it to infarct and thus seemingly shrink. Finally, if the bladder is full during the obstetric ultrasound, it can compress the lower uterine segment together, and make a low lying placenta look like a previa. The opposite is not true, however.

69–D

Meconium, the fetus' first bowel movement, can cause meconium aspiration syndrome when it ends up in the neonate's lungs due to aspiration in utero or at birth. It has also been associated with higher rates of infection during and after delivery of the uterus. Meconium is more commonly seen in pregnancies complicated by events that lead to fetal stress such as with cocaine use, infection, or chronic hypertension. It is also seen more with post-dates pregnancies and with oligohydramnios. It is not commonly associated with preterm labor or delivery.

70–D

All of the other findings on biophysical profile speak to the current status of the fetus. If the mother has taken an opioid minutes prior to the BPP, there will likely be reduced fetal movement, fetal tone, fetal breathing motion, and a nonreactive NST, but the amniotic fluid will be normal. Alternatively, in a fetus with a placenta whose function is diminishing over time, the fetus may acutely look good on the ultrasound, but the amniotic fluid will be low. Using the modified BPP (an NST plus an AFI), both the acute and the chronic issues are examined.

71–B

Until recently, only PGE_2 was used for cervical ripening. Its most common application was in gel form, placed intravaginally every 4 to 6 hours. The next preparation brought into use was Cervidil, an intravaginal suppository also containing PGE_2. This preparation was placed intravaginally and could be left in for up to 12 hours. The suppository was attached to netting and a string for easy removal. More recently, misoprostol or Cytotec (PGE_{1M}) has been studied for use as a cervical ripening agent. At higher doses, there have been case reports and small trials demonstrating increased rates of uterine hyperstimulation. However, this has not been seen with the 25 µg dose. $PGF_{2\alpha}$ (Prostin) is not used for cervical ripening but rather is used postpartum in patients with uterine atony and hemorrhage.

72–C

An intrauterine pressure catheter is placed into the uterus via the vagina for two essential purposes: 1) to measure and time contractions, and 2) to be used as a conduit to infuse normal saline into the amniotic cavity. The first use is important in the setting of a patient who is not making adequate cervical progress during the active phase of labor. The differential diagnosis in this situation includes the three "P"s. Either the fetus (Passenger) will not fit through the pelvis (Passage) or the contractions are not strong enough (Power). In the latter case, the strength of the uterine contractions must be quantified via calculation of Montevideo units and, if determined to be inadequate, uterine contraction augmentation with oxytocin should be considered. The second use of amnioinfusion is to dilute meconium and has been shown to decrease the rate of meconium aspiration leading to meconium seen below the vocal chords upon intubation in randomized trials. Amnioinfusion is also used in the presence of repetitive variable decelerations, indicative of umbilical cord compression, particularly in the setting of known oligohydramnios. However, infusing fluid into the uterine cavity is unlikely to help in the setting of late decelerations, which are caused by uteroplacental insufficiency.

73–D

The cardinal movements of labor begin with engagement as the fetal head enters the pelvis. As the head flexes, the smallest diameter of the head presents and descent is accomplished. The head is in the occiput transverse position until it undergoes internal rotation to the occiput anterior or posterior (the former is ideal) position. As the fetal head is pushed through the birth canal it extends to pass beneath and around the symphysis pubis. Once the head is pushed out, restitution or external rotation occurs and the head can be seen to shift to face laterally.

74–A

Arrest of dilation is defined as no dilation despite 2 hours of adequate forces. Adequate forces is considered 180–200 Montevideo units or greater. Montevideo units are measured as the sum of the pressure differences during contractions from the baseline resting uterine tone to the peak of a contraction measured in mm Hg over a 10-minute period (as measured by an IUPC). Similarly, arrest of descent refers to no descent of the fetus in the pelvis despite adequate forces. The descent of the fetus is measured by station, where station is defined as the number of centimeters above (–) or below (+) the ischial spines. Protracted labor is nonspecific—that is, slow or arrest of progress without a description of adequate forces. Slow slope active course applies to an active phase that is protracted, but again is nonspecific and does not specify forces.

75–D, 76–D

Very specific criteria should be met before an assisted delivery with vacuum or forceps is performed. First of all, the fetal station must be +2 or lower to be a low operative delivery, or 0 to +2 for a mid-delivery. Poor neonatal outcomes have been associated with deliveries above 0 station. In addition, the practitioner must know the fetal position to correctly apply the assisting device, the bladder must be emptied to avoid trauma, and the patient must have adequate anesthesia. Lastly, the estimated fetal weight should not be greater than 4000 grams unless the patient has previously delivered a baby of comparable size without injury (this is somewhat controversial). Shoulder dystocia is the main risk of attempting an assisted delivery of a baby this size in a mother with diabetes. Shoulder dystocia, the inability of the shoulders to be delivered secondary to fetopelvic disproportion, can be a catastrophic event causing great morbidity to the neonate. Rotation to the OP position is not an option as the OA position is preferred.

ANSWERS

77–D

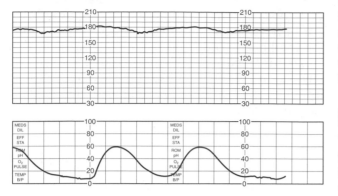

FIGURE 20 Fetal tachycardia. FHR > 160s baseline is worrisome, particularly in the setting of late decelerations. (Illustration by Electronic Illustrators Group.)

A fetal heart rate tracing (FHT) is best read systematically, with specific attention paid to the baseline heart rate, variability, accelerations, decelerations, and timing of the decelerations with contractions. The normal fetal heart rate is between 110 and 160 bpm. Variability has been historically broken into short-term and long-term variability. Now, many providers tend to examine short-term variability only and refer to it simply as variability, which is indicative of fetal ability to withstand insults. The FHT is then evaluated for the presence of accelerations in fetal heart rate and whether the FHT is formally reactive (the presence of two accelerations of at least 15 bpm over the baseline lasting at least 15 seconds in a 20-minute period). If there are decelerations, they are described in terms of their length and how low they descend. Their timing is associated with contractions. If the deceleration begins and ends with the contraction, they are designated early and associated with fetal head compression. If the deceleration begins at or beyond the midpoint of the contraction and does not begin to resolve until after the contraction ends, it is designated a late deceleration. This is a sign of poor placental perfusion during the contraction, which can be related to maternal hypotension, increased placental resistance, or decreased placental-uterine interface. This FHT should be interpreted as tachycardic with a baseline in the 170s, with minimal variability and recurrent late decelerations.

78–A

This is a nonreassuring FHT with evidence of fetal tachycardia, minimal variability, and recurrent late decelerations. This patient is likely having an abruption, which is leading to decreased fetal oxygenation, particularly during the contractions. Because she is remote from vaginal delivery (cervix only dilated 3 cm), an urgent or emergent cesarean delivery should be performed. If she was fully dilated, an operative vaginal delivery would be another option.

79–C

This patient most likely has a placental abruption, which commonly manifests as a placenta that separates easily and has an adherent retroplacental clot. She is unlikely to have a placenta previa because there was no evidence on examination, although a marginal previa is always possible in these situations. A vasa previa, fetal blood vessel lying over the cervix, is also unlikely, as the fetus would not have been likely to be viable given the amount of blood loss experienced by the patient. A placenta accreta, attachment of the placenta deeper than the endometrium and into the myometrium or beyond, is also unlikely and inconsistent with this patient's history.

80–C

There is no systematic evidence that marijuana nor its active ingredient, THC, leads to fetal anomalies. Cocaine has been associated with developmental delay. Benzodiazepines and alcohol have been associated with fetal anomalies, specifically fetal alcohol syndrome. Finally, phenobarbital use in patients with seizure disorders has been associated with both fetal anomalies and developmental delay.

81–B, 82–C

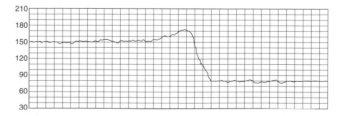

FIGURE 21 The fetal heart tracing shows a prolonged deceleration and bradycardia, a sign of an acute event causing fetal hypoxia. (Illustration by Visual Graphics, Inc.)

The patient's fetal heart tracing is not reassuring and actually quite worrisome. There is a prolonged deceleration that lasts for 6 minutes. The fetal heart rate variability is diminished, which indicates decreased fetal ability to withstand hypoxic insults. Either the decelerations need to be stopped or the fetus needs to be delivered. If there was evidence of uterine hyperstimulation or a tetanic contraction, a SC shot of terbutaline could help relax the uterus. However, there is no evidence of either phenomenon by the IUPC. To accomplish the delivery, an examination should be performed to assess cervical dilatation and determine the most appropriate route of delivery, and also to assess for any evidence of uterine rupture. Signs and symptoms suggestive of uterine rupture include a previously palpable fetal head that is now floating or nonpalpable, vaginal bleeding, or maternal sensation of "popping" or abdominal pain. If the cervix is fully dilated, the fetus can be delivered via an operative delivery more quickly than via emergent cesarean section. However, if the patient is not fully dilated, an emergent cesarean section is indicated, as uterine rupture carries significant morbidity and mortality for both the mother and the baby.

83–C

Indications for cesarean section include malpresentation (e.g., breech or transverse), nonreassuring fetal status (e.g., recurrent late decelerations, bradycardia), outbreak of genital herpes, failure to progress in the active phase of labor, fetal macrosomia, and having had a prior cesarean section or full thickness myomectomy. A patient at 2-cm dilated has not yet entered the active phase of labor and may remain in the latent phase unchanged for many hours.

84–A

In general, amnioinfusions have been best studied with regard to their effect on reducing fetal meconium aspiration. In small studies, it has been shown that infusing 500 cc of normal saline into the uterine cavity in the setting of moderate or thick meconium can presumably dilute the meconium and reduce the amount of meconium seen below the vocal cords after delivery (i.e., reduce the amount/occurrence of meconium aspiration). Amnioinfusion has also been used in the setting of recurrent variable decelerations to help cushion the compromised cord by increasing the amount of fluid in the intrauterine environment, which is the situation in the present case. Amnioinfusion has never been used or studied to cool the fetus down, to measure the contractions, or to increase contractions.

85–B

Injury of a blood vessel without disruption of the overlying epithelium during delivery can lead to a contained (often concealed) bleed called a vaginal hematoma. As blood fills the adjacent space, pressure builds causing vaginal or rectal pain. This is an important diagnosis, as the condition can lead to significant and even life-threatening blood loss.

86–C

A cervical laceration should be suspected when bleeding is noted after delivery despite a firm uterus. A very small laceration or an exposed vessel may be repaired simply with 5 minutes of pressure to the area using a ring forceps. Larger lacerations should be repaired with suture. Of particular importance for larger lacerations is identification of the apex, as these lacerations may extend into the lower uterine segment and be hidden.

87–B, 88–C

The most common cause of postpartum hemorrhage is uterine atony. Risk factors include prolonged labor with Pitocin augmentation, macrosomia, multiple gestation, multiparity, chorioamnionitis, exposure to magnesium sulfate, and a previous history of atony. After delivery of the placenta, IV Pitocin is generally begun as prophylaxis for atony along with abdominal massage of the uterus. If the uterus remains boggy (and inspection of the placenta reveals it to be intact) bimanual massage is next performed. If the patient continues to bleed and the uterus remains boggy, use of other medications should be considered. Uterotonic agents include oxytocin (Pitocin), methylergonovine (Methergine), and 15-methyl-prostaglandin F2α (Hemabate, Prostin). Methergine is contraindicated in hypertensive patients and Hemabate is contraindicated in asthmatics. Therefore, the next medication to use in this patient is Hemabate. Side effects of the medication include nausea and diarrhea.

ANSWERS

89–D

There is no evidence to support the use of PO antibiotics after clinical improvement with no fever for 48 hours, absent uterine tenderness, and normal white blood cell count.

90–A

Septic pelvic thrombophlebitis is an uncommon cause of postpartum fever. Its pathogenesis is likely as follows: infection of the placenta leads to congestion and thrombosis of the myometrial then ovarian veins. The presentation is often similar to that of endomyometritis but with spiking fevers despite 48 to 72 hours of antibiotics. Therapy requires treatment with heparin, though length of therapy is controversial.

91–D, 92–B

Mastitis has an incidence of about 2% of postpartum patients. Presentation includes history of engorgement followed by unilateral breast pain, erythema, fevers, and chills. This is a similar presentation for engorgement in the absence of mastitis, which can cause fever, but pain is usually bilateral and resolves with feeding. The most common organism involved is *Staphylococcus aureus*, spread from the neonate's nose and throat to the breast. Treatment is usually dicloxacillin, 500 mg orally QID for 7 to 10 days (or erythromycin if penicillin allergic). Continued breastfeeding is an important part of therapy, though pain medications or pumping may be required given the level of discomfort this can cause the mother. Fever beyond 48 to 72 hours or a palpable mass suggest abscess formation, which requires surgical drainage.

93–B

The estrogen component in combined OCPs will decrease the quantity and quality of lactation if started before milk production has been established (by 4 to 6 weeks). This is mediated by the negative effect estrogen has on prolactin secretion. Neither barrier methods nor progestin-only methods, including Depo-Provera (DMPA) and Norplant, affect lactation. Progestin-only contraceptives act primarily by thickening cervical mucus and making the endometrium unsuitable for implantation. They suppress ovulation less reliably. Norplant is a sustained-release system of levonorgestrel contained in six silastic rods. The rods are placed in the subcutaneous tissues of the underarm where they slowly release the proges-

terone over 5 years. It has a failure rate of 0.2%. DMPA is injected intramuscularly every 3 months and has a failure rate of 0.3%.

METHOD	WHEN TO START IN LACTATING WOMEN	EFFECT ON BREAST MILK
Condoms, sponge	Immediately after lochia stops (counsel against intercourse prior to this, as it carries a risk of infection)	No effect
Cervical cap, diaphragm	4 to 6 weeks postpartum, after the cervix and vagina have returned to a nonpregnant state	No effect
Progestin-only methods	Initiate immediately postpartum	No significant impact on milk production
Combined methods	Wait 3 to 6 weeks postpartum to initiate	Quantity and quality of breast milk diminished if started before lactation established
IUD	4 to 6 weeks, once uterus has involuted. However, in some countries used immediately postpartum.	No effect
Tubal ligation	Usually done within first 24 hours postpartum	No effect

94–B

In addition to thickening the cervical mucous and altering endometrium, circulating levels of progestin with DMPA are high enough to block the LH surge and, therefore, ovulation. The levels are also high enough to support the endometrial lining. Hence, menstrual flow does not occur. OCP use is contraindicated in women > 35 years old who smoke cigarettes. This patient is 30 years old. OCPs have been shown to decrease the risk of STIs, which is thought to be due to alterations in cervical mucous. Lastly, having multiple sexual partners makes this patient a poor candidate for the IUD.

95–B

There are two commonly used regimens for emergency contraception. The Yuzpe method (combined OCPs) uses two doses of at least 100 μg of ethinyl estradiol and either 1 mg of progesterone or 0.5 mg of levonorgestrel, taken 12 hours apart. The progestin-only method uses 0.75 mg of levonorgestrel or 1.5 mg of norgestrel taken 12 hours apart. Nausea and vomiting is common, especially with the Yuzpe method. Hence, antiemetics are often prescribed. Both regimens are effective up to *72 hours* after intercourse and cause a 75% to 85% reduction in the pregnancy rate.

96–D

Average monthly blood loss with menses increases about 35% with the IUD. Dysmenorrhea occurs in up to 20% of women. Removal rates for pain and bleeding in the first year are 12%. Otherwise, the copper IUD can stay in place for up to 10 years. A history of dysplasia is not a contraindication to IUD use. You should, however, establish that her Pap smear is negative prior to insertion. Finally, IUDs are so effective in preventing pregnancy that using one actually lowers a woman's overall risk for ectopic pregnancy. However, if she does become pregnant with an IUD in place, her ectopic pregnancy risk becomes 5% to 8%.

97–C

Functional cysts result from normal physiologic functioning of the ovary. Follicular cysts, the most common form of functional cysts among reproductive age women, arise from failure of the mature follicle to rupture. Corpus lutein cysts, also a type of functional cyst, are formed when the corpus luteum becomes enlarged and hemorrhagic. Rupture of these cysts can cause acute pelvic pain and hemoperitoneum. Theca lutein cysts arise from high levels of β-hCG and are seen in the setting of molar pregnancy. A cystic teratoma is the most common benign neoplasm of reproductive age women. On the ultrasound, the cyst appears simple without the calcifications seen in teratomas.

98–B

Most follicular cysts resolve within 60 days. For reproductive-age women with cysts smaller than 6 cm, observation for 6 weeks with a follow-up ultrasound is appropriate. Cysts that are larger than 6 cm, persist for more than 60 days, or appear solid or complex on ultrasound are probably not functional cysts. In these cases, exploratory surgery is often warranted. Of note, ultrasound is better than CT scan for imaging the pelvic organs, especially the ovaries.

99–B

Malignant ovarian neoplasms usually involve adhesions and hence rarely undergo torsion. Teratomas are benign and can be large and irregular in shape. They are the most likely ovarian neo

plasm to undergo torsion. Endometrioid tumors, cystadenocarcinoma, and granulosa cell tumors are all malignant ovarian neoplasms.

100–C

All ruptured ovarian cysts will cause acute pelvic pain. Only a corpus luteum cyst can cause sufficient hemoperitoneum to cause hypovolemia. This occurs when a lacerated vessel on the ovary (usually an artery) continues to bleed after rupture.

101–B

The incidence of fibroids is three to nine times higher among African-American women compared to Asian, Hispanic, and Caucasian women.

102–D

The most common symptom of fibroids is abnormal uterine bleeding. This typically occurs as heavy periods of longer duration (menorrhagia), resulting in iron deficiency anemia. Metrorrhagia is characterized by bleeding between cycles, with flow usually less than menses; a common cause of this is an endometrial polyp. Polymenorrhea occurs if similar periods occur at less than 21 day intervals.

103–D

Fibroids may distort the endometrial cavity and fallopian tubes and thus interfere with implantation, causing recurrent pregnancy loss. If sufficiently large, the fibroid uterus can compress a ureter and cause hydronephrosis. Endometritis is an infection of the endometrium and is not a complication of fibroids.

104–B

Fibroids have the potential for excessive growth during pregnancy. This may lead to IUGR, malpresentation, premature labor, and dystocia. If the fibroid blocks the presenting part, a cesarean section may be necessary. Polyhydramnios is commonly due to fetal structural and chromosomal abnormalities.

105–A

The recommended treatment with a 90% to 95% cure rate is metronidazole, 2 grams PO, for both the patient and partner. A regimen of 500 mg PO BID for 7 days can be given to those who do not respond to the one-time dosage. In addition, it is recommended that the patient and partner

ANSWERS

abstain from sex or use condoms for 2 weeks following therapy to avoid reinfection. Patients must be informed that alcohol should be avoided when taking metronidazole, as significant nausea and emesis will occur in a reaction similar to that caused by Antabuse.

106–C

The most likely diagnosis is bacterial vaginosis in which clue cells are seen on a wet mount. However, chlamydia can be asymptomatic and present similarly (in this case, white blood cells would be seen on wet mount). Bacterial vaginosis is an interesting infection that, at one point, was considered sexually transmitted. We now know this is not true. As evidenced by its name, *vaginosis*, this is usually a nonirritating entity and many women remain asymptomatic. These women do not need to be treated for asymptomatic infections (though this is controversial) unless they are pregnant (as there may be an increased risk of preterm labor and preterm rupture of membranes). The diagnosis is made by the presence of a malodorous discharge, clue cells (epithelial cells stippled with bacteria) on wet mount, a vaginal pH that is basic, and the presence of a fishy odor with addition of KOH ("whiff test").

107–C

Taking broad spectrum antibiotics predisposes the patient to the development of vaginal candidiasis. Other predisposing factors include use of oral contraceptives or steroids, and the presence of diabetes.

108–A

Gonorrhea and chlamydia can cause cervicitis, urethritis, and PID. *Trichomonas* infection can cause vaginitis and urethritis. Although candidiasis can cause dysuria, this is generally due to irritation rather than an actual infection of the urethra. Note that the most common cause of urethritis is a urinary tract infection, which is associated with a very different group of microorganisms.

109–E

The postcoital form of contraception, named the Yuzpe method after its founder, consists most commonly of two Ovral pills given in two doses, 12 hours apart. Ovral is composed of 50 μg of ethinyl estradiol and 0.5 mg of norgestrel. Lo-Ovral consists of 30 μg of ethinyl estradiol and

1.0 mg of norgestrel. Alesse consists of 20 μg of ethinyl estradiol and 1.0 mg of levonorgestrel. The goal is to give two doses 12 hours apart, with each dose consisting of at least 100 μg of ethinyl estradiol. In this question, the Alesse dosing achieves this, whereas the Lo-Ovral does not. An IUD placed just after coitus will work as contraception; however, in this setting of possible exposure to STIs, this is not the optimal management plan, given the potentially increased risk of PID. Vaginal misoprostol can be used as an abortifacient early in pregnancy but not periconceptually. Depo-Provera has not been studied as a form of postcoital contraception.

110–A

Given the 15% cross-reactivity between cephalosporins and penicillin, it is not a good idea to give a cephalosporin to this patient who has a penicillin allergy when alternative treatments exist. In this case, the ceftriaxone would normally be given to cover *Neisseria gonor-rhoeae*, which can also be covered with one-time doses of ofloxacin, ciprofloxacin, and the 2-gram dose of azithromycin. If ofloxacin or ciprofloxacin are used, the patient also needs coverage for *Chlamydia trachomatis* with either a one-time dose of azithromycin or a 1-week course of doxycycline.

111–D

This patient appears normally responsive to questions and is without a specific indication for a psychiatry consultation. Alternatively, a social services consultation to arrange follow-up care, possible counseling, and support groups is useful. The face x-rays should be performed to rule out an orbital fracture, and a chest x-ray to rule out a rib fracture. The HIV prophylaxis should be offered, though patients often decline.

112–D

HPV, human papilloma virus, is the cause of condyloma as well as cervical cancer. Unfortunately, there is no particular way to prevent its transmission other than barrier methods such as condoms. Chlamydia, gonorrhea, and HIV can all be prevented with prophylactic antibiotics, and hepatitis B can be prevented by giving HBIgG.

113–E

The Bartholin cyst is the most common cystic growth in the vulvovaginal area. It usually occurs in young women and requires treatment for pain, enlargement, and infection. Fibroma is the most common benign solid tumor of the vulva. It typically occurs along the insertion of the round ligament into the labium majora. Epidermal inclusion cysts are usually asymptomatic and present as a small hard lump containing sebaceous material. Hidradenomas are benign growths from apocrine glands. Nevi are common in the vulva and can be very varied in appearance. They need to be followed closely and biopsied or excised for acute changes in size, color, or shape.

114–A

This patient had a Bartholin gland abscess, which was initially treated by drainage and antibiotics. She now presents with a likely reinfection of the cyst, secondary to inadequate treatment at the initial presentation. Insertion of a Word catheter into this cystic cavity to form a fistulous tract will allow the gland to drain appropriately. A biopsy and/or excision procedure would be justified if there is a concern about an underlying malignant process. Marsupialization is indicated in recurrent Bartholin gland enlargement. This is a procedure where a portion of tissue is removed in an elliptical fashion and the edges of the skin and cyst wall are approximated to form a pouch. This allows for continued drainage and reepithelialization of the involved area.

115–B

In postmenopausal women with unilateral Bartholin gland enlargement, the possibility of an underlying malignancy needs to be considered. The possible types of malignancies include adenocarcinoma, adenoid cystic carcinoma, and squamous cell carcinoma of the vulvar. A biopsy of the cyst wall is warranted in this patient, in addition to placement of a Word catheter.

116–C

The most common cause of Bartholin gland enlargement is an infection. These infections are generally polymicrobial with anaerobic and aerobic organisms. Cultures of cyst contents are positive for *N. gonorrhoeae* in approximately 10% of the cases. Nevertheless, all patients should be screened for STIs at the time of presentation with a Bartholin gland abscess. Fibrosis after an infection can lead to cyst formation from accumulation of the gland's mucinous secretions.

117–D

Hidradenitis suppurativa is a chronic refractory infection arising from apocrine glands affecting the skin and subcutaneous tissue. Deep-seated, painful subcutaneous nodules are observed in the areas containing apocrine glands, such as the vulva and axilla. Occlusion of apocrine ducts from chronic infection results in progression of disease to multiple draining abscesses and sinuses. Dermatologic diseases that typically involve other areas of the body can affect the vulva too. Vulvar psoriasis generally appears in the intertriginous areas as red to reddish-yellow papules that bleed easily. Acanthosis nigricans rarely involves the vulva but it is a raised, pigmented papillary lesion that can become quite extensive. Behçet syndrome is a triad of oral ulcers, genital ulcers, and ophthalmologic inflammatory changes, with possible involvement of the ocular mucosa. Squamous cell carcinoma is a slow-growing cancer that can present quite variably and is frequently painless. The basic tenet of vulvar lesions is to biopsy for diagnostic confirmation.

118–E

Vulvar vestibulitis is a syndrome consisting of pain on palpation of the vestibule or attempted vaginal entry; physical findings are of inflammation and erythema localized to the vestibule. It can be a chronic problem and is often multifactorial in origin. Typically, surgical specimens reveal areas of inflammatory changes, often characterized by an abundance of plasma cells and lack of polymorphonuclear leukocytes, with the vestibular stroma most prominently involved. There is no evidence of HPV changes on her Pap and biopsy. Similarly, she does not have yeast vulvovaginitis on the wet mount. Lichen planus lesions tend to be intensely pruritic and appear as chronic violaceous papules. In addition, some women with lichen planus can develop a desquamative vaginitis, resulting in burning dysesthesia of the vulvovaginal area. Contact dermatitis usually presents with pruritus, and in severe cases with evidence of excoriation, erythema, and edema.

119–B

First-line therapy for vulvar vestibulitis is topical steroid application. If an infectious cause is identified, concurrent treatment with antibiotics must be initiated. Amitriptyline, in addition to steroids,

ANSWERS

can be useful for patients in whom psychological factors appear to have a role in disease manifestation. Topical estrogen is used for management of atrophic vaginitis. Local care with sitz baths and compresses can confer significant relief from the "pain-itch" cycle of vulvar irritation caused by contact dermatitis, and may be helpful for vulvar vestibulitis as well.

120–D

In the absence of a documented infection, addition of a broad-spectrum antibiotic is not recommended. In women with HPV disease, recombinant alpha-interferon injections into the vestibular glands have been effective in treating vulvar vestibulitis. CO_2 laser ablation of the vestibular glands has been shown to be ineffective and, conversely, can cause significant scarring and worsened dyspareunia and pain. Spontaneous remission has been reported in up to 30% of women (within 6 to 12 months of the initial complaint), but it seems unlikely to be the case here. In a small percentage of women, elimination of dietary oxalates (coffee, chocolate, tea, peanuts, spinach) can alleviate the pain. Gland excision and perineoplasty has produced relief in 75% to 90% of women who fail medical management and should be discussed.

121–A

If the first line of antibiotics fails, the appropriate treatment is to expand coverage to triple-antibiotic therapy. Laparotomy and adnexal surgery is reserved for TOAs that are unresponsive to antibiotic therapy or grossly ruptured. Usually a unilateral salpingectomy is performed for unilateral TOAs. For bilateral TOAs, bilateral salpingectomy or even a concomitant total abdominal hysterectomy may be necessary.

122–B

The two most common sequelae of PID are infertility, which is estimated to occur in 20% of all PID patients, and ectopic pregnancy, for which there is a tenfold increased risk. Fitz-Hugh-Curtis syndrome, an ascending perihepatitis, is an occasional complication of PID. Toxic shock syndrome (TSS) occurs rarely. It has been associated with menstruation and tampon use and with postpartum and postabortal endometritis. However, neither TSS nor bacterial vaginosis are sequelae of PID.

123–D

Both gonorrhea and chlamydia can cause a mucopurulent discharge. Currently, a first-stream urine test is only available for chlamydia. The treatment for chlamydia cervicitis is a 7-day course of doxycycline, 100 mg PO BID, or a one-time 1-gram dose of azithromycin. This patient should also be treated presumptively for gonorrhea with ceftriaxone, 250 mg IM once.

124–B

Risk factors for PID include young age, multiple sexual partners, non-Caucasian and non-Asian ethnicity, unmarried status, recent history of douching, and cigarette smoking. IUDs have been considered a risk factor for PID. However, with current IUDs it seems this risk only exists around the time of placement. OCPs have been found to be protective against PID. The mechanism is thought to involve alterations in cervical mucous. The best protection against PID is provided by barrier contraceptives.

125–B

A review of the menstrual cycle demonstrates that after ovulation, progesterone rises dramatically as it is secreted by the corpus luteum. This rise helps the endometrium to become more glandular and secretory in preparation for a possible fertilized ovum to implant. If ovulation does not occur, then you do not see this rise in progesterone. Measuring estrogen is not a useful test in this situation, as it is difficult to interpret and to specify which result would signify anovulation.

126–D

The nonspecific diagnosis for this patient is dysfunctional uterine bleeding (DUB). This diagnosis of DUB is made when other conditions, anatomic lesions, and cancerous states have been excluded. The treatment for DUB secondary to anovulation involves many options. No treatment is an option for anovulation if the condition occurs infrequently. However, a more chronic anovulatory state (which is an estrogen-dominant state) can put a patient at risk for developing hyperplasia or carcinoma, so therapy with progesterone is recommended. In addition, a patient can become quite anemic from this chronic blood loss. All of the treatments listed will likely help to control the patient's cycles, limit bleeding, and add back some progesterone to protect against hyperplasia or carcinoma.

127–B

Uterine fibroids, also called leiomyomas or myomas, are a local proliferation of uterine smooth muscle cells and are very common. They can grow slowly or quickly over time, causing increasing symptoms. However, most women remain asymptomatic even with large fibroids. Symptoms include menorrhagia, pelvic pain, pelvic pressure, or pelvic fullness. The patient described could have any of the other diagnoses listed as well, but all would be much less common for this presentation.

128–E

Approximately 25% of endometrial cancer cases occur before menopause. Abnormal bleeding in a woman older than 38 to 40 years of age, especially if they have risk factors, mandates an endometrial biopsy. Known risk factors for endometrial hyperplasia and carcinoma include exposure to estrogen therapy without progesterone; tamoxifen therapy; diabetes mellitus, nulliparity; a family history of endometrial, colon, or breast cancer; early menarche (before age 12) and late menopause; obesity; and hypertension. In much younger women, abnormal bleeding is generally not related to cancer, though hyperplasia can occur. In addition, breakthrough bleeding on oral contraceptives during the first 3 to 6 months is quite common.

129–A, 130–A

Endometrial polyps are an overgrowth of endometrial glands and stroma. Less than 1% are associated with adenocarcinoma. Removal is recommended, both to establish that no cancer is present as well as to eliminate the symptomatic bleeding. Removal can be accomplished in several ways. Hysteroscopy can be done in the office or the operating room, allowing the gynecologist to visualize the endometrium and if needed to remove polyps or lesions. A hysteroscope is a metal instrument and camera that is inserted into the vagina and cervix to allow visualization of the uterine cavity. Through a separate port, fluid is instilled into the uterus to dilate the uterus and act as a medium for the operative procedure. The operative hysteroscope will often be followed with curettage (scraping) of the endometrium so that the entire endometrium is sampled and can be evaluated by pathology.

131–A

In performing diagnostic and operative hysteroscopy, several distension media are available. It is important that the operator knows and understands the complications of each medium so as to prevent such complications or recognize them immediately should they occur. High viscosity fluids such as Hyskon and dextran have been associated with anaphylactic shock, bleeding diathesis (through interference with platelet function and factor VII), and pulmonary edema. Low viscosity and hyperosmolar fluids such as glycine and sorbitol are associated with hyponatremia, which can lead to cerebral edema and death.

132–B

Cervical polyps are generally benign focal overgrowths of cervical tissue. Their removal is usually quite easy and can be done in the office. Polyp forceps are used to grasp the polyp in its entirety and the polyp is then twisted until it is removed. Bleeding is generally minimal and can be resolved with pressure. The specimen is then sent to pathology to confirm that the polyp is benign.

133–A

Continuing with OCPs until conception is desired is the best option. You have not ruled out endometriosis, which is a real consideration in this patient, for which OCPs may have some additional value aside from pain control. In addition, if she only has pain with menses, she may use OCPs continuously, stopping only several times a year to induce withdrawal bleeds. Prolonged discontinuation of OCPs will likely result in recurrence of her symptoms. There are no contraindications for the use of oral contraceptives after age 35 unless there are concomitant risk factors that increase the risk of thromboembolic events, such as cigarette smoking. OCPs actually reduce the risk of ovarian cancer by twofold to threefold.

134–C

For patients with progressive dysmenorrhea who have failed primary therapy with NSAIDs and OCPs, the next step in management is laparoscopy for diagnosis and treatment. Antidepressants like SSRIs may be efficacious in premenstrual dysphoric disorder (PMDD) or chronic pelvic pain. Therefore, making a formal diagnosis will help guide therapy. Total abdominal hysterectomy, with removal of tubes, ovaries, and appendix, may be considered in patients with severe

ANSWERS

endometriosis who have completed childbearing and for whom medical as well as less invasive surgical approaches have failed. Endometriosis can be treated with a GnRH agonist. However, confirmation by direct visualization is usually required prior to initiation of treatment.

135–A

Primary dysmenorrhea is unusual in women with irregular cycles. In fact, it usually begins within 6 to 12 months after the onset of ovulatory (regular) cycles in young women. Treatment of primary dysmenorrhea can be accomplished with either NSAIDs or OCPs, with similar response rates. NSAIDs are more effective if therapy is initiated prior to the onset of menses and continued for 3 to 5 days. Before the diagnosis of primary dysmenorrhea is made, secondary dysmenorrhea should be ruled out. Generally this can be done with a careful history and physical.

136–D

Cervical stenosis is usually seen in patients with a history of prior surgical procedure to the cervix (e.g., cone biopsy, LEEP). It manifests with colicky lower abdominal pain and scant or light menstrual flow. A fixed, retroverted uterus and nodularities on the uterosacral ligaments are characteristic, albeit not exclusive, of endometriosis. Diffuse enlargement and tenderness of the uterus are typical findings of adenomyosis that can be best appreciated at the time of menstruation. Dysmenorrhea is a common complaint among IUD users, but no characteristic size, shape, or flexion of the uterus associated with IUD dysmenorrhea. NSAIDs are usually effective in managing IUD-related dysmenorrhea. In addition to colicky lower abdominal pain, primary dysmenorrhea is often accompanied by nausea, vomiting, headaches, diarrhea, anxiety, syncope, and abdominal bloating.

137–A

The first three on the list are the most likely diagnoses prior to physical examination. Mayer-Rokitansky-Küster-Hauser syndrome is agenesis or dysgenesis of the müllerian system, whereas this patient has evidence of a normal uterus, cervix, and upper vagina. The fact that a hymeneal ring is not visualized makes transverse vaginal septum unlikely. Distal vaginal agenesis is also unlikely because the obstruction is relatively thin. Thus, the most likely diagnosis is imperforate hymen.

138–D

Patients with abnormalities of the genital tract and pelvic organs are at risk for renal anomalies as well. The most common of these include horseshoe kidney, unilateral renal agenesis, and ectopic or accessory ureters.

139–C, 140–B

Diethylstilbestrol (DES) is a progestogenic agent used in patients who had recurrent miscarriages from the 1950s up to the mid-1970s. There were case series of young patients with vaginal adenocarcinoma, also known as clear cell carcinoma, that were eventually associated with the use of DES by their mothers. As more evidence came in, associations with uterine anomalies, other genital tract anomalies, and cervical incompetence in pregnancy were discovered. The last patients were treated with DES about 25 years ago, so the legacy of this drug will dissipate over the next few decades.

141–D

The clinical picture is highly suggestive of endometriosis; a cystic adnexal mass with low level echoes, although nonspecific, has a high likelihood of being an endometrioma. There is some controversy over the optimal treatment for mild endometriosis, but adhesive disease and endometriomas greater than 2 cm are best managed with surgery. In this symptomatic patient, a diagnostic laparoscopy, with subsequent laparoscopic surgery versus laparotomy (depending on the intra-operative findings), is the best next step.

142–D

The object of surgery in endometriosis is to ablate, electrocauterize, and/or excise all visible lesions, and restore anatomic relationships while preserving the reproductive organs to allow for future fertility. For all stages of endometriosis, laparoscopy offers similar results to laparotomy with less morbidity and decreased costs. Radical or definitive surgery in endometriosis includes total abdominal hysterectomy, usually with bilateral salpingo-oophorectomy, and is reserved for patients who have failed conservative therapy and have completed childbearing.

143–B, 144–C

Medical therapy of endometriosis with hormones is generally done in a stepwise fashion. The first step is cyclic oral contraceptives. If this fails, the next step is continuous oral contraceptives. If there is no pain relief from continuous oral contraceptives, a diagnostic and therapeutic laparoscopy should be performed in patients without a definitive diagnosis. In patients who have already been diagnosed, the next step is treatment with a GnRH agonist (Lupron), which sends the body into a premature menopausal state. In this patient who has been treated with cyclic OCPs, but never a continuous regimen, the next step in her management after the surgery would be to attempt to control her pain with this way. Some patients will get relief from the surgery itself, and if they are interested in fertility, will decline any hormonal treatment whatsoever. For acute pain relief, NSAIDs are the first-line therapy. Opiates should only be used in the emergent setting where a patient needs pain relief for a defined time period prior to surgery or for a particular hormonal treatment to work. If opiates are used chronically, the patient is likely to develop an addiction.

GnRH analogs produce a hypoestrogenic state similar to that seen in oophorectomized women. Side effects are related to the low estrogen state. Long-term users of an GnRH analog should be consideration for "add-back" therapy, given concerns about its role in bone loss. Danazol, another agent used in the treatment of endometriosis, has been shown to have a negative impact on serum lipids. However, this has not been demonstrated with GnRH analogs when used for 6 months or less.

145–C

Medications that antagonize dopamine cause elevated prolactin, because dopamine suppresses prolactin secretion by the pituitary. Clozapine is the only dopamine antagonist in this list. Medications that antagonize dopamine include antipsychotics (such as phenothiazines), tricyclic antidepressants, estrogen, MAO inhibitors, and opiates.

146–A

In the setting of hyperprolactinemia with visual disturbances, a pituitary lesion is likely. A pituitary mass or an enlarging pituitary can compress that optic chiasm and lead to bitemporal hemianopsia. Retinal hemorrhages are due to severe hypertension or, in infants, rotational acceleration ("shaken baby syndrome"). Lateral nystagmus is typically due to vestibular pathology. Amaurosis fugax is transient monocular blindness due to occlusion of the retinal artery by emboli arising from the carotid arteries.

147–B

The next diagnostic step is to perform a progestin challenge test. This is done by giving oral progesterone for 10 days and then observing for a withdrawal bleed after the course is completed. Absence of a withdrawal bleed indicates hypoestrogenism (hence no endometrial lining). The serum FSH would then help determine if the hypoestrogenism is hypergonadotropic or hypogonadotropic.

148–B

Atrophy of the vaginal mucosa suggests a low estrogen state. Pregnancy is extremely unlikely in this setting. Sheehan syndrome is hypopituitarism due to ischemic injury to the pituitary gland. This is rare, and in women it usually follows severe obstetric hemorrhage. In addition to hypoestrogenism, patients have hypothyroidism and corticosteroid deficiencies. Premature ovarian failure is possible, but unlikely in a 22-year-old woman. Mild to moderate hypothalamic dysfunction causes hypogonadotropic hypogonadism, which is being increasingly recognized as a common cause of menstrual cycles irregularities among female athletes and dancers as well as in patients with eating disorders.

149–C

The goal of intrauterine insemination is to overcome low sperm counts by decreasing the barriers (cervix, cervical mucous) sperm must cross to reach the ovum. If this fails, the next treatment is to directly inject a single sperm into an egg. This can only be done with IVF. This couple would not benefit from ovulation induction because she is ovulating normally.

150–D

Retrograde ejaculation occurs when sperm are propelled into the bladder rather than the urethra. This diagnosis can be confirmed with evaluation of postejaculatory urine. A varicocele is the abnormal dilation of veins in the spermatic cord. The associated rise in testicular temperature is thought to impair semen quality. Mumps orchitis and radiation exposure both result in abnormal sperm morphology.

ANSWERS

151–A

In general, 80% to 85% of couples will achieve spontaneous pregnancy within 1 year; 90% will do so within 18 months. Couples who have not achieved pregnancy after 1 year of appropriately timed, unprotected intercourse warrant an infertility evaluation.

152–B

Clomiphene citrate acts as an antiestrogen by competitively binding to the estrogen receptor in the hypothalamus. This leads to increased pulsatile GnRH, which causes increased FSH and LH release from the pituitary and subsequent ovarian follicle growth and ovulation.

153–A

In patients with adult-onset congenital adrenal hyperplasia (CAH), they may or may not have elevated DHEAS and testosterone. The initial screening test for adult-onset CAH is a 17-hydroxyprogesterone (17-OHP). If it is extremely elevated, >800 ng/dL, it is diagnostic for 21-hydroxylase deficiency. If the 17-OHP is mildly elevated between 200 and 800 ng/dL, the next step is an ACTH stimulation test. Markedly elevated levels after the ACTH stimulation test are also diagnostic.

154–A

An elevated LH/FSH ratio is a classic indicator for diagnosing PCOS. Many clinicians still use it. However, if her other laboratory tests are normal and she has irregular menses and hirsutism, a clinical diagnosis of PCOS could be made.

155–D

The treatment of hirsutism is multifaceted. Spironolactone acts to inhibit androgen production and as a direct inhibitor of 5α-reductase, the enzyme that facilitates the peripheral conversion of circulating testosterone to the much more potent androgen dihydrotestosterone (DHT). Finasteride also inhibits 5α-reductase. Dexamethasone acts to suppress ACTH secretion and, in turn, adrenal androgens. Oral contraceptives are important in these patients both for menstrual regulation as well as to affect the hormones that lead to hirsutism possibly including ACTH, DHEAS, ovarian androgens, and the gonadotropins (LH and FSH). Bromocriptine is not used in patients with hirsutism, but rather in cases of hyperprolactinemia, particularly in association with pituitary microadenomas, to suppress prolactin production.

156–D

Patients with hyperandrogenism have a high association with insulin resistance and type II diabetes. One classic physical finding in these patients is acanthosis nigricans, a velvety thickening on the back of the neck. Thus, it is important to screen these patients with a fasting glucose and a 75-gram glucose loading test. If the patient had an elevated DHEAS suggestive of an adrenal tumor, a CT followed by a check for urinary catecholamines would be indicated. A patient with elevated fasting prolactin of unknown cause deserves an MRI to rule out a pituitary tumor.

157–A

Absence of testes (gonadal agenesis in XY individual) means that neither müllerian-inhibiting factor (MIF) nor testosterone are produced. The uterus and cervix form from the müllerian ducts but breasts do not develop because there is no peripheral conversion of testosterone to estrogen. In 46, XY individuals with absent GnRH secretion or 17α-hydroxylase deficiency, MIF is produced but not sex hormones. In müllerian agenesis, ovarian estrogen secretion is normal.

158–B

This patient is hypoestrogenic. A serum FSH would reveal whether this is due to a hypothalamic or pituitary defect (low FSH) or to gonadal failure (high FSH). A 24-hour cortisol is used to diagnose Cushing syndrome. A serum testosterone can be helpful in diagnosing the cause of hirsutism in females. Levels above 200 ng/dL suggest an adrenal mass.

159–A

Primary amenorrhea is defined as the absence of menses in women who 1) have not undergone menarche by age 16, or 2) have not had a period by age 14 in the absence of normal growth and development and appearance of secondary sex characteristics. Although 15 years is relatively late for menarche, it is not outside the realm of normal. A normal physical examination excludes an anatomic or outflow tract abnormality.

160–D

Kallmann syndrome is the congenital absence of pulsatile GnRH. As a result, the pituitary does not release FSH or LH. The resulting phenotype is a uterus present (no MIF), but breast development absent (no estrogen).

161–B

There is an 8% risk of multiple gestation with clomiphene citrate. Ovarian hyperstimulation and possible subsequent torsion are complications of ovulation induction using gonadotropins such as Pergonal. Premature ovarian failure is not a complication of clomiphene citrate use.

162–A

Polycystic ovary syndrome is a constellation of symptoms that usually includes infertility, menstrual disturbances, hirsutism, and obesity. Patients with PCOS are at risk for hyperinsulinemia and insulin resistance. They also manifest abnormal lipid profiles, which place them at risk for coronary artery disease. Because chronic anovulation causes elevated estrogen levels, these patients are at risk for endometrial and breast cancer, not ovarian cancer.

163–C

Pelvic surgery and salpingitis can cause tubal occlusion, and hence are risk factors for ectopic pregnancy. IVF can result in ectopic pregnancy if the fertilized embryos are pushed up into the tube when they are placed in the uterus. Gonadotropins stimulate multiple ovarian follicles to mature, but do not change tubal function or patency.

164–C

Clomiphene citrate is the first-line treatment for mild hypothalamic amenorrhea. A patient who has failed gonadotropin induction (a more powerful form of ovulation induction than clomiphene citrate) needs IVF. Asherman syndrome is the presence of adhesions in the endometrial cavity and is a rare complication of endometrial surgery. Cervical stenosis can be treated with cervical dilators.

165–A

Oral contraceptives (OCPs) are widely accepted in the management of the transition to menopause and are the best choice for this patient. OCPs will relieve her menopausal symptoms, suppress irregular bleeding, and provide her with a predictable bleeding pattern. Many perimenopausal women, despite irregular cycles, are ovulatory and OCPs will provide effective contraception. At age 50, they can be switched to the combined HRT regimens. A continuous combined HRT regimen will provide vasomotor symptom relief, but it will not manage the irregular bleeding and could actually worsen erratic bleeding. Unopposed estrogen therapy and transdermal estrogen therapy without progestins is not recommended as it increases the risk of endometrial hyperplasia/cancer. Progestin therapy can relieve menopausal symptoms, particularly hot flashes, and can be used for patients who have contraindications to estrogen use. There is, however, a high incidence of unpredictable bleeding.

166–C

It is not uncommon for a woman to report breakthrough bleeding during the first year of initiating HRT. This patient, however, had no bleeding for 15 months and then reported several episodes of postmenopausal bleeding. A Pap smear alone is not sufficient to evaluate postmenopausal bleeding. Observation is contraindicated for the same reason. An endometrial biopsy needs to be performed to evaluate for possible endometrial abnormalities such as atrophy, polyps, hyperplasia, or cancer. Although it has 90% sensitivity for identifying endometrial abnormalities in women with postmenopausal bleeding using an endometrial thickness cutoff of 5 mm, ultrasonography cannot define the pathology. Nevertheless, it is a helpful test, particularly when performing an endometrial biopsy is not possible, or before deciding to proceed with a hysteroscopy, dilation, and curettage.

167–B

Continuing her current regimen would not address the issue of unpredictable bleeding. A cyclic sequential HRT regimen, on the other hand, has the advantage of providing the patient with predictable withdrawal bleeding periods with a lower incidence of breakthrough bleeding. There is no medical indication for performing a hysterectomy. Clonidine is an alternative therapy for hot flashes in cases where estrogen and progestins are contraindicated. Increasing the dose of progestin would probably not help her, as her bleeding is from an atrophic endometrium.

ANSWERS

168–D

Osteoporosis is defined by a T-score > 2.5 standard deviations below the mean. The T-score is the standard deviation above or below the peak bone mass of young adult women of the same ethnicity as the patient. In postmenopausal women, hypoestrogenism is an important predictor of low bone mineral density. Acute vascular thrombosis, however, is a contraindication for continuation of HRT. Addition of alendronate, a bisphosphonate, to a diet supplemented with calcium and vitamin D can be instrumental for managing bone density loss. Raloxifene is not an alternative as it has been shown, like estrogen, to increase the risk of thromboembolic events threefold. Ginseng is thought to have estrogenic properties, but to date no studies have been conducted to demonstrate its effects on bone remodeling.

169–D

Alpha-adrenergic antagonists such as Prazosin reduce urethral closing pressure and would exacerbate urge incontinence. Anticholinergics such as tolterodine or oxybutynin inhibit detrusor muscle contraction. Beta-adrenergics like metaproterenol and muscle relaxants relax the detrusor.

170–C

This patient's symptoms and high postvoid residual are consistent with overflow incontinence. Detrusor muscle contractions are mediated by cholinergic receptors via the parasympathetic pelvic splanchnic nerves. Neurologic deficits such as lower motor neuron disease, autonomic neuropathy, spinal cord injuries, and multiple sclerosis can cause detrusor insufficiency, which leads to bladder overflow. Diabetic neuropathy can cause overflow incontinence in this manner, or it can blunt the sensation of a full bladder, causing progressive overdistension, eventually leading to overflow incontinence. Pelvic masses may lead to outflow tract obstruction that can in turn cause bladder overdistension. Bladder neck hypermobility is associated with stress urinary incontinence.

171–B

In the United States, the most likely cause of vesicovaginal fistula is surgery or pelvic irradiation. Women with vesicovaginal fistula present with painless, continuous loss of urine. You confirm the diagnosis by instilling methylene blue dye into the bladder and seeing if the dye leaks onto a sanitary pad.

172–B

Micturition involves 1) stretch receptors in the bladder wall sending a signal to the CNS to begin voiding; which triggers 2) inhibition of the sympathetic fibers from T10–L2 (hypogastric nerve), causing relaxation of the urethra and external sphincter; and then 3) activation of the parasympathetic pelvic splanchnic nerves to contract the detrusor muscle.

173–B

Vaginal pessaries provide mechanical support of the pelvic organs. They are placed in the vagina and hold the pelvic organs in their normal positions. Using a pessary requires a very motivated patient as they require routine removal and replacement for cleansing. A cervical cap is a contraceptive. It does not provide pelvic organ support. Prazosin (alpha-antagonist) would relax sphincter tone, worsening incontinence. Improved management of chronic bronchitis will not reverse pelvic organ prolapse.

174–B

Common surgical procedures for stress incontinence fall into three main categories: 1) anterior colporrhaphy which is designed to close an open bladder neck; 2) bladder neck suspension procedures to correct hypermobility; and 3) sling procedures to correct intrinsic sphincteric weakness. Although this is quite technical, you should be aware that surgery is commonly used to treat stress incontinence, that urethral dilation would only make matters worse, and that a hysteroscopic myomectomy involves the removal of fibroids from the uterus and is a different procedure altogether.

175–A

Kegel exercises result in increase in resting and active pelvic muscle tone and have been shown to be effective in treating mild stress incontinence. Medical treatment for stress incontinence involves alpha-adrenergics, which increase sphincter tone, not anticholinergics such as Ditropan. This patient does not need hormone replacement as she is not menopausal.

176–A

A woman who has pelvic organ prolapse but is asymptomatic does not need treatment. However, she is a high risk of developing symptoms and may require treatment at that time.

177–B

The most common reason for vulvar pruritus is yeast dermatitis. Vaginal discharge from bacterial vaginosis and trichomoniasis, common vaginal infections, can cause vulvar irritation, dyspareunia, and pruritus. Estrogen deficiency is a common reason for vulvar pruritus in the postmenopausal woman. Finally, acute contact dermatitis caused by perfumed soaps, laundry detergents, tight-fitting or synthetic undergarments, or vaginal hygienic products can also cause intense vulvar pruritus.

178–D

Symptomatic relief while awaiting biopsy results could be achieved with a topical steroid cream. Local measures to diminish irritation such as cotton underclothing, avoidance of strong detergents/soaps, and use of bath salts can also help control the itching. Testosterone gel or cream in combination with a topical steroid would be appropriate treatment for lichen sclerosus et atrophicus. Imiquimod is indicated only for the treatment of condyloma.

179–B

The colposcopic findings are consistent with the diagnosis of VIN. Vulvar dysplasia will appear as multifocal discrete whitish, thickened lesions. Vulvar dystrophies such as lichen sclerosus et atrophicus typically appear thin, with areas of scarring or contractures. Skin fissures may be present because of excoriation. Condyloma will appear as solitary or clustered, pedunculated, papillary lesions. Melanoma is the most frequent nonsquamous cell carcinoma of the vulva and presents as irregularly pigmented, variegated lesions that can be flat, ulcerated, or nodular.

180–B

Various modalities exist for treatment of premalignant changes in the vulva. Circumscribed VIN II–III lesions, like those described in this patient, can be treated with a wide local excision procedure.

Skinning vulvectomy or CO_2 laser therapy are forms of therapy for superficial multifocal disease. Topical steroid or testosterone creams are not treatment options for vulvar dysplasia. Trichloroacetic acid is effective treatment for small condyloma acuminata lesions.

181–C, 182–B

Pap smears are a screening tool for cervical cancer. The procedure involves scraping cells from the transformation zone of the cervix, but is not a biopsy. Thus, the results received can be open to interpretation and how one manages a patient with dysplasia can be controversial. In general it is agreed that all patients with a Pap smear suggesting high-grade squamous intraepithelial lesion (HGSIL) proceed directly to colposcopic exam with directed biopsies. Also, most practitioners agree that patients with low-grade squamous intraepithelial lesion (LGSIL) proceed directly to colposcopic exam with directed biopsies. This would certainly be the case in this patient who is a smoker. The follow-up for a patient with a first-time result of atypical squamous cells of undetermined significance (ASCUS) is more controversial. A good rule of thumb is to proceed directly to colposcopic exam in a patient with risk factors for cervical cancer or at risk for noncompliance with close follow-up. In a patient with a history of normal Pap smears with one risk factor, repeating the Pap in 4 to 6 months is also reasonable.

183–C

Atypical glandular cells of undetermined significance (AGUS) is a very different entity from ASCUS. First of all, there are two types of cervical cancer: squamous and adenocarcinoma (glandular). The spectrum of dysplasia associated with squamous cell cancer includes ASCUS, LGSIL, and HGSIL. AGUS is considered a dysplastic entity associated with adenocarcinoma of the cervix and endometrium. The percentage of AGUS patients with a significant lesion is much higher than those with ASCUS. Thus, colposcopic exam, endocervical curettage, and endometrial biopsy (in older patients) is required.

184–B

The serotypes 16, 18, and 31 are correlated with cervical cancer. The serotypes 6 and 11 are associated with condyloma only.

ANSWERS

185–A

The diagnostic test of most value is an endometrial biopsy with a diagnostic accuracy of 90% to 98%. A physical examination rarely reveals evidence of endometrial carcinoma or hyperplasia. A Pap smear is not reliable, as <50% of women with endometrial carcinoma have an abnormal Pap result. Currently, more data are needed before transvaginal ultrasonography can substitute for a tissue diagnosis in the workup of postmenopausal bleeding, though an endometrial thickness of <5 mm in a postmenopausal woman is consistent with atrophy. A wet mount would only evaluate for bacterial vaginosis, yeast, or *Trichomonas*. A CT would be useful if the clinical examination was limited secondary to habitus or discomfort.

186–E

Endometrial hyperplasia classification is based on the findings that only cytologically atypical lesions progress to cancer. Hyperplasias are classified as simple or complex based on architecture, and designated as atypical hyperplasia on the basis of cytology. Progression from hyperplasia to cancer occurs in 1% of women with simple hyperplasia and in 3% of women with complex hyperplasia. Eight percent of women with simple atypical hyperplasia progress to carcinoma; 29% of those with complex atypical hyperplasia develop carcinoma.

187–D

Treatment for endometrial cancer typically involves surgical staging, hysterectomy with bilateral salpingo-oophorectomy. Postoperative radiation is considered for advanced and/or poorly differentiated endometrial carcinoma. Progestins may be used to treat hyperplasia with or without atypia in select patients with either medical comorbidities (who are, therefore, poor candidates for surgery) or in those who desire future childbearing. Close follow-up study with endometrial biopsies is indicated in these patients. A D&C is of no diagnostic or therapeutic value in this patient with endometrial cancer. Observation and rebiopsy is inappropriate here.

188–B

In endometrial cancer, both grade and depth of invasion discriminate the risk of nodal disease.

As grade becomes less differentiated, there is a greater probability of deep myometrial invasion and, subsequently, pelvic and para-aortic lymph node involvement. Greater depth of invasion (>50% myometrial involvement) is associated with a higher probability of extrauterine tumor spread, treatment failure, and recurrence. Nevertheless, regardless of grade, 1% of women with endometrial involvement have pelvic or para-aortic lymph node metastases.

STAGES	CHARACTERISTICS
IA G123	Tumor limited to endometrium
IB G123	Invasion to <1/2 myometrium
IC G123	Invasion to >1/2 myometrium
IIA G123	Endocervical gland involvement
IIB G123	Cervical stromal invasion
IIIA G123	Invasion of serosa or adnexa or positive peritoneal cytology
IIIB G123	Vaginal metastases
IIIC G123	Metastases to pelvic or para-aortic lymph nodes
IVA G123	Invasion of bladder and/or bowel mucosa
IVB	Distant metastases including intra-abdominal and/or inguinal lymph node

HISTOPATHOLOGY	GROUPED BY DIFFERENTIATION OF ADENOCARCINOMA
Grade 1	<5% nonsquamous or nonmorular solid growth pattern
Grade 2	6% to 50% nonsquamous or nonmorular solid growth pattern
Grade 3	>50% nonsquamous or nonmorular solid growth pattern

189–A

Ovarian cancer primarily spreads by direct exfoliation of malignant cells by either rupture or penetration of the ovarian capsule and implantation on other tissues. The disease then spreads along the circulatory path of peritoneal fluid flow and the lymphatic drainage system. Tumor involvement of the omentum, paracolic gutters, and cul-de-sac may be quite extensive. Hematogenous metastases are rare in ovarian cancer; therefore, parenchymal involvement of the lung, liver, and brain is rare.

190–C

Ovarian cancer staging is done clinically via exploratory laparotomy and evaluation of all areas at risk for metastatic disease. A rigorous staging procedure is necessary because postoperative therapy is based upon anatomic staging as well as other factors, such as histologic subtype of the tumor. The technique for surgical staging of ovarian cancer involves multiple cytologic washings or aspiration of ascites, removal of the adnexal mass/tumor, complete abdominal exploration, removal of the remaining ovary(ies), uterus, and fallopian tubes, omentectomy, pelvic and para-aortic lymph node sampling, and biopsies of the peritoneum including the diaphragm.

191–C

She has stage IIIC ovarian cancer. Stage III disease is defined as tumor involving one or both ovaries with peritoneal implants outside of the pelvis and/or positive retroperitoneal or inguinal nodes; or tumor limited to the pelvis but with histologically verified malignant extension to the small bowel or omentum. The presence of superficial liver metastasis also equals stage III. In stage IIIC the tumor implants are at least 2 cm in diameter and the retroperitoneal/inguinal nodes are positive for cancer. Unfortunately, ovarian cancer most commonly presents as stage III disease. The 5-year survival for stage IIIC epithelial ovarian cancer is 18%, with an overall 5-year survival rate of 31%. Survival rate has been shown to be influenced by the histologic grade of the tumor and the extent of residual disease after surgical debulking.

192–E

Pedigree analysis can estimate a family member's risk of ovarian cancer. Patients with a family history suggestive of hereditary ovarian cancer syndrome (where more than two first-degree relatives have ovarian cancer or related cancer) have a 30% to 50% chance of developing ovarian cancer (JAMA 1993;269:1970–1974). Ms. C's daughters are at increased risk of developing ovarian cancer given their family history. Routine screening involves the combination of annual or biannual pelvic examinations, CA-125 levels, and transvaginal ultrasonography. However, no screening technique, even in high-risk patients, has significantly reduced mortality from ovarian cancer. Prophylactic oophorectomy can decrease the risk of ovarian and breast cancers but it does not remove the risk of peritoneal carcinomatosis. BRCA1 screening can also be considered in her daughters. Studies suggest that the BRCA1 mutations occur in 5% of women diagnosed with ovarian cancer prior to age 70. BRCA mutations are being studied extensively to elucidate their roles in breast and ovarian cancers. BRCA1 is a tumor-suppressor gene on chromosome 17q21, whereas BRCA2 cancer-susceptibility gene is located on chromosome 13q12–13. BRCA2 mutations also increase the risk of ovarian cancer but to a lesser extent than BRCA1 mutations.

193–C

HPV has been linked to the development of cervical dysplasia and squamous cell carcinoma of the cervix. Molecular analyses reveal that HPV DNA is integrated into the host cell's DNA in over 90% of cervical cancer cells. HPV serotypes 6 and 11 are associated with condyloma; whereas serotypes 16, 18, and 31 are correlated with the development of preinvasive and invasive cervical squamous cell carcinomas. Sexual-behavioral risk factors such as multiple sexual partners, early age of onset of sexual activity, and a history of STIs place women at increased risk for cervical dysplasia and cancer. Sexual partners of women with cervical cancer have been found to be at increased risk for HPV-associated diseases and penile cancer. Abnormal Pap test history, cigarette smoking, and infection with HIV are all risk factors for cervical dysplasia. HPV prevalence is variable depending on the population studied, but it is highly prevalent in a population of young sexually active individuals. HPV testing can be highly sensitive but lacks the specificity to be useful as a screening test for preinvasive and invasive cervical cancer.

194–C

Cervical carcinoma is a disease that is staged clinically and primarily by pelvic examination. It can be modified by findings on chest x-ray, intravenous pyelogram, or CT that demonstrate ureteral obstruction or a nonfunctioning kidney, but not by operative findings. Clinical stage is the most important prognostic factor in cervical carcinoma. This patient has a 4- to 5-cm nodular lesion of the cervix that does not appear to involve the parametrial tissues, the rectovaginal

TABLE 49. Staging Cervical Cancer	
Stage I.	Confined to the cervix
	IA. Microscopic disease
	IB. Clinically identifiable lesions
Stage II.	Extracervical, but not to the pelvic walls or distal third of the vagina
	IIA. No parametrial involvement
	IIB. Parametrial involvement
Stage III.	Extension to the pelvic wall or distal vagina
	IIIA. Not to the pelvic wall
	IIIB. To the pelvic wall
Stage IV.	Beyond the true pelvis
	IVA. To the bladder or rectum
	IVB. Distant metastases

ANSWERS

septum, or the pelvic sidewalls. She has a stage IB2 cancer of the cervix.

195–E

When a patient is clinically unstable, intravenous access needs to be obtained and aggressive resuscitation started with fluids and blood products. In this case, where the source of bleeding is diffuse from a tumor on the cervix, one can try to apply pressure to the cervix with a vaginal pack while resuscitation is ongoing. Consultation with interventional radiology for possible embolization of hypogastric vessels is appropriate. If the bleeding is not controlled with these less invasive measures, one will have to go toward an exploratory laparotomy and a modified radical hysterectomy, where paracervical and parametrial tissues are removed. A simple abdominal hysterectomy has little role in the therapy of invasive cervical cancer, though it may be performed for women with preinvasive or microinvasive disease. A radical trachelectomy is a conservative variant of a modified radical hysterectomy for young patients with early invasive cancer of the cervix who desire future childbearing. Progestins have no role in controlling bleeding from a cervical tumor.

196–C

Invasive cervical carcinoma was recently added to the CDC class C list of AIDS-defining illnesses. HIV-infected patients are at increased risk of cervical neoplasia and recurrent vulvovaginal candidiasis. In fact, recurrent or difficult to treat vulvovaginal candidiasis, multiple episodes of PID, and cervical dysplasia have been added to the CDC list of class B diseases, which formerly were known as AIDS-related conditions (ARC). Screening of HIV-infected women for abnormal cervical cytology is a controversial topic, with a conservative management option being closer intervals of Pap examinations—for example, performing Pap smears every 6 months times two followed by annual exams, presuming normal cytology. The impact of gynecologic conditions on progression of disease in HIV-infected patients has been recognized by these changes in the CDC classification of HIV disease.

197–C

The most likely diagnosis in this 29-year-old woman is a simple cyst. Cysts can present in any location on the breast and can grow rapidly, causing acute onset of pain and discomfort. On palpation, cysts tend to be smooth, round, and mobile. A fibroadenoma usually presents as a painless, discrete, firm, mobile mass. It is the most common benign breast tumor, occurring most frequently in young women. Fibrocystic disease, also called fibrocystic changes, describes normal physiologic changes of the breast during the menstrual cycle. Some women with fibrocystic disease will complain of pain or even of a "lump" in the breast. Clinical examination findings vary from findings of a discrete, tender mass to large prominent glandular changes in the breast(s). The involved areas fluctuate in size and tenderness through the menstrual cycle. Cystosarcoma phyllodes is an uncommon tumor that presents as a well-defined, firm, rapidly growing lobulated mass. Fat necrosis describes changes in the breast, usually following a traumatic event, which can be confused with malignant lesion. There frequently is a discrete, hard mass that is fixed to the underlying breast tissue without associated tenderness. If a clear history of trauma to the breast is elicited, it is reasonable to observe the lesion for resolution. Otherwise, a fine-needle aspiration should be performed. Unfortunately, only 50% of women recall a history of trauma to the breast. Fat necrosis has also been seen after radiation therapy or segmental resection of the breast.

198–D

Aspiration of the palpable cyst is a reasonable course of action. She should have immediate relief of discomfort following decompression of the cyst. The fluid is characteristically clear with a yellow or brown tint and can be sent for cytologic study. It is reasonable to observe the patient for a short period prior to an aspiration procedure. An excision is not warranted at this stage. One would proceed to diagnostic imaging with ultrasonography if the patient declined a diagnostic aspiration or fluid was not obtained on aspiration. Ultrasound is not only a useful tool for evaluating women with breast cysts but also ideal for guiding fine-needle aspirations of deeper, nonpalpable lesions. Mammographic imaging is limited in young women with radiographically dense breasts, though cysts will usually present as smooth, round densities scattered through the breast. Ductography is useful in a patient with abnormal nipple discharge, and in particular, in evaluating for the presence of intraluminal lesions within the duct. At present, MRI does not have a role in clinical screening for breast cancer, given its cost and accessibility.

199–E

The event most likely to have transpired is early (less than 6 weeks after complete aspiration) recurrence of the cyst. Indications for excisional biopsy of the cyst are early recurrence, recurrence of the same cyst after two aspirations, or the presence of an underlying mass on examination of the breast following cyst aspiration. In the absence of a history of fevers, chills, and erythema or induration on the breast, it is unlikely that the patient has an abscess or a cellulitis.

200–A

Breast cancer risk factors have been investigated extensively and relative risks calculated. Risk factors include menarche before 12 years old; older than 35 years at first pregnancy; nulliparity; older than 55 years at menopause; family history of breast cancer in mother, sister, or daughter (with greater risk if the cancer was diagnosed premenopausally, or was bilateral, or was present in two or more first-degree relatives); prior history of cancer in one breast; personal or family history of ovarian or endometrial cancer; being Caucasian (in U.S.); living in an industrialized nation (except Japan); and history of fibrocystic changes of the breast with papillomatosis, proliferative changes, or atypical epithelial hyperplasia.

BREAST CANCER RISK FACTORS	RELATIVE RISK
Nulliparous vs. parous	3:1
Menarche before age 12	1.3:1
First birth after age 34	4:1
Menopause after age 50	1.5:1
First-degree relative with	
Unilateral premenopausal	1.8:1
Bilateral premenopausal	8.8:1
Unilateral postmenopausal	1.2:1
Bilateral postmenopausal	4:1
Proliferative fibrocystic change	2–5:1
White vs. Asian	3:1

CASE PRESENTATIONS

DIAGNOSIS

INDEX

INDEX